Earthbound Christian

Earthbound Christian

*Flourishing Within Limits in the
Age of Infinite Growth*

CALEB CRAY HAYNES

Illustrations by HANNAH GIBSON

WIPF & STOCK · Eugene, Oregon

EARTHBOUND CHRISTIAN
Flourishing Within Limits in the Age of Infinite Growth

Copyright © 2026 Caleb Cray Haynes. All rights reserved. Except for brief quotations in critical publications or reviews, no part of this book may be reproduced in any manner without prior written permission from the publisher. Write: Permissions, Wipf and Stock Publishers, 199 W. 8th Ave., Suite 3, Eugene, OR 97401.

Wipf & Stock
An Imprint of Wipf and Stock Publishers
199 W. 8th Ave., Suite 3
Eugene, OR 97401

www.wipfandstock.com

PAPERBACK ISBN: 979-8-3852-5693-8
HARDCOVER ISBN: 979-8-3852-5694-5
EBOOK ISBN: 979-8-3852-5695-2

Unless otherwise noted, Scripture quotations are from New Revised Standard Version Bible: Anglicized Edition, copyright © 1989, 1995 National Council of the Churches of Christ in the United States of America. Used by permission. All rights reserved worldwide.

Scripture quotations marked NIV are from the Holy Bible, New International Version®, NIV® Copyright © 1973, 1978, 1984, 2011 by Biblica, Inc.® Used with permission of Zondervan. All rights reserved worldwide.

For
Emily, Story, Daily.
Thanks for being earthbound with me.

I arise today
Through the strength of heaven,
Light of sun,
Radiance of moon,
Splendor of fire,
Speed of lightning,
Swiftness of wind,
Depth of sea,
Stability of earth,
Firmness of rock.

. . .

Through a mighty strength, the invocation of the Trinity,
Through belief in the threeness,
Through confession of the oneness,
Of the Creator of Creation.
—St. Patrick's Breastplate

Contents

Preface ix

Acknowledgements xiii

Introduction xv

PART ONE—*Only Human*

Chapter 1 | Eco-Hypocrite 3

Chapter 2 | Eco-Confessions 15

PART TWO—*Tall Buildings in a Single Bound*

Chapter 3 | Skydiving in the Anthropocene 37

Chapter 4 | Coffee, Curtains, and the Human Condition 61

PART THREE—*Games, Cake, and Money*

Chapter 5 | The Infinite Game 87

Chapter 6 | American Doughnuts 105

PART FOUR—*The Boundary Layer*

Chapter 7 | Deeper Than the Holler 125

Chapter 8 | Subatomic Salvation 143

PART FIVE—*Jesus Drives a Station Wagon*

Chapter 9 | Humble Power 167

Chapter 10 | Dancing in the Moonlight 189

Epilogue 205

Bibliography 215

Preface

Then God said, "Let us make humans in our image, according to our likeness"...

Then the Lord God formed the human from the dust of the ground and breathed into their nostrils the breath of life, and the human became a living being.

GENESIS 1:26 AND 2:7[1]

UNLIMITED, UNRESTRAINED, UNLEASHED, UNCHAINED, UNBOUND, and, of course, free are all best-selling words. There is an emotional tug to each of these terms upon our spirit. Somewhere deep within us is something primal that wants to fly, to break free, defy gravity, and to know the experience of, at last, being untethered and unfettered from all our limitations and pain.

I can't help but wonder if that's part of "the heaven" inside of us. In other words, it's the part of us, if we could name it, that is designed for eternity, that is reflective of the "otherness" of God, who is also the One we are created in the image of.

It's said that common among human experience are flying dreams. I know I've had these. Dreams where, free of all constraints, I soar above the earth like a human rocket, unhinged from everything. Ultimate unrestraint. Could this be a special clue within our human spirit that inherently desires to be more than who we presently are? We crave to become.

But there is another part of us. An earthly part. A creaturely part. We are beings who live on the ground. At home on the earth. Earthlings. Humans from the humus. *Ha adam* from the *Adamah* as it says

1. Personal translation.

in the ancient Hebrew.[2] We are people created from a scoop of soil in the hands of the Creator. We are, in our most basic form, "of earth." In this earthiness we are finite, limited, and gravitationally bound. Yet, this earthbound life is not one reflective of some "fallen state of humanity" but of the Creator's design. Something within us craves this grounded life. There is an intimacy with the natural world that we hunger for and return to in efforts of reconnecting or recharging each season as we go for a hike, take a trip to the nearest coast, soak in the mountains, or even explore the desert.

So, is it possible that we are both? Bound to heaven . . . and bound to earth?

When we are *bound* for something, we are saying that there are no other outcomes than for our joining-up with that thing. Destiny may be another way we name this. To be bound for a place means that within our existence lies a path laid out for us that desires to be present with that place.

This is not to be mistaken with modern theological ideas of predestination but rather about the kind of home God has created us for.

It's not uncommon for Christians to talk about being heaven-bound. Being heaven-bound is usually thought about as where we are going after this life is said and done. But what if Scripture indicates heaven is arriving *here* on earth? "*On earth as it is in heaven,*" is how we learn to pray. What does it mean to be heaven people who are earthbound?

And really, what does any of this have to do with how we live our lives today? What does it have to do with how we care for the planet today amidst ecological crises? What does being heaven-bound or earthbound have to do with my ordinary busy life as a parent driving between the grocery store and taking kids to soccer practice?

Heaven and earth are our two spectrums; they are the polar ends that create what's needed to be human. Without both ends there is no energy, no flow.

Our lives are answering the question: What does it mean to be a people who are created to flourish and multiply while living within earthy boundaries? What does it mean to be a people created from the material

2. Gen 2:7.

ground, yet animated by the very breath of God? What does it mean to be a people of heaven and be a people of earth?

While there are plenty of books out there that talk about what it means to be Christian and heaven-bound, the pages ahead are set aside to explore what it means for us to also be earthbound. We will not do the work here of deciphering Christian doctrine about "the last days," analyzing post-millennial versus pre-millennial end times theories, or explore here the myriad of ways that Scripture informs us of how heaven is coming to earth.[3] Rather, we'll be exploring here what it means for a heaven-bound Christian people to be living intentionally earthbound in harmonious ways, within the web of life that God has placed us.

On the surface we might call this "eco-friendly living"—that's just a name used to describe a bit of cream on top. Underneath awaits for us a life that is far more rich and flavorful. It is a life of meaning, tethered to the goodness that is God's gravitational plan for humanity and all of creation.

Too often when we think of a life that is limited, a feeling of imprisonment can rise within us, but this is not a book about being trapped, stuck, or suppressed. We live in a time when people do not like the idea of limits. Everything from our stocks to our fitness goals to our personal growth resonates with the idea of becoming limitless. What if what's behind so much of our discontentedness and despair today *and* what is behind these ecological crises facing the planet is our inability to see that flourishing occurs within limits?

It would not be a leap to suggest that many of us have been culturally predispositioned to think that orienting our lives around limitations is inherently bad. As a parent, I've watched as my children have had to navigate a world with a million more options than I had growing up. From streaming shows, unlimited music, the world wide web, and now to AI and smart devices sitting on our counter . . . my kids are growing up in a world that seems to have fewer limits every day. Yet, when I consider the things that make my children better people, learning values of patience, growing in the fruits of the spirit, living bodily healthy lives,

---

3. I explore some of this thread further in my book *Garbage Theology*, and theologian N. T. Wright explores this beautifully and extensively in his work, *Surprised by Hope*.

and becoming better friends, these limitless choices rarely do them any favors. In fact, as my kids fight over which show to watch together amidst their almost limitless choices, my wife and I laugh at how that was never the case for us growing up when we watched whatever show was on the one kid's channel that we had! Nothing to fight about there! Sure, this is just a funny micro-example, but it represents a major defining issue of our time: chasing human well-being through the unceasing pursuit for more while living within the limits of God's creation.

Today, the systems that hold power in the world continue their march upon God's creation, and they require an unquestionable ethos that demands "more" infinitely.

Pause and consider. If creation's flourishing (that includes you) is not something that can occur within limitations, then one might conclude that there is a fundamental flaw within God's created design. Would God create a cosmos and world marked by boundaries and limits, skin and bones, shores and mountains, that is fundamentally unable to flourish? Of course not!

This is a book that wrestles with the difficulty of living in a time, place, and culture that is increasingly at odds with our humanity and the natural world. It is a book about being the kind of people God intends for us to be. Here, I hope you will find that our own flourishing is intimately connected to the flourishing of all creation.

Acknowledgements

I'M SO THANKFUL FOR our Creator and the gift of being part of creation. Without this air, this soil, these birds singing in this willow, and this humble back porch, there would be no book in your hands. These words are part of what's grown here (alongside some tomatoes, pumpkins, and blueberries).

There aren't enough words to truly thank my wife, Emily, for her love and patience that she has offered in this process. When you're wearing this many hats and also birthing a book into the world, it's a family affair. I'm so thankful for her wisdom and care that saturates these pages in hidden ways.

Story and Daily, my two rascals who mostly have me around their fingers. Their childlike joy and presence, continually offering the gift of parenting and pushing me to become better, inspired so much of what's written here. (As you'll see.)

There are so many others who I owe massive gratitude to, as our stories are intertwined. My sister in-law Hannah, for sharing her amazing talents with us through these brilliant illustrations. They're just so wonderful to include and help bring these stories to life. My friend Noah for lending conversation, coffee, and poetry. Laurie Braaten for all his wisdom and insight. To my other friends who I mention in these pages and who are a part of the community that surrounds me, thank you!

A special thanks to my friends at Nazarene Theological College–Manchester. My time there was so precious and exceptional. Many of the seeds that grew this book came from that special place.

I'm so thankful for the friends that I've gotten to know and work alongside of in the mission of caring for God's creation. I'm so thankful for Erin Grimm who has been a friend and major support in the creation of this book. There is also deep gratitude for the wonderful thinkers like

Wendell Berry, Norman Wirzba, Robin Wall-Kimmerer, and others who have faithfully exegeted this conversation in ways no one else could, and in which I'm just riding their waves!

Last, but definitely not least, I have to thank my roots. My family, my parents who love me despite my peculiar wildness, and my humble country beginnings.

Finally, I'm so thankful for you picking up this book, friend!

Introduction

THE STORY GOES LIKE this. Early in the life of the earth, four and a half billion years ago, an enormous collision occurred. Earth was struck by what researchers refer to as Theia (an ancient planet about the size of Mars); it received a planet-sized punch to the side of the face, bursting rocky fragments into space. Impacting Earth at about nine thousand miles per hour, the impact formed massive dust clouds in the aftermath of this cosmic coming-together. Over the course of time, this debris of dust, rock, and gas leftover from the impact swirled together, coalescing into discs, clumps, and eventually into the body known today as the moon. All of this made possible through that everyday miracle we so easily take for granted: gravity.[4] Swinging around our orbit, catching glimpses of each other, the earth has been dancing with the moon for ages, like starstruck lovers.

In the thirteenth century, Italian friar and Christian mystic St. Francis of Assisi sang the praises of God: "Praised be You, my Lord, through Sister Moon and the stars, In the heavens you have made them bright, precious and fair." In Genesis, we read that on the fourth day, "God made the two great lights—the greater light to rule the day and the lesser light to rule the night—and the stars. God set them in the dome of the sky to give light upon the earth, to rule over the day and over the night, and to separate the light from the darkness."[5] As Christians, we believe that this great light of the moon is part of the divine design and we praise the Lord for it!

Today, in our artificially lit evenings, we often take the light of the moon for granted, something the civilizations that came before us would

---

4. Canup, "Origin of the Moon," 708–12; Hartmann, "Satellite-Sized Planetesimals," 504–15; Taylor, *Lunar Science*, 137–57.

5. Gen 1:16–18a.

never do. For as far back as we can trace, humans have looked to the moon for information on seasons, agriculture, animal migrations, and many secrets of the human–creation relationship we are in.

In fact, science today confirms this relational dependency we have with our tagalong celestial sphere. Without the moon, light in the darkness wouldn't be the only thing we were missing; without the moon, our entire planet would be an unstable place to live. We know that the moon's gravity gives us the tide, which over millenniums have become critical for marine life and the greater ecosystems of the earth. Further, the moon has gravitationally pulled on the earth for so long that our days lengthened to twenty-four hours, thus saving us from chaotic conditions on the planet. Perhaps most importantly, the moon stabilizes the earth's axial tilt right around that important 23.5 degree sweet spot (thought to be the result from its bout with Theia). Without the moon keeping us in check, life as we know it would be nonexistent, seasons would be altered, extreme climate shifts would occur, and all this would make agriculture nearly an impossible feat. Kudos to the moon.

It's the gravitational pull that makes the moon gracious. Gravity is the gift that keeps giving. It is the love language that makes all of life as we know it possible. If the moon is the body that embraces, gravity is the outstretched arms reaching out, holding us in the embrace.

Gravity is also the force that informs us of these "necessary for life" limitations. It says, "go here and no further." It is the pull and push. You can consider gravity as that which tells you to stop jumping on your bed *or* as the one who assures you that your bed will be there when you come back down.

These earthly limits, these great lights, this gravity, are all part of God's intentional grace-filled setting for our lives. And we're bathing in it. It's all around us, setting us firmly on the ground in this garden called Earth, right where we belong.

In the adventure ahead, we will be exploring the ramifications of being part of civilizations that push, with all their might, to transcend gravity. What are the naturally occurring consequences of a certain percentage of the earth's population becoming utterly captivated by overcoming our limitations?

A quick scroll down the news reminds us that we are making great strides in overcoming any and all barriers to having an easy life; and the next scroll of your thumb will leave you looking at mass flooding, extreme heat, drought, terrifying tsunamis, crashing ecosystems, and the loss of topsoil like we've never fathomed possible, all happening in real time.

We are witnesses to technological advancements, online shopping, smart phones, fast food, and faster cars that make our lives comfortable, yet continually fail at "making a life." Yet, we pursue them ceaselessly.

How long can we press up against gravity before the moon can no longer hold us in check? How will we be saved from ourselves?

As a Christian, I believe in Jesus. The pages ahead are not about inviting Jesus into your heart but about inviting Jesus into the rest of your body and life. It's about being the kind of human you were created to be. Finite, in a body, feet on the ground, produce-eating, flesh and bones, dirt-under-your-fingernails, human . . . yet, eternal, deeper, rooted, created in the image of God. This is about believing in Jesus so much that you follow Jesus. But be warned, Jesus doesn't do much climbing the ladder. Rather, Jesus' path is incarnational. Jesus comes and it's gravitational.

Here's what I want to know: Does Jesus show us the way out of these environmental crises? Does being human inherently mean being in a tumultuous relationship with the earth? Does being created in the image of God leave us with any clues about being earthlings? Are humans meant to walk on the moon or purchase bean burritos for $1.29? Is it possible to flourish within limits? Let's explore what it means to be earthbound and Christian together! Are you ready?

Part One—Only Human

Chapter 1 | Eco-Hypocrite

BECAUSE I'M HUMAN, TOO . . . I'm also a bit of a hypocrite. Just like you. If you're anything like the rest of us, this whole climate crisis and quest for healing the earth feels gargantuan. Meanwhile, we're just human, right? For many years now, I've been on a personal mission to do everything within my grasp and power to help save every piece and part I'm able to. I've started organizations, mobilized programs, written books, planted trees, given webinars, sifted through mounds of trash, advocated for legislation, preached, podcasted, and prayed. And, as it happens, there's still loads more to do. The work is wider and the dig is deeper.

    At some point, you begin to see things from a different altitude. But what I've found is that perspective isn't from somewhere higher but someplace lower down. It is revealed through our confessions, foibles, utter failures, and archaeological findings. Perhaps the lessons I've learned here are lessons close to each of our hearts. In an age of what appears to be "environmental Armageddon," what if the tools creation needs for healing aren't necessarily just more technology, more advancements in infrastructure, and smarter AI, but something that is as close as your own humanity?

When I scroll down my environmentally obsessed social media feed, what I regularly view is post after post selling us a bit of guilt over something that we enjoy. *Do you enjoy football? Well, have you seen the gargantuan footprint of energy consumption and waste that football produces annually through stadiums, equipment, maintenance, travel, and fans? Do you enjoy candy bars? Did you know, the majority of chocolate bars are key contributors to deforestation and soil loss? Do you like new shoes? Let me tell you about the conflict, resources, and extraction required for petroleum-based non-renewables and the leather industry, cattle industry, and ensuing deforestation!*

How will we change the world and solve global environmental problems with a narrative that says, "Stop doing every single thing you enjoy because it's killing the earth!"? It doesn't take a marketing expert to know that's a tough sell! So, we end up with a movement that is driven by shame on one side and fear on the other. Fear of there being no tomorrow if the earth keeps hemorrhaging at our current rates of consumption. *So, shame on all of "you" playing a part in that!*

The issues of earth care for the people of earth are nowhere close to being this binary today. We live lives that are inseparably intertwined with every leaf, bug, and blade of grass, along with every gigabyte spent on TikTok and the sushi we had for lunch. Millions of decisions make up the special relationship between humans and the humus we depend upon. This, my friends, is how I believe God saw fit to order it all. And if you've really seen it, then you know why it's called "very good."[1]

So, what do we do when the lives we live are part of larger systems that degrade God's good creation? Is it possible to be a flourishing human being, have a society that is healthy, happy, and whole, and *not* be causing environmental degradation?

POSERS AND PROPHETS

Traveling is well known to be one of the most wasteful decisions we can partake in, which recently is making me into quite the clown. I'm sitting in London Heathrow during one of those too-long-to-sit-still but too-short-to-leave the airport layovers. I'm surrounded by

---

1. Gen 1:31.

everything I can't afford. Louis Vuitton, Gucci, Prada, and a Starbucks line that reaches back to America! It should be noted that I'm here in the UK because of my studies on the intersection of theology and ecology. So, whether it's the fact that I seem to be too poor to be in this terminal or that I am here on an environmental mission . . . either way I feel like a poser. Flying is basically the worst personal decision I can make as someone who cares for the environment. I suppose that makes me the largest eco-wannabe in London today or maybe the only one with a "legit" excuse to fly. I'll let you decide.

If you're an enneagram nerd, let me "out" myself and say that I'm a "nine." Conflict is not my jam, but I've learned to navigate it well enough. If you know my wife, she's an "eight." That's code for "conflict is her jam!" I could fill an entire book on the adventures of everyday struggles I've had a front row seat to with her over the years (and that may just happen one day when I write my bestseller on *How to Hide Inside Yourself While Your Loved Ones Jump Outside Themselves* . . . it's a working title). Just to be clear, her ability to be confrontational is not a curse but is her gift to the world.

One such memory is from a flight that Emily and I were on. Towards the end of the journey, our flight attendant comes by to collect the trash. Emily reaches down to collect her aluminum can and begins to hand it over but hesitates and asks if the airline recycles. It was a legitimate question as any item that you gave them went into the same trash bag. Admittedly, it was suspicious. The attendant, who was already wearing the "I'm not living my best life" badge on her sleeve, responded with what I'll call a *sassy "yes,"* and proceeded to snatch the can from my wife's hand. Needless to say, she was unable to attain the can from Emily, who was now absolutely *certain* that this can was *not* going to be recycled. Emily decided the safe decision was to keep the can and put it in her bag to recycle it at home.

One would think that was the end of it, but this flight attendant was also among the feisty variety of people, probably of Amazonian or Viking descent. The attendant, now firmly planted within the aisle, began declaring that my wife must surrender the can to her possession. (Now was the point at which I had to decide whether it was more viable to pretend to be asleep or be engrossed in my book. Further, it should be stated that we were now bordering on an absurd interaction.

People were simultaneously melting in their seats, yet glued, unable to look away. It was the equivalent to a juicy soap opera meets *Survivor*, hours into a boring flight.) Thankfully, the second attendant was now approaching the situation and worked to coax her coworker off of her last stand. In the end, that aluminum can safely made its way home with us to our secure recycling bin in Nashville. Ecological disaster averted!

I love this story because it continues to remind us of the absurdity of it all. This, often, is what it feels like to care for creation. Battles over aluminum cans, lunch leftovers, light bulbs, to-go cups, and carpooling. When we think of "doing our part" for the earth, I think we can safely say that these thoughts don't get us out of bed in the morning! This story also reminds me that, yes, it can sometimes feel like a fight because, for at least the part of the planet I live on, caring for creation is an afterthought. So, when I go about my day, eat at a restaurant, decide what products to buy, what business to support, and the best way to consume in the world, it's like swimming upstream—because so much of our culture and the way we do business is not "set up" for caring.

Creation care is just that. Caring. And caring occurs in tiny, unglamorous, meek, and generally unnoticed ways. Care finds its sweet spot in the intentional helping of a neighbor, smile for a stranger, or visit with a widow. But the most important part here is the word "intentional." True care becomes part of what we are *intentionally* doing in our world. This is a huge part of what I love about my wife, her intentionality. Her being exudes purpose. She's never done something "half-assed" in her life.

Here's why this is important, because you and I live within strong currents. Perhaps the chief among those is the current of over-consumerism.[2] The current requires virtually nothing from us to stay within it. At the end of the day, we must consume to live. Further, through marketing and ease-of-access, we can be spoon-fed everything we consume without ever leaving our flotation device. So, whether you're on an airplane or in the grocery store, it takes a great deal of intentionality to be a good stewardess of creation.

---

2. Yes, "over-consumerism." It's important to note that consuming is not inherently bad. In fact it is essential to life. Yet, our current global ecological crises are driven directly from our *over*-consumption.

I think if we're honest though, when just recycling the aluminum can incites a conflict, when the current often seems so strong, and when it's often difficult to believe our personal choices matter anyway, it's pretty hard to keep the eco-faith.

Perhaps we need to admit a couple of things before we can get anywhere else.

Our first confession is that we are all some form of hypocrite. There is no escape from it. Sometimes I wonder if being human is admitting to being hypocritical. At any given time, even with the best intentions, odds are, something we are doing is somewhat contrary to caring for the earth and our human siblings. Even the people and places we love, we regularly hurt.

Second, many of us humans lack a great deal of eco-intentionality, especially when it comes to certain areas of how we choose to live our lives. And that level of intentionality can be hard and exhausting. If you grew up learning that the highest value is "keeping the peace," "not rocking the boat," and to keep things going as easy as possible, then you're going to be challenged by what it means to heal God's creation today. If you happen to be among those who have conflated "niceness" or "goodness" with not fighting for the "small things," then you may struggle with the work ahead.

Third, it can feel like a leap of faith today to continue doing all the many actions of care without seeing results. So, what does it mean that "faith" is actually a big part of this whole earth care package?

Good. So, now that we're all feeling a bit more human, let's move on!

Sitting here in Heathrow, being literally trapped inside the flow of this airport current of consumerism as it tempts me to dive in, I smile thinking of what it could be. What would all this become if this were an airport filled with humans who were primarily interested in healing the planet, who were intentional, taking ecologically healing leaps of faith? What if this airport were full of Emily-level intentionality? We would change the world! . . . Oh man, I'm definitely going to check out this Harry Potter store!

RIBBONS

Sometimes I think there's no such thing as a life easier than mine. I have food in my cabinets and a refrigerator that I can raid at any time. I have a comfy, cozy bed that I can lay my head down each evening and drift away in. I have a home with an indoor controlled climate that allows me to be temperate at all times. I have a closet full of clothing options for any day of the week. Beyond the essentials, there are also the perks. You know, the flat-screen with my favorite show on, the ice cream, the sea salt chips with sour cream, the water park, the minivan that totes us wherever we need to go, and the ready-made access to pretty much anything I need via sitting on my couch with Wi-Fi in hand. Welcome to paradise.

December 1st, 2008, I was living in Germany helping start a new local church movement. On this particular day, I noticed that everywhere I went, people were wearing little red ribbons on their shirts. I thought, "Hmmm, that's a bit strange." Talking with my German friend Janika, I asked, "What's up with red ribbons? Why is everyone wearing them?" She told me that it was World AIDS Day! "Wow," I thought; how could I not already know about this!

"So, what are the ribbons for? Why do we wear them?"

"To show that we care," she said.

"Right," I said. The pragmatist in me wanted more, "but what should we *do* today?" I waited to hear about some call to action that the ribbons represented or something we were going to do as a church. She thought for a second and laughed, "We just care!"

We both had a good laugh at this. Probably because, in a way, we both saw the underside of it all, especially as two people who were giving our lives to start a faith community called "church in action!" We knew that there was really no such thing as "just caring" without doing something.

We are a society that has gotten *very* good at wearing the ribbons. We have a ribbon for each occasion, strapping it onto our profile picture or collar or social media post or car bumper at just the right time of the year. This type of caring usually has a couple slogans that go with it, something like, "You have my thoughts and prayers." "Thinking about you." "Sending love." And my Southern favorite, "Bless your heart."

Who could have imagined that we could ever become so proficient in the language of caring and so distant from the act of it? Why is that?

Can I just admit that caring is hard? Because caring requires me to stand up. Caring requires me to move myself in ways that, frankly, don't advance my comforts. Caring means putting the needs of others up there with my own, and sometimes even above my own.

Let's be honest, it's easier to just wear the ribbon.

This sums up one of our greatest struggles with solving environmental issues today. We are almost incapable of caring about something that isn't more concrete, that isn't right in front of us. When we talk about the consequences of climate change, they are almost always distant and far off. But the actions they require of us are immediate and in the now. It is very difficult to motivate people to dramatically change their lifestyles today for outcomes that are seemingly in a distant time and space.

For many of us then, caring for the earth just feels hard. Perhaps it wasn't always this way. In a different time in history, when humanity lived closer to the soil, closer to the water we drank and bathed from, closer to the plants we consumed, maybe it wasn't so hard then. But today—wow, it's a lot. I've spent a good portion of my life at this point just trying to convince other people to care for our common home. On the outset, you wouldn't think it would be such a tall order. Yet, it certainly can be.

Why is that? We live in a different time. We live in an age when many of us, especially here in the Global North, are pretty isolated from the natural world, at least in comparison to previous ages. We are housed, insulated, light-fixtured, screen-tertained, and fed from a microwave and a drive-through window. In some ways, to really care would mean to be in conflict with much of what makes up our everyday lives.

So, let's all say it together: *"This is hard."*

It can be hard to avoid plastic every single time we go out for food, groceries, or any home good. It can be hard to lower my carbon footprint when I have to drive everywhere I need to go, turn my kitchen lights on, cook dinner, and cool my home.

Do I want to travel the world? Absolutely! Who doesn't want to see Paris? And what better way to "get away, rest, and refuel" from life's work than travel? But what do we do when these "getaways" become the number one carbon-intensive consumer choice I can partake in?

We could go down the list and talk about the kind of diets and practices we have. In reality, there is no choice that you or I make that doesn't have an ecological impact. Everything you do changes the earth.

Yet, in the wake of something so enormous as global environmental degradation and warming oceans, to a changing climate, how much will my personal home thermostat really affect? I mean, come on! Can't we all just be left alone to wear our ribbons, watch Netflix, and eat Ben & Jerry's? To be honest, that sounds kind of like a good time!

Here is something that I have observed over the years. Many people who possess a healthy base level of knowledge in understanding our environmental crises, who have all the means necessary to make great personal choices toward caring for our common home, often continue to make poor day-to-day decisions when it comes to caring for creation.

What's up with that?

What I've learned is that there are a couple of possible explanations. Either, despite what they have heard, in the wake of climate change and the array of environmental problems, some people don't believe what they do with their small lives matter in the grand scheme of things. In a recent conversation, it was retorted to me with a sarcastic laugh, "Yeah, what I do here really matters, meanwhile large corporations are spewing tons of carbon into the atmosphere!" (We love talking about the responsibility of big corporations as our excuse to not take responsibility for our own actions.)

Or, deep down, despite having all the information and resources to live different kinds of lives, the temptations of culture are just too alluring. The meat is too juicy, the entertainment too catchy, the toys too shiny, and we're just on a watermelon-sugar high. Altering our lifestyles to help the earth loses out every time to the weekend shopping spree and Steak 'n Shake.

Maybe if we're honest, I wonder if it's a bit of both? A bit of doubt and a bit of addiction?

There's another group of people I'll mention here though. These are the people doing it. They're traveling with reusable cutlery in their car glove boxes, repairing old scooters in their makeshift, wooden-pallet garages and driving them to work; they're raising chickens, goats, living off the land, and protesting the chains of injustice. Yet, even in the midst of it all, ecologically induced depression and anxiety sometimes haunts them, providing a secret undercurrent that cast shadows for their life.

So, I can't help but wonder if we're all thinking about it backwards.

What if we're still going about ecological care from the completely wrong direction?

What if we're looking at it from the top rather than the bottom?

What if the whole thing requires joy, but we're trapped by the grief and incapacitation of it all?

Could it be that we need a little more permission to be human?

What if I told you that *being human* is the secret sauce to caring for the earth in all the right ways?

PERMISSION FOR PARADES

It's completely natural that we all struggle so much with earth care. Not just in the "this is hard" sort of way, but in the way that being "eco-friendly" confronts so much of the *way* we've done life for so long. If we're honest, we have a lot of fondness attached to the way of things. It's more than just something being hard, it's about taking the things that we like, the things that are *familiar*, and then calling them bad! This would be wildly difficult for anyone.

One of my all-time favorite things is to wake up on Thanksgiving morning and watch the Thanksgiving Day Parade. Do I understand that this parade and the Friday that follows are the epitome of our Western consumer culture? Yes, but can I just say I have a lot of fond memories for all that consumer chaos? (See, you thought I was just blowing smoke with all that hypocrisy talk!) I know I am, for sure, not supposed to say this, but there is just something about the holiday hubbub that is kind of fun and nostalgic! Lights, shopping, even the ridiculous ads and letters to Santa, the weary M&M commercial with Saint Nick—you know the one. What a ridiculous mark of the age that we live in!

I think it's totally normal to have nostalgia for all these things. Something about it is comforting, in the way that it is familiar, that it reminds us of times past, family, growing up, or just the life that we knew that feels safe. Ultimately, we are creatures that are capable of loving almost any place. It's no surprise that we come to appreciate all the things and parts of culture that we do, regardless of whether they are actually good for us. So, as someone who spends his waking life hoping to help other people alter theirs toward a holistic earth-friendly posture, maybe shaming, guilting, and demonizing even the most consumeristic thing that someone enjoys is not a great way to go about it.

Maybe today, what you need is just some permission. So here we go, from me to you.

You, my friend, have permission to *not hate* consumerism.
You have permission to authentically enjoy and cherish *stuff*.
You have permission to look back with fondness and a degree of nostalgia on the unique culture that made you.
That is OK. And, I would add, normal.

[Insert deep breath here.]

Does that mean you condone any harm that consumerism caused and is causing? No, of course not. Does that mean that you desire to see human and nonhuman creation endure suffering at the hands of sweatshops, planned obsolescence, or wastefulness? No way.

It's OK to give thanks for your story, even if it's not perfect. It's part of how you got "here." And here is where we are. There's nowhere else to start but here.

I still watch that parade full of theater dancers, Black Friday ads, pop singers, and balloons with my girls on Thanksgiving morning. Do I know it's one big, three-hour advertisement telling me to "Shop at Macy's"?

Yeah, I know.

Yeah, this is part of it. But I know we won't support it. I know that our family does more than just wearing ribbons. We may watch it (for now). We may see it. We may even get a waft of its fruity scent and enjoy the colors. But as for me and my house, we won't be eating it. We're not buying what they're selling.

We can experience some enjoyment without having to possess the experience. And there may yet come a time when we finally do say, "You know, we're done with this." When we're on the other side of that which used to bring joy but no longer does.

Here's one last bit of permission.

Consider whatever it is that causes you to struggle with caring for the earth because it's in conflict with something you have affection for. What are some things about our consumeristic culture that you really enjoy, yet they have negative environmental impacts? What has been part of your story, but something is nudging you to leave it behind? Jot a few of these things here:

Now, one by one, give thanks for the joy that each thing brought you.

With God our Creator's help, receive the permission to mature and grow from who you were and where you started to who God is shaping you to become, a human created in the image of God living your life on a place called Earth.

Would you be willing to take steps toward letting these things, patterns, collections, habits, tools, or traditions go for the life of the world?

So if anyone is in Christ, there is a new creation: everything old has passed away; look, new things have come into being!

2 CORINTHIANS 5:17

God, I confess that I have fallen short of your divine intention for my life. That in times when I should have cared more, I couldn't have cared less. In times when I could have spoken up, picked up, cleaned up, and mended—I didn't.

God, admittedly there are times when I don't care.

Or rather, I don't want to care. Times when I fear that I have utterly failed at caring.

Deep down, I want to care deeply, but so much gets in the way.

I confess that I often feel powerless to care. Like swimming upstream against corporation and culture, waste and wealth, powers and principalities.

God, cleanse the thoughts of my heart by the inspiration of your Holy Spirit. Give me a new mind set on your healing activities amidst a groaning creation. Transform my apathy into empathy. Help me to see myself within the setting you have set me, as your means of grace in this place and time.

In my weakness, Lord, be made Strong.

In my smallness, be Great.

In my human frailness, be Sustainer.

Just as we are your hands and feet,

Oh Christ, be our Head.

Spirit be our Breath.

Creator be our Heart.

Amen.

Chapter 2 | Eco-Confessions

Some approach "being eco" as if it were just a knowledge gap. All you have to do is learn all the tips, find out how to be a conscious consumer, and be trained on how to become a policy advocate. I should say, if you learned all that, it would certainly be amazing—and, just maybe, your brain would turn a nice eco-green color! But we know that a lack of knowledge isn't the only thing that matters because, frankly, the permafrost is still melting.[1]

Many of our ecological problems today are inadvertently due to a knowledge overdose. As agrarian author Wendell Berry suggests, our ironic downfall may be that we are experts in everything.[2] Expertise *does not* translate into correct action. (And if you watched the 2024 Olympic breakdancing competition, you know what I'm talking about!) We know so much about what is going on around the entire world and it's just . . . too . . . much. War in the Middle East, wildfires out west, heat waves up north, the tsunami in Asia-Pacific. It's all more than we can handle. Back home, we've got a lineup of heated political debates about gun control, abortion, racial discrimination, and the

1. Younger, "NASA Helps Find Thawing Permafrost."
2. Berry, *What Are People For?*

never-ending decisions about what they're teaching our children in schools. We're often absorbing all this "news" as we drive to and from work in the morning or while we're making dinner. "After all of that, on top of it all, you're telling me I've got to be an environmentalist as well?!" OK, maybe that is putting it bluntly, but perhaps that's how it feels for you. So rather than being in action, we're in apathy and exhaustion. Rather than feeling equipped, we're feeling immobile. It's no wonder that apathy becomes a dominant feeling toward earth care, because it feels just too big. What can I *really* do about all of that?

What if we had a different posture around informational intake? One confession that's hard but freeing—"I don't know." What if "I don't know" is a valuable posture in life?

> If we're being transparent, there will always be . . .
> news that we're not "up on,"
> great books we haven't read,
> wonderful music we haven't listened to,
> places we've never been,
> and loads of education that we'll just never have.

Out of all the confessions, "I don't know" is a harder one. To admit that we are lacking. No one wants to receive *that look*. You know, the look that people give other people when they're aghast that you haven't watched the latest episode of whatever the new "hot show" is or heard of "that artist." That's a confession we all struggle with, to say that we haven't seen it and we haven't heard it. We don't have all the information or answers, and we don't really know what the outcomes will be. We don't have it all figured out. Maybe this is why the tree of the knowledge of good and evil looked so delicious. We want to be all-knowing.

As parents, that fruit is more tempting than ever. Our sweet little children look up to us as the source of all knowledge and we wear that hat for as long as we can. But like all parents, at some point, we face a critical decision when those late-night questions start rolling in from your seven-year-old.

Where did God come from? Is Gran-Gran in heaven right now watching us? Why don't turtles have eyebrows? (Questions may vary!)

"Wow, Honey . . . I don't know."

CHAPTER 2 | ECO-CONFESSIONS 17

I wish I knew. I want to know. But I'm also a little frightened to know. Mystery has a way of keeping us humble and grounded, doesn't it? Not knowing can remind us of our human limitations. I am not the all-knowing one.

Information is a form of control, and we like being in control. Being in control is comfortable and secure, but admitting our ignorance is neither of those things. Saying "I don't know" may be the spiritual practice we all need in an age when technology and AI become our tools to know all things.

I wonder if there isn't something sacred about the limitations to our knowledge?

Is the human brain capable of knowing all things? If it were, would that be good? Would we be happy? Would life be simple then? Would we need each other? Would we become like a giant brain-shaped meteorite crashing to the ground in blinding informational glory? Could our knowledge become our own undoing? It feels like a backwards inquiry, but for the first time in history, maybe it's an important question. Because today, through this keyboard, screen, and Wi-Fi connection, I could spend the rest of my days drinking knowledge from a bottomless cup.

I'm sure I'm not the only one who gets that ominous notification from my phone that tells me how much screen time I've had this week. Every time I see that weekly update, I choke and gasp, "I was on my phone how long!?" In an age when we can scroll forever, how many scrolls will we consume? How many will consume us? If you have set these limits on your device, you're all-too-familiar with that white screen that states, *"Time Limit. You've reached your limit on Facebook."* ... *"Ignore Limit for Today."*

Acquiring knowledge is necessary for life. Further, it's part of what makes humanity special, our quest for betterment through more knowledge! I'm not advocating for mental atrophy or forgoing opportunities for continued learning and discovery. Yet, if we aren't careful, we may consume so much of it that we wake up the next morning naked, covering ourselves with fig leaves, with a data hangover.

Because there are no set limits on information. We can have as much as we like. Back in the day, it at least required a deal of effort to get the kind of knowledge we can have in moments now. My children know that if they want to find out the answer to a question, they can always ask Alexa. We are venturing into the ages where mom and dad no longer are the keepers of information. It's scary territory, especially for dads like me who would prefer to be the keepers of all knowledge! The technological power of AI is right there ready to quench our information-thirst and play Imagine Dragons to our heart's content.

Here's the deal: we already have more information than we have the ability to respond to.

The state of our planet is the perfect example. When it comes to how to care for planet Earth, we already have so much of the information that's required to heal this brokenness. The data may tell us what's wrong, even how to act, but it doesn't get us there, it doesn't move us.

Really, I think the action happens in our gut. It's within our gut that we are moved to compassion in the world, which is precisely how the ancient Hebrew people understood it. And, of course, thousands of years later, we're discovering the "gut-brain axis."[3] So, maybe there really is something to "digesting information!"

I suppose this is my "bone to pick" with knowledge, that we treat it as our great purpose, the end goal, or as our theologian friends might say, the *telos*. But that's the very mistake we've been making all along. Today, there are more educational degrees in the western world than ever before, and yet so much societal injustice and brokenness still exists. To reiterate, we know that knowledge and information aren't inherently bad, education is a wonderful thing, but we cannot make it our lives' "be-all and end-all." If we *acted* on half of the knowledge we already possessed, we'd change the world.

This is why the incarnation, Jesus the Christ on earth, is always the Word (the *Logos*) jumping off of the page for us. The Word made Flesh. Jesus is always leading the way for us. If we're going to follow Jesus, our words must take on flesh. By all means, keep growing, be a lifelong learner, attain knowledge! Just make sure that knowledge gets a body. And don't be afraid to say, "I don't know," and when you say it,

---

3. Clarke, "What Is the Gut-Brain Axis?"

maybe pause and look for a friend, look for Indigenous wisdom, pray ... and then maybe ask Alexa.

Here is a way to think about it and some guiding questions.

In the age of limitless information, where do we draw the line? What outcomes are we gaining from what we are learning? Is what we are learning changing the world for the better? Making us better humans on earth? Or, is it scrolling for scrolling's sake? Are we intoxicated with too much information?

Does the knowledge we're seeking help us become better people? Live better in our communities? Does the knowledge we're gaining help us love God, neighbor, or nonhuman creation better?

In the age of informational overload, maybe those questions can help to thin out our knowledge intake in order to let some air in and space to breathe and digest. Just maybe that's where we'll find a new awareness of Spirit.

JABRONI

If you've known me at any point since middle school, my favorite way to throw a little shade is to call someone a *jabroni*! So much so, my brother-in-law gave me a hat with the word stitched on it. I guess I had that coming! Ever since Dwayne Johnson, *The Rock*, strutted around a nineties' wrestling ring throwing that dis down, it's been stuck in my head. It always makes for a playful way to say, "Hey man, not cool! Know your role. Don't be a jabroni."

Sometimes it's not playful though. Sometimes there are *real* people doing *real* jabroni things out there. I like the word because it always feels like it can go both ways. And sometimes people you know, and even people you don't know, need to be called out on some ridiculous things. Yet, as time passes, I find myself asking more and more: "Am I the jabroni?"

Recently, in one of those down-home country moments, we were at my parents' place with some of our friends taking a hayride, like you do. Our kids were having a great time meandering around back country roads while lying in itchy hay being pulled around by a tractor. We slowly wound our way up and down old hills taking spectacles at the hillbilly collections decorating the front yards. If you didn't know, it's called "country clutter" for a reason. When you live out "in the sticks" while still amidst the culture of stuff that we do today, it's not so easy to rid oneself of that clutter as in the city. Often, all that paraphernalia just ends up hanging around your property. Old rusted cars and tractors setting out in yards are half decoration and half essential! Barrels, buckets, toys, and chairs are statues frozen in time, as if touched by the White Witch in Narnia from some age long gone, waiting for the breath of new life.

We slowly crept along back roads, and our kids were getting an eyeful of this special part of country culture. As we rolled by one John Bunyon-looking fellow down in the holler amidst his yard-belongings, burning some items in a barrel, our kids took the opportunity to yell a few things akin to, *Hey! Hey! You're killing the earth! Polluter! Don't pollute!*

Needless to say, I face-palmed hard, made eye contact with my friend, and inquired, "Are our kids bullies!?" My wife caught it first: "They're eco-bullies!"

We couldn't help but laugh! Our children, in their upbringing, had been well-equipped with the important knowledge of earth care, but such knowledge in the hands of eight- and nine-year-olds always has the potential to become a taunt on the playground.

Admittedly, they were little eco-jabronis.

As funny as it was, the moment gave me pause. No one wants to be eco-bullied. (Or bullied at all!) If I feel bullied, or pushed, or made to feel like crap, that's probably not going to motivate me to change my life. This is the critical differentiation that Brené Brown sharply points out for us between guilt and shame.[4] In her research, she highlights that shame is never helpful—in fact, it is quite harmful if we ultimately feel unworthy or unlovable through it.

Yet, quite unlike shame, guilt is a critical part of growing as a human. We need guilt in order to mirror back the things we might consider changing about ourselves. If we didn't have guilt, we would

---

4. Brown, *Daring Greatly*.

ultimately never accept the fact that we've done something wrong in life and turn the other way.

So how do we navigate this? How do we not eco-bully anyone? How do we not become the jabroni? How do we uphold social responsibility and promote doing things "better" while remaining in relationship with folks whom we don't always see eye-to-eye with? Our culture has a tendency to "cancel" anyone with these relational inconsistencies. However, if we've eco-canceled certain people or groups, we've likely burned their invitation to the party simultaneously. In the end, we don't want to exclude a group of people that are needed, in their own unique way, to care for our common home for all of our collective well-being.

We learn here that compassion must come alongside information. Is it possible that too much good information can turn us into unfriendly neighbors when we lack a spirit of compassion and empathy?

YOU CAN'T SAY THAT

I like to consider myself a fairly "up on the times" guy. Which, as I type that, admittedly it sounds like something an out-of-touch great-grandpa would say. I'm convinced that one of my wife's favorite pasttimes is telling me, "You can't say that."

After growing up in the countryside, my twenties and thirties were spent in the clearings, figuring out how much of the rural-bubble values of my past are worth passing on and which ones may need to evolve. (Which is really everyone's quest, isn't it?) For instance, where I grew up, there's only one restaurant (which is connected to our gas station and post office). So, guess where we ate? I love that little place; I grew up there, and it holds many memories. But if you're attempting to scope out where to get the best salad in Maury County, you might want to keep looking.

I've gotten a lot of things wrong. Being a middle class, middle-aged, white American man, my life is a field of mines. (I know everyone is playing their tiny violin for me!)

Today, some of us are being told that everything we have ever done, ever believed or valued, is . . . wrong. I don't know about you, but it's just not the nicest feeling. I think if we're honest, no matter how "wrong" the thing was, no one enjoys the correction, even if they welcome it. It hardly matters what social issue we're being brought to the altar for; once your eyes are open, the light can be painful in the beginning. Because how we've lived up until that point is just that, our life. The things we've consumed, said, valued, the way we've spent our time and recreation, the rituals we have, all of these things are part of the cultures of being who we were. Despite finding out that the things we bought, or the ways we lived our lives, or the things we used to say, caused harm in the world, change can still be difficult and close to the chest. So, on a side note, yes, there are immense wrongs in the world that should be altered in the function of society, but don't forget to be gracious with our human siblings (and with ourselves) as we navigate a new life.

Sometimes, it feels as if we live in the age of hyper-correction. We've discovered that much of the food we eat isn't good for us or the earth, how the clothes we wear have chemicals in them and oppress workers so we shouldn't wear them, and perhaps that our business has a gnarly carbon footprint.

I was recently having lunch with my friend Jerry for his birthday. "Jerry, it's your birthday, where do you want to go?" In truth, I knew where he wanted to go, because it's his favorite place. "Caleb, lets go to Wendy's!" he says. There I was, ready to take him almost anywhere in town, within reason. Nope, he wants fast food. Jerry wants Wendy's.

Wendy's is bad for everyone. From us, the people who are eating it, all the way to the abusive relationship with soil, animals, and atmosphere, to the field workers and the underpaid burger flippers.

For my friend Jerry, he really likes Wendy's. Wendy's is familiar, safe, affordable, and perhaps even nostalgic. It's connected to deep neural pathways forged for over fifty years, and that's OK. If we're being honest, we all have a "Wendy's." Some of us have a lot of them. There may be lots and lots of places and guilty pleasures for you.

So, here's a question. *What would it take for you, what information would you have to have, to alter your lifestyle choices and not "do Wendy's" any longer?*

There have been many studies on human behavior and the "why" behind the ways people choose to move about in the world. Again, we know that sheer information is only helpful to a point. We can understand that Wendy's isn't good for us or the world, but that information alone will not be enough to stop most of us from eating there if that's what we've learned to enjoy. (I recently heard of a comedian sharing that he would give his kids a punch in the arm every time they drove by a McDonald's and that seemed to eventually do the trick!)

When it feels that all my words, actions, and lifestyle choices are under the microscope and social critique of the masses, it may inadvertently make me feel *less emboldened* to make change and *more embarrassed* of my humanity. Worse, I might get offended and double down on what I enjoy, despite the evidence that it is not good for me or my home. Could it be that, even though the intentions of those around me pointing out my needed areas of improvement are good, I become more defeated or defensive than delivered? Is this anywhere close to something you've experienced when it comes to our call to care for creation?

There's this passage of Scripture in 1 Corinthians where Paul is in deep contextual dialogue with the church-folk of Corinth. Some pretty nonkosher things have occurred there like, for instance, some guy "hooking up" with his stepmom, and so Paul has paper to pen. In this time and place, there are some popular sayings or "maxims" around how people live and Paul, similarly, is "up on the times!" So, in the sixth chapter, Paul starts lining them up. He quotes a series of what would have been familiar axioms that the Corinthian believers knew. But Paul doesn't just quote them, he gives addendums to them; he qualifies them.

"*Everything is permissible for me,*" but not everything is beneficial.

"*Everything is permissible for me,*" but I will not be mastered by anything.[5]

I wonder if these are still the words we need today?

---

5. 1 Cor 6:12.

It's one thing to give yourself permission to cherish the memory of some thing or time that "the world" gave to you, but it's something else entirely to give "the world" permission to have mastery over you.

Here is what I mean. For the Corinthian believers, in the vein of "everything is permissible" and in the effort of being masters of their own lives, they were becoming mastered by their desires and the "freedom" they sought. What was thought to be liberty had become a vessel for captivity.

You know you're mastered when you can't say "No." When you can't turn it down. When you can't change course. When you can't turn and go the other way . . . because you're a servant to something else. Mastered.

We should all be continually considering who our master is. Who or what has a hold of us. Sure, everything is permissible! But not everything is beneficial. Not everything is good. Not everything is an expression of loving God.

Honest confession, there is a part of me that has a hard time when I see people frequently traveling around the world for fun. Jealousy and eco-anger make devilish dance partners. Sure, it's hard to see the people around you making decisions that you know are greatly harming the earth. Whether it is witnessing the ongoing purchases of new cars or gadgets, the continual eating out, or the consumption of harmful products, it becomes hard to watch. After analyzing the research, reading the books, listening to the interviews, and viewing the footage, I don't just see a purchase or a meal; I see faces of people enslaved, open-pit mines, pesticides, cancer rates, bee colony collapse, negative birth outcomes, melting glaciers, food scarcity, polluted rivers, and another super-cell hurricane making its way inland. I see how all of these are connected with our seemingly "insignificant" choices. (Yeah, I know that's a lot to consider for a trip out to Trader Joe's and a burrito.)

If I'm honest, I've been angry, resentful, envious, and indignant at times. This comes after years of doing *every single thing* I can to draw down my ecological footprint, to not participate in excessive a healthy atmosphere for tough eco-conversations with your friends, neighbors, or faith community?

> *God, we ask that you grant us the gift of embodying grace with those around us. A grace like yours. A grace that isn't violent, yet isn't passive, but a grace that is transformational. Show us the way forward. Your way.*
> *Amen.*

ECO-EPISTLE

Wrestling with the difficult tension of a hurting creation, eco-guilt, the avoidance of shame, and a spirit of love, I found myself turning to the New Testament epistles and Paul's letters to the churches.

How did apostle Paul navigate this? How did the early church move from the old ways into the new way of Christ and all the struggles that lay therein? There was so much that the early church had to "leave behind" in their old ways of doing things. Could the New Testament have more to teach us about discovering new ways of living in order to be good news for the world?

To this end, I will borrow Paul's Letter to the Philippians and offer an eco-paraphrase. For clarity, *this is not Scripture*, but I'd like to explore a way forward for us using the spirit and words of Paul's writing.

> *Servants of Christ Jesus,*
>
> *To all the saints in Christ Jesus who are members of God's good creation:*
>
> *Grace to you and peace from God our Father and the Lord Jesus Christ.*
>
> *I thank my God for every one of you. You are always in my prayers, as I pray with joy for your partnership in the good news of keeping creation. I am confident of this, that the one who created you in his image will continue to complete it until the day of Jesus Christ. It is right for me to think this way about all of you; we are all part of God's cherished creation and, as believers, we are called into the special work of stewardship as partners in God's grace towards the creation. For God is my witness, how I long for all of you with the tender affection of Christ Jesus to fulfill*

your calling here on earth. And this is my prayer, that your love may overflow more and more toward God, neighbor, and all that God has made, with knowledge and full insight to help you proclaim the gospel in all creation, so that in the day of Christ you may be pure and blameless, having produced the harvest of righteousness that comes through Jesus Christ for the glory and praise of God.[6]

This paraphrase helps to frame the spirit in which we are meant to dialogue with one another in the church. Sure, Paul also had some stern words in the epistles, yet each letter is saturated with generosity and the love of God. Paul had a kind of perspective on the situation that few did. Amidst the grief, the urgency of the gospel, the murderous threats towards the church, and even his own imprisonment, he was gracious beyond compare.

How might we take hold of a posture of love, grace, and honesty with one another as we approach dialogue on the essential work of stewarding God's creation, as we were created to do?

Once visiting a college campus, I had the joy of being in a large room packed with students in a dialogue on creation care. It was so much fun! For almost two hours, we wrestled with questions around all the tangible struggles of why and how to implement these acts of care in our lives. We talked about the implications of how all our choices in life are tethered to the well-being of human and nonhuman creation around the world. There is complexity to our choices when we embrace the reality of how we shop, eat, and commute to work are interconnected with the commandment to love our neighbor.

Close to the end of our time, a young man several rows back cautiously worked his hand upward. The mic was passed around and he held a brief pause then asked, "Are you saying that if I go out and eat a cheeseburger tonight or fly home for Thanksgiving (because I live very far away) that . . . I'm going to hell?"

I could tell by his posture that this student's inquiry was very sincere. There were no snarky tones present, simply genuine authenticity.

---

6. Adapted from Phil 1:1–11.

I thought it was a very brave question on his part. I love this question because it got straight down to it; it went straight to the thing so many were likely already turning over in their minds. It's a great question because he connected some important dots for us, that what we believe about salvation is entangled within this conversation. But it also broke my heart because of the anxiety, fear, guilt, and maybe even shame that was there.

My response to him was from a foundational truth I've found myself returning to over and over.

Here is the thing. At the end of the day, I don't care for creation because I think it's the right thing to do, or because of all the bad things that are happening in the world, or because of fear, or anxiety, but I care for creation because I am Christian. Being good stewards of what God has made is an outpouring of who I am as created in the image of God, a wonderful part of God's salvific work through me to the world. If God is walking around with an eco-scorecard, we're all in trouble.

THE ECO-SCORECARD

For the first time in history, we can come close to seeing what an individual's ecological footprint actually is. We can look at income, square footage, number of cars owned, distance traveled, and foods consumed to get a pretty clear image of what a personal imprint and toll upon God's creation is. How much does our personal life impact this great big planet called Earth?

Yet sometimes this new awareness can spiral us into states more reflective of panic than peace. So, we wage war even harder on environmental injustice. Our weapons of combat are riding bikes, eating more beans and less meat, hang-drying laundry, being picky about the brands we buy and the things they are packaged in; we are adjusting our thermostats, unplugging appliances in a flurry, shortening our showers, constructing our rain barrels, and calling our senators. So, why don't we feel more at ease about things rather than more anxious? The answer, of course, is right there.

If the ecological care in your life is marked by "waging war on environmental injustice," your spirit will inevitably feel less like harmony and more like you're having a heart attack. In other words, if the posture that you approach earth care from is out of a battlefront or savior complex, the harder the fall will be in the end. As we know, love is the true engine of restorative justice in the world, not fear.

There is a quote that often gets attributed to the eighteenth-century founder of Methodism and rock star preacher John Wesley. While it's unlikely that he actually said this, it represents his fiery "all you can" spirit!

> *Do all the good you can,*
> *By all the means you can,*
> In all the ways you can,
> In all the places you can,
> At all the times you can,
> To all the people you can,
> As long as ever you can.[7]

This is what we hope for in regard to caring for God's creation, that justice might permeate every "all" of our lives. In fact, at some point, speaking of "creation care" is unhelpful because, in doing so, we are separating and making it something else "to do"—when we are simply speaking of care as "intentionality." It's about *the way* in which you're "to do" all the things you already do.

Can we exhibit this "all you can care" in a non-anxious way? Without a mental breakdown along the way?

How do we simultaneously acknowledge the seriousness of earth's current state of brokenness and not either be apathetic, burnt out, or just frozen in place?

You can't grow a tree without growing deep roots. Without those deep roots you're susceptible to storms and many hazards. But with them, you give life and shade to all those around you. In other words, you've got to have the base notes. The foundation. Could the rootedness of our care lie in our most basic confession of faith?

The words we need here date back to our earliest creedal saying, "Jesus is Lord."

"Jesus is Lord" is what we are always setting in front of ourselves to remember as the people of God. Not because we're going to get in

---

7. Attributed to Wesley, "Rule of Life."

trouble if we forget it (although inadvertently, we might!), but because it puts *everything else* in perspective.

This is about what happens when we move from creedal statement to something "written on our hearts." You see, when we confess that Jesus is Lord, we are simultaneously confessing that we are not. When Jesus is Lord, there is power to put our scorecards away. We put them away not because we aren't going to do anything about the injustice in the world, not because nothing we do matters (because if we were apathetic, we couldn't rightly confess that Jesus is Lord), but because we aren't the savior.

Only through this faithful rootedness will we be able to look at something as big as climate change in the eye, respond in all the healthy ways one can respond, and still not end our days in a ball of hopeless despair. Our confession of Jesus as Lord of heaven and earth is our necessary reminder that "He's got the whole world in His hands" (a song I return to again and again with my children and entire church)! I don't drive a Prius, grow a pollinator garden, eat locally, use bamboo toiletries, plant trees all around my neighborhood, and continually annoy my state representative because I am going to save the world . . . but rather as an act of hope, confessing that Jesus is saving the world and I get to participate in that coming kingdom here and now! My life, the loving of all my neighbors within creation, is an act of love toward God who is the central Actor within this salvific drama, however it plays out.

Now to answer that question that people are always asking, "How do you balance hope and despair and all the many things that can make up living 'eco-friendly' in a time such as ours?"

We confess that Jesus is the Christ. Our part is to be faithful. Our part is that we get to join in with what Christ is already doing in the world. Hope then is something we experience as we both confess this *and* find ourselves participating in the compassionate work of being Christians on earth.[8]

---

8. For more on the conversation of hope and environmental care, see Wirzba, *Love's Braided Dance*.

For thousands of years, no human has ever had to deal with all the things that you have to deal with today. Never at any other point in human history has someone had to make as many choices as you and I make in a single day. Never before has the decision to buy a phone or a piece of fruit been so entangled with global economics, deep carbon footprints, or human slavery the way it all is today. The entanglement of responsibility and choices set before us doesn't seem fair at all.

If we can summarize part one of our journey together, it is grace.
Grace to be human.
Grace to be vulnerable.
Grace enough to have gotten it wrong, to have messed up along the way, and to have missed the mark when it comes to caring for God's creation.
Grace for each other.
Grace enough to see the great situation that lies ahead and acknowledge our limits.
Grace as we "lean on the everlasting arms."
Grace as gravity has its way with us.

For my eco-readers out there, I realize you may be ready to scream and cast stones. Because it certainly feels that the last thing the earth needs today is for wealthy Westerners talking about cutting ourselves some slack. But what we must catch is that if we don't change from a place of anxiety and shame and approach this critical work as loving, frail, authentic, finite human beings who are marked by the grace of God, we won't be able to sustainably approach it at all. If we are experiencing unsustainability in our very spirit, we certainly won't be able to approach sustainability in our bodies within the world.

Would you be willing to choose one new thing? Sometimes we feel as if we've got to be like a juggler in a circus, throwing seven objects into the air all at the same time. There is no such thing as doing everything all at once, and those who do balance many practices at once have become proficient at it over time. Let me encourage you to pick one new eco-practice to learn and begin working on.

Work at it for thirty days. Chew it. Hold it. Wear it around. Talk about it. Be playful with it. Plant it. Process it.

Then, before you know it, you're suddenly getting better at it! Watch how it grows. Watch how it becomes second nature. Afterwards, add on a second habit to begin forming. Out of all the eco-habits that began as difficult for me, I can barely remember any of them. Because in the arc of time, what began as hard has long been forgotten by muscle memory.

Changing diets, shopping habits, or daily routines are all on the table!

One great example of this that comes to mind is the temperature in our home. For some people, they really can't imagine keeping their HVAC at 67 or 68 degrees in the winter or 78 degrees in the summer. Yet, after allowing your body to acclimate, it becomes just the normal comfortable temperature. Humans are incredibly adaptable; it's just that in our new culture of comfort, we have the money and technology to force the natural world to adapt to us instead.

What are you going to do? Try not to move on from this point in the book until you've chosen.

In part two, we move further up and further in to understand this odd struggle that now exists between many of our lives and the rest of God's creation. Hope you've got your parachutes!

> *Lord, to say that we've done things the wrong way would be an understatement; a failure to confess the whole of our sin. We confess, Lord, that we've been guilty on many counts and occasions. Forgive us for any way in which we have become the jabroni, even in spirit or posture or ways unknown or unseen. Infuse us, Lord, with your graciousness that is reflected unto us through your ever hopeful creation. Like trees faithful to bring forth green leaves every spring, help us to come out of cold seasons into seasons of new life. Help us, Lord, to photosynthesize your love. Help our branches embrace, our fruit be nutritious, our roots be thirsty and deep, and our shade be a refuge for the community of creation. God, help us to be the kind of human you desire us to be.*
> *Amen.*

PART TWO

Tall Buildings in a Single Bound

Chapter 3 | Skydiving in the Anthropocene

THERE IS A ROCK on my front porch with painted pink flowers and some large letters. It says, "Escape the Ordinary." I have no idea where it came from; quite literally, it recently just appeared there. We have more than a couple of sweet neighbor ladies who frequently drop things off for us; I suspect perhaps it was one of them. I've rolled the cute little rock-phrase over and over again in my head. Escape the ordinary.

Escaping the ordinary is our cultural obsession, isn't it? We generally want to be anything but ordinary, regular old humans. In fact, we so want to escape the ordinary that we've built entire economies upon just that principle. Everywhere from hardware stores to shopping malls are helping us fulfill our dreams of escaping the ordinary as they sell us new, shiny, and fun toys. There's even someone out there writing it on rocks and selling them for profit.

It does make you stop and wonder, what is so bad about ordinary?

When my dad turned sixty, it was "do or die." So, he decided to try both and booked a ticket to go skydiving. Upon hearing about his existential quest for meaning, I didn't like the fact that he was going alone, so I went, too. If I'm honest, it was also a bit of a personal challenge. Jumping out of an airplane for the first time is 100 percent not as sexy as it sounds or looks in movies. Sitting in a little rusty airplane with a four-foot ceiling, two benches with no seat belts running parallel down the plane, as you climb to the jump point. If you've never gone skydiving, you should know that unless you're certified, you have to skydive tandem. Tandem means that you are attached to the front of the "person in charge" by harnesses, like the small children you see secured to the chests of their parents at the zoo. Loosely strapped, straddling a bench, I lean over my shoulder and yell above the wind (the plane door is left open): "So, should we tighten these straps up a bit?!" When you're climbing thousands of feet into the air on a plane with no door or seat belts, your body loosely attached to a stranger you're going to jump out and free fall two hundred miles per hour with, there's a moment when you begin rethinking all your choices that somehow led you up to this point. At least that's what I did. The guy on the other bench was like "Oh yeah! This is awesome!"

What they don't tell you is that almost every single certified professional that you're going to be attached to will be making jokes the absolute entire time until the moment right before you roll out of the airplane. Like a flipped switch, once you finally enter the correct altitude and distance, it's "go time"; everyone is taking their job seriously now and you've got to get out of the plane rather quickly. The only way to achieve this is by tandem butt-scooting toward the opening in the plane, a three-by-four-foot hole out of which nothing but oxygen stares back at you. My "professional" suddenly zipped us tight, reminded me to bend backwards like a banana and just fall out! So, I did.

CHAPTER 3 | SKYDIVING IN THE ANTHROPOCENE

Skydiving is perhaps the most appropriate singular embodiment of the absurdity of the Anthropocene.

"Anthropocene" is a word that geologists began using many years ago to dialogue about how our planet has left behind the steady and familiar Holocene epoch (which has been the gracious environment we've been soaking in for the last ten thousand years) and moved into a new age.[1] What this new term Anthropocene communicates is that humans have dramatically altered the physical structure of our planet, so much so that we've now pushed ourselves out into a new time and thus a new place. It is an age so influenced by eight billion humans that it's named after us ("anthro" means human).

The term Anthropocene has now taken on deeper dialogue and a more robust meaning since its earlier geological debut. John Green notably explores the topic in his book *The Anthropocene Reviewed*. Chapter by chapter, Green cleverly offers a "review" of the different aspects of this new age we find ourselves living within. He writes about air-conditioning, Piggly Wiggly, Diet Dr. Pepper, teddy bears, Monopoly, and Super Mario Kart in amusing and thought-provoking ways.[2] There are a million and one oddities present within the created world today whose only unique purpose is to orbit around us humans. The world has been reshaped.

The planet we live on today is *not* the same planet in which our ancestors dwelt. Our world would be unrecognizable for them. For our ancestors, their relationship with creation was one of vulnerability, not domination. It was one of survival and humility, certainly not overconsumption, and certainly not exploitation. How could they exploit the land that they so depended upon? How could we?

On a visit to Washington DC, I once had the joy of exploring the Smithsonian National Museum of Natural History. Walking through,

---

1. "The overarching context of this report is this: human influence has become a principal agent of change on the planet, shifting the world out of the relatively stable Holocene period into a new geological era, often termed the Anthropocene," says the Intergovernmental Panel on Climate Change (IPCC). IPCC, *Global Warming of 1.5 °C*, 53.

2. Green, *Anthropocene Reviewed*.

I began to feel the sensation of being simultaneously small within the scope of history, and yet, being a part of the arc of time that is so much larger than myself. As I climbed the steps, I found myself entering the fascinating yet nerdy area of geology—the history of rocks, minerals, and space dust. As I enter, a sign reads, "Without any doubt, this is the oldest material you'll ever see. It is older than the Solar System itself." Behind a glass case inside a vial under a microscope was milky liquid with tiny diamonds that were acquired from a meteorite in the sixties. The material is a remnant from a dying star that accumulated into the cloud that is believed to have given birth to our solar system! (Feel free to marinate on that last sentence for a moment before moving on!)

I stood there for the longest time looking through the glass at the substance. If this is true, even though I'm seeing and reading it, I can hardly comprehend it. Imagine if we only believed in the things we could comprehend.

A few rooms over are artifacts we feel more familiar with: diamonds and jewels. A necklace and diadem that Napolean gave to his wife. The notorious Hope Diamond that has made its global tour for centuries, from rulers to thieves, aristocrats to museums with its deep blue purity. After moving room to room, up and down across the Smithsonian—ancient fossils, human skeletons, dinosaurs, mummies, insects, a tracing of the diverse span of existence that we've been able to measure over eons—something occurs to me. I have the realization that, while this is an attempt at presenting the journey of natural history, what we are really viewing are all the ways in which the natural world has evolved over deep time, particularly in the wake of human beings' increasing involvement.

While history has never been static, the earth has also never been static. What point in history you're referring to determines which "Earth" we are talking about, because the surface, substructure, atmosphere, and temperature of this place we call home is continually moving, inhaling, exhaling, and becoming. Yet, with loads of measurable data today, it is more clear than ever that humanity as a whole has set our planet on a disastrous course that is unnatural. Unnatural in that, for as far back as we can look (which apparently goes all the way back to stardust), nature has unfolded in a certain pattern and at a certain pace. As Christians, we might call it God's divine order in creation. For ages, every ecological change the earth has undergone has been through natural biological development, maturation, and slow transformation. Therefore, it's striking to see how "unnatural" Earth's history has become.

As I walk through the museum, I can tell that great labor has gone into conveying this very message on several exhibits, especially the ones about deep time and human involvement. Looking at the long pattern of the earth's climate, we know that the planet should now be entering into a new ice age. Yet, instead of cooling down, we have been warming up as greenhouse gas has accumulated in the atmosphere at extreme rates since the industrial revolution began. As modern mining injures the rocky substructure of the earth, burning petroleum depletes the ozone layer, and factory farming kills off biodiversity, it doesn't take a scientist to bring these findings to a conclusion. The natural order is interrupted.

Back out on the street, leaving the natural history museum, it's unmistakable how unnatural DC feels. Concrete monuments and statues erect on every corner acknowledging the heroes of our progress. It makes one wonder, what is this "progress?"

For my wife's and my fifteen-year anniversary, we took a family road trip in the Northeast where we explored New York City for a few days. On the first evening, we arrived and decided it would be fun to head straight toward Times Square, see the sight of it and find food. If you've ever stood on the streets of Times Square, you already know. When you look out your Manhattan window, you see something different than just Earth. We could've been on Coruscant for all I knew![3] *What planet are we on?*

I can't say I was surprised to discover that our children didn't really love being there. Our oldest daughter, who was eleven, turned to us after no time at all asking if we could leave and find somewhere quiet to go. In fact, a couple of months later, I chatted with some

---

3. In the *Star Wars* universe, Coruscant is a city-covered planet known as the Imperial City.

friends about their NYC trip and going to Times Square with their kids, who were teenagers; they also expressed how much they disliked the experience.

What is this place we have made? Lights and screens that grapple for your presence and claw at your money. Shop after shop, stores become the incarnation of the tale of a luring house made of sweets, operated by a witch who is looking to eat you up. Just like in the story of Hansel and Gretel, it may not be safe for those who are childlike.

There are no falling leaves to catch your fall here. No room for the sun to find your cheek between these towers. No air to find for your lungs between the taxis and smog. In this concrete jungle we've created for humans, while flashy and alluring, is the very place in which it might be most difficult to . . . *be human*.

Our world in the Anthropocene is the culmination of humanities' creation, which is, ironically, becoming the undoing of humans. It is a world that places the human race at the very center, only to find that our existence, at least as many of us have curated it within the Global North, is unsustainable. It's an existence that finds itself in the shallows, devoid of that which would allow the depth of human flourishing.

We've all been complicit in the making of this Anthropocene. Some much more than others. I must confess that flying up into an airplane just for the joy of jumping out into the sky and free falling with our fragile human bodies could be the crowning image and logo of a human-centric age. The ultimate high that might end in death—up in the clouds, slicing through the invisible barriers between being human and being angelic. Our privilege has temporarily blurred the lines for us between what's real or artificial. For eternal seconds, we're unsure if we are falling or flying. Since the dawn of the industrial revolution, a question resurfaces: "Are we gods?" This question lurks on the lips of our hearts as we soar above and over all that which was previously known to be our human limits as we break each record set by our ancestors, as we go where no human has gone before.

Since the days of early Genesis, we have climbed up to grab and consume that which was not meant for our consumption. It's our consumption assumption.

This is why the redeeming story of Jesus begins with resistance and fasting in the desert. Jesus resists craving, glory, and worldly power. Jesus refuses to jump and soar through the air on the wings of angels, quoting, "Do not put the Lord your God to the test."[4] God is the One who glorifies, which is exactly why the resurrected Christ, in the end, ascends into the heavens.

In the Anthropocene, I wonder, are we within the greatest age of temptation for cravings, glory, and power? Have we put the Lord our God to the test by jumping both feet into an existence that seeks to unsustainably surpass each and every gravitational gift we have been given?

SYCAMORE GAP

One of my absolute favorite movies growing up was *Robin Hood, Prince of Thieves*. We're talking pure gold with Kevin Costner, Morgan Freeman, Alan Rickman, a Sean Connery cameo, and Christian Slater! Yeah, I know, it's a lot of dudes . . . welcome to the nineties, right? Something about that film became comfort food. We all have stories that reconnect us to core memories and familiar seasons of life.

One of my favorite scenes occurs as Robin and his new friend, Azeem (Freeman's character), are walking through England's hills and dip low into a picturesque gap with a giant tree keeping watch at the bottom. It's an iconic site and moment marking the return of this character to his home, as Robin defends a boy from being taken by the Sheriff's men and the tree from being chopped down.[5]

I love that scene. It's filmed at a spot along Hadrian's wall, which is a rock wall built by the Romans thousands of years ago in Northumbria, spanning from one side of England to the other. After hearing the place was on my bucket list, a dear friend took a day road trip with me to visit the site during some time spent in the UK. It was magnificent. It was like seeing history in real time and is a memory I'll always have.

---

4. Matt 4:7.
5. Reynolds, *Robin Hood*.

Today, there is a shadow following that memory. In 2022, in the middle of the night, someone hiked out to Sycamore Gap, chain saw in hand, and felled the ancient tree that had so long stood watch there.

Utterly heartbreaking.

Why do we do this? What is that urge that comes from our bellies to our hands in order to express power over the natural world? What is this "human verses nature" urge that rises up in us? Why cut down an old tree that has spent its life looking after you and your ancestors?

For some, this posture is a game, a sport. It is the urge to "power-over" nature. In a time when many of us aren't required to push our bodies up against the soil, toil in the heat, and sweat for our bread, the terrain of the natural world looks to us as a recreational test of our limitations. Over three hundred bodies on Mount Everest are frozen testaments to this.

How far can we go? It's clear that some of us are out there on the mountain for different reasons. Not for an adventure, setting out to have a good experience *within* the natural world, but something else. Some people are out to prove something, to defeat something, to best a challenge, or even to best ourselves.

At times, I've found myself glued to the show *World's Toughest Race: Eco-Challenge Fiji*, hosted by Bear Grylls. The description is in the name! It's "adventure racing" in its most difficult form. Teams of four gather from countries all over the world to compete in a race across Fiji, hacking through jungle trails, rafting, sailing, diving, climbing, and biking for a total of eleven days. Once you get a couple of episodes in, it's hard to look away! Part of me is in awe of the impressive condition that these humans are in, and the other part of me sits there eating Chex Mix, thinking, "I could definitely do that!" (Being ridiculously overconfident occasionally is also a common human trait, right?) In reality, the people who have trained hard enough to put themselves through these courses are the "superhumans" of our time. After forty-eight seasons of *Survivor*, it's probably safe to say that we are absolutely fascinated with the question of "how far can humans push themselves?"

How tough are we?

How high can we really jump?

How long can we stand on this ledge?

CHAPTER 3 | SKYDIVING IN THE ANTHROPOCENE

In total honesty, a big part of me really wants to "get out there" and see what I can do! Perhaps, in an age when many of us spend too much time behind desks and screens, we crave to test ourselves—that is until we get winded on the stairs at the airport and reality sets in.

It is important to state that there is nothing inherently wrong with pushing our limits. There is something within us that craves this at times. Something about being human drives us toward bettering ourselves and becoming more than we were.

Yet, it's important to first return to those guiding questions from earlier before taking that fourteen-day trek into the jungle:

Is this really benefiting me?
Is this bettering my community or the earth?
Is this making me a more loving person?
Is this an outpouring of Christ in me?

Or is this about something else?
A quest to fulfill a craving that can't be satisfied?
An addiction to the climb?

Only you can answer those questions.

If there is one thing that feels consistent with human history, it's that we are going somewhere! We are a people who are growing in every way and all ways. (From what we know, we are even taller than we used to be![6]) From our ideas to our technology, to our ability to run a mile in under four minutes, we are not the people we used to be.

It *was* like this . . . but it's not like that anymore.

We know more, we've grown, we are maturing, we have more data, we know what worked and what didn't. While the eighties had some cool hair styles and fun music, it's not the eighties anymore, and thankfully, we wear seat belts now. Why? Because a lot of people died.

---

6. Hatton, "Why Did Humans Grow."

"You have heard it said . . . but I tell you . . . ." Once, it was eye for an eye, but now we say "love our enemy."[7]

In ancient times, to take an "eye for an eye" was a huge leap forward in society as a mechanism of justice. It was to say, let there be equality, a semblance of accountability and justice at work within your community. Then, thousands of years later, God returns saying, "OK now, we're ready to go further; I tell you, love those who persecute you." No doubt we are not the people we were, we are not in the same places, and all the walls have moved. It's part of the DNA of creation. It is the be-fruitful-and-multiply-ness of it all. It is the "creationivity," as I like to call it.[8]

But what happens when that proclivity toward creation continues, except through a posture of greed, selfishness, and then oppression? What happens when we use all our creativity to overcome the very limits God gave us in the first place?

GRAVITY

By such deductions the law of gravitation is rendered probable, that every particle attracts every other particle with a force which varies inversely as the square of the distance. The law thus suggested is assumed to be universally true.

$$F = G(m_1 m_2)/R^2$$

Isaac Newton

If we didn't have gravity, the earth would have no atmosphere and no life. There would be no guacamole, no salsa, and utter devastation. Gravity holds the air, water, and everything else in place. Gravity is everywhere, in and through all things. Everything in the universe has gravity. If you have mass, you exert gravitational pull. Of course, it may be very small compared to something as large as the moon, but friend, you've got gravity. Gravity can slow time, bend light, and make a pebble feel like a boulder.

---

7. Matt 5:38–44.

8. "Creationivity" is a word I use to describe what God gifts creation with in early Genesis. It is the creative gift of creation being able to participate in creating more . . . creatively! See Haynes, *Keeping Creation*.

CHAPTER 3 | SKYDIVING IN THE ANTHROPOCENE

Sometimes we even state that something has "gravity" to it. What we mean by this is that it's serious, important, or has weight. It calls to mind the Hebrew word *qabod*. Most commonly translated as "glory," *qabod* is also translated as "heavy." In Scripture, when we read about the *qabod* of the Lord, what is being conveyed is the power of the presence of God. It's about the significance of the physical manifestation of God's presence. When God shows up, it's gravitational! No wonder when the presence of God appears in Scripture people, immediately find themselves on their knees, from the prophet Ezekiel to Paul. Paul writes that

> at the name given to Jesus
> every knee should bend,
> in heaven and on earth and under the earth,
> and every tongue should confess
> that Jesus Christ is Lord,
> to the glory of God the Father.[9]

I wonder if that doesn't ultimately have to do with gravity's intended purpose. To pull us into postures of worship, not as a power-over kind of force, but as a loving invite, which is at the heart of this Philippians passage. Gravity invites us into postures of kneeling as it conveys the glory of God.

Yet, centuries into the "discovery," many aren't sure if gravity is a curse or a gift. It keeps us from leaping tall buildings in a single bound, but it also keeps us from accidentally throwing toddlers into space. Pretty important, I'd say.

I like to think of gravity as a boundary that helps keep things in check. Gravity is a law of nature that keeps our feet on the ground. We may often think about gravity like the leash that the dad has his three-year-old on at Target so he doesn't disappear. What if gravity is the line that keeps everything inbounds? Like part of the rules of the game? I always think about that scene in *Back to the Future 2* when Marty and Doc are flying through the air on the flying car highway. Can you imagine the chaos? We can't even navigate good driving on the ground! I know, I live in Nashville! (Although, by the time this book hits the shelves, flying cars are set to be on sale if you have a

---

9. Phil 2:10–11.

million dollars lying around.[10]) Gravity is a critical ingredient necessary for creation's thriving and human well-being. But, as we know, that didn't stop the Wright brothers!

Once those bros broke the flight barrier, it seems like we've been spreading our wings every day since. Today, you may just step outside for a moment and see multiple passenger planes, jets, news helicopters, or the neighbor kid's drone flying overhead. The sky is a busy place. We live in a new time when, if you have enough money and are among the wealthy elite, you can just hop up to outer space for a little drive. Take that gravity! What are the consequences of blazing past this universe-wide barrier?

On the surface, there are several negative ramifications. The most glaring result for the earth today is the tons of extra carbon emissions collecting in our atmosphere warming the planet. All those airplane flights up there spew an absolutely wild amount of carbon into the thickening blanket of our atmosphere.

Also present are all the secondary emissions that result from flying, which are the outcomes of a global-scale economy unlike anything seen in history. If people can go everywhere anytime, there must be more *things* for people to *consume* in each place they go. Think about how every exit on the interstate has a McDonald's, Cracker Barrel, or Starbucks. Now think of that travel trend globally. Consider every global drive-through order being fulfilled. Many once self-sustaining local economies have become almost entirely dependent on the tourism industry that has flooded their community. What does it mean that these places become even further dependent on humans continually traveling, spending, and consuming?

What if there are some even deeper ramifications to breaking that gravity barrier? What if there are sub-level consequences that we don't frequently name? What if part of who we've begun identifying ourselves as are creatures that can do *anything we can put our minds to*? What if we've begun to identify ourselves by the barriers we break and the boundaries we overcome? What if we're identifying ourselves by what we can *do* rather than who we can *be*?

Many of us are familiar with that kind of slogan. We're taught these life mottos growing up, like football players chant before they

---

10. *Science and Space News*, "Flying Cars Are Coming."

go back out onto the field: "Clear eyes, full hearts, can't lose!"[11] But wait, losing is a real thing; people lose all the time. In fact, just about every game has winners and losers. For you to win a game, someone has to lose it.

If we really can "do anything we put our minds to," what are the outcomes of such a posture? Can we just "try harder" and "achieve" anything we want? Is that the right question? If we were able to do such things, what horrors might we unknowingly unleash into the world? What have we already unleashed? What are the ramifications of coalescing our very identity as a people with ideals that buttress the narrative, "the sky is the limit," or, "if we can dream it, we can achieve it"?

What could possibly go wrong?

BABEL AND BRICKS

And they said to one another, "Come, let us make bricks and fire them thoroughly." And they had brick for stone and bitumen for mortar. Then they said, "Come, let us build ourselves a city and a tower with its top in the heavens, and let us make a name for ourselves; otherwise we shall be scattered abroad upon the face of the whole earth."

GENESIS 11:3–4

Human technology is a gift. It's an outflow of who we are created to be: creators. Sometimes, I sit on my back porch and stare in awe as one of those human-made "giant birds" fly thousands of feet over my head with hundreds of people on board. Our ingenuity and ability to create, build, and engineer cannot be denied. Looking back over just the last few hundred years, we have even amazed ourselves at what we've been able to achieve!

From steam engines, to typewriters, to the Nintendo Switch, we've made some impressive things. Our technology and creativity can offer much beauty in the world. We can only imagine how many lives have been saved or made better through modern technology. No, technology itself has not been our pitfall but our gift. Humanity's

---

11. If you haven't watched the show *Friday Night Lights* yet, what are we even doing here?

shortcoming has always been much deeper than that, found in our unsatiated desire for more. Our stumbling block might be best described as simply the quest for more blocks.

The story of the Tower of Babylon (or "Babel"—the Hebrew form of the name) is our oldest biblical record of human technology and how far it will take us. It's a technological story about bricks.

Today, these rectangular hard objects are everywhere and may not seem that impressive. But in the days of ancient Mesopotamia, bricks were a revolutionary technology. Before the days of flat, uniform building blocks, there were just stones. To build something required not just finding all of these big rocks but also stacking them. If you ever tried to build a large structure with a group of uneven rocks, you already know where this is going! It was hard, more labor intensive, and the finished product was often subject to the material available. (Even so, through years and years of hard labor, there are still some magnificent "pre-brick" structures surviving.) So, you can see how the brick was a giant leap forward in technology and civilization. The ability to make bricks gave humanity opportunities that we never had before. We would be strolling through shopping malls and hitting up Home Depot before you know it! But first, we had to build this tower.

Before there was Google Translate and Duolingo, we all spoke the same language, at least according to early Genesis. We had the bricks, we had the mortar, we had the language—it was time to do something big. How far could we go? How high could we climb? What couldn't we do if we all got in on it? "Let us make a name for ourselves," we said. So, we did. Brick on brick, we built; we began to climb, higher and higher, up to the heavens, unlimited! But then something disruptive happens:

> The Lord came down to see the city and the tower, which mortals had built. And the Lord said, "Look, they are one people, and they have all one language, and this is only the beginning of what they will do; nothing that they propose to do will now be impossible for them. Come, let us go down and confuse their language there, so that they will not understand one another's speech."[12]

---

12. Gen 11:5–7.

According to this narrative, God confuses our speech so that this great tower can no longer be built. What's the deal, Lord? I mean, aren't we created in the image of a Creator? Isn't this our jam? Why would you stop this? This verse in the middle of this story truly confounds us: *"This is only the beginning of what they will do; nothing that they propose to do will now be impossible for them."*

What is so wrong with that? Wouldn't that be a good thing?

The whole story reminds me of my children stacking their blocks just as high as they will go. I've seen it a hundred times. Smiles, excitement, joy, thrill that always ends in screams, tears, frustration, and somebody getting hurt. It would seem blocks can only be stacked so high before things go wrong. God sees something coming that we don't see.

Is it possible that the same technology that allowed us to advance and grow in the first place might also become our undoing? Is it possible that at some point, we might cross a line from technology that flows out of a posture of love and need to one of excess, comfort, and even greed and domination?

For the people of Israel, when you looked up "bad guys" in the dictionary, there was a picture of Babylon! From 2 Kings to Jeremiah to Isaiah and into the New Testament, Babylon is the image of that which is not of God. Finally, in Revelation, Babylon is named as the civilization that is the opposite of the kingdom of heaven, "practicing a politics of oppression and an economics of greed and exploitation."[13] You see, the Babylonian way of life is a means to talk about a life turned inward. It is a life captivated and clawing after whatever it is that you crave until you get it, for better or worse. Genesis 11, this ancient tower building story, is a lens to help us see many things more clearly.

It's not hard to see how this great tower has been built in our society. Just consider the "technological advancement" we call plastics. We've "progressed" to the point in which we've created a polysubstance that cannot be properly returned to God's soil as biodegradable. In our climb to go higher, we surpassed the brick with something strong yet pliable.

---

13. Pointed out in Linthicum, *Building a People*.

But at what cost? For the first time since the inception of plastics, we are getting a truly sober look at the ramifications of ongoing plastic distribution, night and day, for decades on end. Oceans and waterways have more plastic than fish.[14] The soil that we depend on for life has become a great victim of microplastics. With every single-use bag and brush, we participate a bit more in the Babylonian economy.

We are discovering how our bodies are swimming in a world of microplastics. These tiny plastic particles are in our soil, water, and air. Microplastics have been found in our bloodstream, in our heart, lungs, liver, kidneys, in our placentas, and inside our testicles.[15] There are plenty of educated guesses and ongoing study into the ramifications of these plastics within every organ of our bodies. It's sufficient to say, none of them are good.

These hard facts about plastic pollution and contamination are ones that every producer of single-use plastics knows very well. Yet, they are undeterred in their production for more. This kind of economy is one that takes and offers empty promises of giving back. It's an economy that feeds those on top of the tower and keeps those at the bottom hungry and enslaved.[16]

Turning the page to the second book of the Bible, the very next thing that happens is that this technological advancement of brickmaking is now the work of God's people enslaved in Egypt. The Egyptian empire has turned Israelite bodies into brick factories. Bricks, what once was a thing of beauty as humans expressed the creativity imbued within them from creation, became the ultimate symbol of oppression.

It's no wonder that, for the next forty years after their exodus from Egypt, the people of God lived in tents and tabernacles. The collective memory of bricks for God's people carried trauma.

Much later, David and Solomon really want to build God one of those big homes, but we learn that God, unlike Pharaoh, is not

---

14. Zhao, "Distribution of Subsurface Microplastics."

15. Carrington, "Microplastics Found"; Leslie, "Discovery and Quantification of Plastic"; Jenner, "Detection of Microplastics"; Ragusa, "Plasticenta."

16. See theologian Michael Northcott. He suggest that "global borderless capitalism is responsible for 'Babylonian captivity' of the earth in the Anthropocene" (*Political Theology*, 5).

CHAPTER 3 | SKYDIVING IN THE ANTHROPOCENE

interested in that. We find that the story of God freeing God's people from slavery *is also* a story of being liberated from an enslavement to technological "progress." God's liberation frees us from the chains of endless expansion and dominating empires. Exodus is a story of liberation from a kind of development that takes lives. It's a story of a freed people who set out toward a new land, ecologically life-giving, described by flowing milk and honey.

In his book *Starry Messenger*, astrophysicist Neil deGrasse Tyson points out that, other than salt, milk and honey are the only two foods humans have that don't originate from the death of something else.[17] Milk and honey are the exceptions to the rule that foods require killing. Which, as a Christian, should make your imagination run wild! "The land of milk and honey" is the very mark of how God's people come to know the promised land. Could it be that the kind of place God has in store for us is a land where life flourishes, we eat and are made well without violence?

I'm struck by the scene, thousands of years later when Jesus is leaving Jerusalem, he turns around to the disciples and, within earshot of the religious establishment, says, "See these great buildings? Not one stone will be left on another."[18] It makes you wonder, how much of Babylon did Jesus see in Jerusalem?

What if Jesus wasn't just prophetically referencing a future battle, the one in AD 70 that not only left the temple destroyed but something else as well? Does Jesus know a deeper truth? Is Jesus also referencing God's fulfilled kingdom on earth that will be the ultimate undoing of the kind of structures that carry injustice?

The stones that have been used to build injustice . . .

The stones that support the empire's work of captivity . . .

The stones that attempt to house religion yet abuse God's people . . . will come down.

I wonder, how much of what is built or defined as progress around us today is more like Babylon than the kingdom of heaven?

---

17. Tyson, *Starry Messenger*, 122.
18. Mark 13:2.

COTTON

Have you ever seen cotton grow? A field of white hair bearing their heads at the tips of short stalks. It always amazes me for some reason that cotton comes from a plant, rather than being sheared off the back of some domestic animal. Shearing would certainly be an easier way to get it, if it were possible!

The cotton engine, or better known as the cotton gin, was invented in 1793 by Eli Whitney (as you may remember from a deep grade-school memory buried in your mind). Harvesting cotton was historically not that profitable and very tedious. It begins with harvesting the cotton off the plant, and then you'd have to separate the cotton fibers from seed, typically using a rolling pin and working them out. This new engine by Whitney was groundbreaking in that it did the work of separating seed and fiber quickly. Further, you could sell the fiber and also the oil created by the seed. So, not only did this new technology save a lot of time and probably some carpel tunnel, but it was also suddenly a means to really cash in on a typically overlooked crop. Human advancement at its finest, right?

What happened next, for thousands of people, was anything but progress. Landowners in the South took this new lucrative opportunity to grow cotton and capitalized on it through the abuse of their human siblings. While the cotton industry was soaring, it still needed grown, picked, and sorted, and who was going to do all that work? We can now look back and see that what immediately followed this new technological revolution was the growth of slavery in the American South. We now know that the invention of the cotton gin became one of the key catalysts causing the Civil War.[19] It wasn't just about cotton, and it really wasn't about enslaved people either, it was about the economy. Much of the Southern economy became dependent on African slave labor and cotton fields. Once the cotton boom occurred in the late 1700s, the number of enslaved people tripled to over three million during the next sixty years.[20] This one crop economy planted the seeds of cotton, white supremacy, and the trans-Atlantic slave trade.

19. Kelly, "What Were the Top Causes."
20. Digital Public Library of America, "Cotton Gin."

CHAPTER 3 | SKYDIVING IN THE ANTHROPOCENE

We look back on a story like this and there is a river of sin leading all the way up and down what happened there. Greed, envy, lust, rage, laziness, gluttony, and hubris.

Today, this co-occurrence between slavery and technological advancement is still happening globally. Let us not, in any way, downplay the horrific reality of slavery in the South or attempt to compare that equally to other situations. The cotton gin, however, is a vivid example of a larger and broader dilemma. It is a dilemma that exists for close to forty million people worldwide today. It is the intersection between the metals in your cell phone and families in open pit mines elsewhere in the world, but also, more than ever, between social media applications and vulnerable individuals.[21] It is the relationship between the fish on your plate and the young person sold into slavery.[22] There is an undeniable thread between what we are so quick to name as technological development and the suffering of human and nonhuman creation.

The co-occurrence of violence and "advancement" is clearer than ever in the wake of the AI takeover. In the span of just months, artificial intelligence has been integrated into most forms of common software all the way to general appliances. Deep fakes (computer-generated images of people, which are only getting harder to recognize) should give us great pause about the ethical dilemmas to come. Yet underneath every single question that we dare ask these robotic gods, are real ecological footprints. Even a small answer from a program like ChatGPT requires about a bottle's worth of fresh water. It's estimated that in just a few years time, AI integrations will have consumed 6.6 billion cubic meters of water.[23] For reference, one cubic meter of water is 1,000 liters. One twenty-four-foot round swimming pool (about four feet deep) holds over 50,000 liters. If we do the math, that's 132,000,000 swimming pools of water consumed for our AI data needs in a couple of years' time—and growing. In a time of global freshwater scarcity, this is a serious problem. A Bloomberg

---

21. Knight, "Impact of Technology."
22. Goodman, "Your Seafood"; Leschin-Hoar, "Was Your Seafood Caught?"
23. Li, "Making AI Less 'Thirsty.'"

report found that two-thirds of these new data centers are being built in places already facing high water stress.[24]

Equally as troubling is that these data centers operate twenty-four hours a day and require increasing fossil fuels. In a time when we need to be seeking sustainability more than ever, the need for more energy to meet the demand for AI growth is skyrocketing.[25] In a five-year period, Google reported that their emissions had increased by 48 percent due to the rising use of AI.[26]

One example is the textbook environmental racism occurring in Memphis, TN—my home state. Elon Musk's company xAI has been busy creating what's been named "Colossus," touted as the world's largest supercomputer. In a race to construct this monstrosity as quickly as possible while attempting to get away with ecocide, the company has targeted one of the "blackest and poorest" communities on the south side of Memphis.

Here, neighbors have long been in the struggle against industrial plots to harm the environment. Now, with an extremely high demand placed on the aquifer along with thirty-five methane-powered turbine generators emitting copious amounts of toxins into the air, these residents are physically taking the brunt of this technological progress.[27] As they face the threat of continual output of atmospheric tons of the carcinogen formaldehyde and also nitrogen oxide into the air they breathe, the results will be reduced lung function, asthma, and cardiac issues.[28] This will lead to higher death rates, preterm births, and child hospitalizations in an area of Memphis already gripped with extremely bad air quality.[29] The rapid growth of AI represents the kind of technology that we should mindfully proceed with extreme caution, especially in reference to when and how it's implemented.

I've sat in many meetings and social gatherings where AI is carelessly used for both work and entertainment. In one moment, we're using it to help solve the most basic thought problems and the next

24. Nicoletti, "AI Boom Is Draining."
25. Goldman Sachs, "AI to Drive 165% Increase"; United Nations, "Artificial Intelligence."
26. Rahman-Jones, "Google's Greenhouse Gas Emissions."
27. Strebig, "Elon Musk's xAI Supercomputer."
28. Wittenberg, "How Come I Can't Breathe?"
29. Marsh, "World's Biggest Supercomputer."

thing we know, we're leveraging it for every question we come across. Meanwhile, for kicks and giggles, we're prompting AI to create images and videos so that we can enjoy the temporary false reality of a pig dressed like a princess who can, of course, fly. All the while, data centers churn, dirty energy burns, and water runs (and our creative spirit atrophies).

Sure, AI can be helpful in a few instances, and like any technology, perhaps it may be leveraged in the right scenarios to bring about a better life. Yet, by and large, that's not how it is being used. AI is frequently being used to do our creative work for us, our research for us, streamline our production, make us more money, and generally as a tool of infinite growth ideologies (more on that in a bit). The result? If we're not careful . . . we will be quickly on the way to a society that loses critical thinking skills, loses our tether with the kind of tasks that make us human, all while finding ourselves estranged from a healthy planet.[30] It's difficult to see AI as an advancement toward human flourishing. Rather, it seems to perpetuate systems of dominance and obsolescence at the expense of our human and nonhuman neighbors.

Wendell Berry writing on advancing technologies says that it can

> be defended, but I observe that the defenses are invariably quantitative—catalogs of statistics on the ownership of automobiles and television sets . . . are always kept carefully apart from their related statistics of soil loss, pollution, social disintegration, and so forth. That is to say, there is never an effort to determine the *net* result of this progress.[31]

The question is, are we taking holistic stock of the ramifications of our continual "progress"?

Consider the vast adoption and widespread use of tractors. Tractors have certainly been key tools in the feeding of thousands of people. Yet, prior to the tractor, agriculture still occurred. Through this new technology, we began further outsourcing our relationship with the land. At the beginning of the twentieth century, the majority of people were engaged in some form of local food production. Fast forward just a hundred years later and that has dropped to about 1 percent of the population who are our marked "farmers" in the West.

30. Jackson, "Increased AI Use."
31. Berry, *What Are People For?*, 186.

Now, that 1 percent are most often trapped in the faltering system of industrialized, mechanized, and subsidized agriculture, stuck in monocropping, smothered in pesticides, and struggling to make ends meet.

Children no longer grow up learning how to care for the land. Local native land knowledge is all but gone. And those tractors? So many decades in, they have ironically functioned as tools of devastation for our topsoil. We've plowed, compacted, and plowed again until now we face desertification of our topsoil and the oncoming threat of hunger.[32] Those tractors are often, by and large, just cogs in the greater machine—not participating in sustainable agriculture but busy with the industry of monocropping corn, soybeans, and other single crops that just feed that economic engine with its ethanol, corn syrup, cornstarch, citric acid, and cow feed.

The crops that comprise the majority of American agriculture, sucking up land and water, are more product than produce. It's more about feeding our economy than feeding our children with this grain we grow; it's padding the pockets of large corporations. Despite all the data that urges us to once again localize our agriculture, engage in polyculture, integrate livestock grazing, and simply grow directly edible produce, the money pipeline says otherwise.[33]

Today, our system only needs a very small percentage of poor, hardworking farmers to keep the cogs turning. Somehow, an industry such as growing food can simultaneously be in short supply of laborers and yet have more demand than ever. This is critical considering that it is estimated we will need to increase our global food production by 70 percent by 2050.[34] How will we overcome this deficit? How will we outsource this hurdle?

Immigrants from South America make up the backbone of US agriculture.[35] These immigrants are economically and socially marginalized, underpaid, undervalued, and in many instances have been

---

32. Check out this amazing documentary on soil health and our global ecological crises: Tickell, *Common Ground*.

33. Another great documentary worth your time here is *Eating for Tomorrow* directed by the Brockway brothers.

34. United Nations, "World Must Sustainably Produce"; Reiserer, "How to Feed."

35. Gutiérrez-Li, "Feeding America."

trafficked or trapped in their circumstances.[36] Just like the Israelites in Egypt and Africans in colonial America, the many immigrants in the US have become modernly enslaved for our agricultural needs.[37] Are we looking closely enough to see the patterns?

We can either continue climbing higher into the false hopes of a Babylonian economy, or we can begin the imaginative work of freeing one another and the earth itself from these chains of domination disguised as progress. True progress will only be found through discovering a new and healing relationship with the soil under our feet and the souls we share this planet with.

What if "the good life," the life of flourishing that God desires for us, is a life that is slower? A life that is closer to the soil? A life lived with the land? A life more physically integrated with the ecosystems that we depend upon? How absurd that we would consider putting more and more distance between ourselves and the earth would somehow *better* our lives? It has only impoverished us, offering higher healthcare bills and weakened bodies from too many years traveling on our butts rather than our legs!

Is it possible for us to continue having advancements in technology without negatively impacting every person, place, and thing? Is this "leap forward" benefiting me, my community, or the earth? Does this make us a more loving people? Or is this about something else?

Here's a burning question:
Can nature be improved upon through technology?
I'm inclined to say, no.

God's natural systems, already present here, are the best tools we have.

Is there such a thing as science and technology that aids humanity by fostering harmony between us and nonhuman creation?
Absolutely.

---

36. Fasih, "Hidden Exploitation." Silva, "Feds Bust 'Modern-Day Slavery.'"
37. Le, "Modern Slaves."

Technology, if it is to be called "good," if it is advancing us at all, should be improving our relationship with the natural world. This technology should be extensions of love in the world. Technology worth adopting is one that helps all humans live better lives, in mutual care with creation. Helpful progress looks like removing barriers (not creating them!) such as pollution or creating access to healthy produce, so that the natural world can achieve what it already does so well—offering air to breathe, food to eat, a joy-filled environment . . . and don't forget, most importantly, coffee to drink!

> *God, you have endowed us with creativity as those created in your image, the Creator. Guide us, we pray, into humility with our creations. We pray for the courage necessary to face down that which we have created that is not of you or your kingdom. Give us strength to tear down the blocks of injustice that oppress our human siblings and your good creation in the effort of benefiting the few. May we be recipients of the tools of your kingdom, so that the structures we build here on earth may advance into heaven as expressions of love and grace.*
>
> *Amen.*

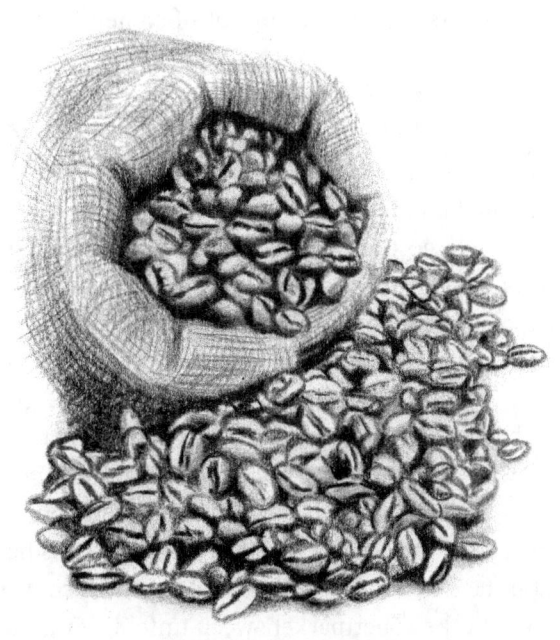

Chapter 4 | Coffee, Curtains, and the Human Condition

If we surrendered
to earth's intelligence
we could rise up rooted, like trees.

Instead we entangle ourselves
in knots of our own making
and struggle, lonely and confused.

So like children, we begin again . . .
to fall,
patiently to trust our heaviness.
Even a bird has to do that
before he can fly.

RAINER MARIA RILKE

When was the last time you ran out of something? Sure, we run out of toilet paper all the time . . . ketchup, bread, fuel. We're used to running out of things. But we're not as familiar with being unable to go out and get a refill. When something "runs out" it's not usually a big deal because, well, there's more to be got. Yet, the moment when the idea is planted that there may not be any more of something, well, that's when people go berserk! Which brings us to the great age of Beanie Babies in the 1990s and special people hoarding toilet paper during the global pandemic of 2020. The moment the idea of scarcity rears its head, you better look out!

Recently, we decided to take a family trip to the grocery store. Something that doesn't happen often due to the increase in time, energy, and "I wants" that are endured. Yet, it's a meaningful teaching moment to occasionally have with our kids. Turning our buggy down the aisle, we take in the sight of a couple with two carts hastily raking Gatorades off the shelves. The four of us ceased our conversation and stopped to watch the supermarket sweep unfold. My girls, who don't spend a lot of time in stores shopping, have their jaws to the floor. About that time, the lady turns, sees us, brings forth a smile, and says, "These are all on sale today, can you believe they're just one dollar?"

It's comical because, if we're honest, we've all been there. When our favorite item happened to be heavily discounted upon our arrival, and the next thing we knew, with pounding hearts and sweaty palms, we scoop every last one into our cart while looking over our shoulder at who else might be coming down the aisle! Something about the very act of hoarding a deal makes us feel as if we're doing something illegal. "We made out like bandits," we exclaim while loading the car, and we proceed to tell the next five friends we see about it!

Dollar Gatorades are not an example of true scarcity though, and anyone who has experienced true scarcity may (rightly) be offended at that thought. In a climate-changed world, we're about to witness levels of scarcity that we are not prepared for.

Noah is one of the most thoughtful people I know and an amazing barista to boot. His superpowers include a deeply mystic heart and the ability to taste every flavor note in a cup of coffee. With our Western eyes, it may seem like two unconnected senses, yet as soon

CHAPTER 4 | COFFEE, CURTAINS, AND THE HUMAN CONDITION 63

as we pull out of our binary-brain tendencies we, begin to see that it doesn't have to be "this" or "that," does it? His ability to be non-dual is likely what helps him hold a deeper awareness for what his body is experiencing.

Emily and I are there sitting on stools in his micro-apartment for a visit while he shares with us a coffee bean story. There are many different varieties of coffee beans out there in God's creation. Just like wine, they are all affected by sun, shade, rainfall, and temperature. As we talk, in a moment of mourning, Noah tells us about one of his favorite coffee beans. He shares that this particular variety doesn't have much time left. The life cycle of this bean crop is almost gone, and there won't be any more of it. Ever again.

In the twenty-first century, it's hard for us to comprehend "ever again." Let those words roll on your tongue.

Never again.

Like, ever ever? In the age of drive-through pumpkin spice lattes that you can set your calendar by, you mean to say that there is a kind of coffee we can't have anymore?

Yes.

We are in the beginning stages of comprehending the finitude of many things that we love (and are addicted to). The scientific community has named the year 2100 or as early as 2050 as potential "doomsday" dates for coffee extinction. As the climate changes and temperatures further fluctuate, this causes disturbed rain patterns and general "global weirding," as climate scientist Katherine Hayhoe names it. So, for coffee plants, who are highly sensitive to all these conditions and only grow along a certain "coffee belt," it doesn't just mean a sad goodbye to one kind of coffee bean today, but potentially a global goodbye to coffee in the near future.[1]

Noah knew what he was grieving. Sitting there on a stool in his kitchen, that's when I really tasted what was steaming within my cup. I was drinking this bean, these flavor notes, this certain crop that had

---

1. Clarke, "Is Coffee Going Extinct?"; Meister, "What Does Climate Change"; Morrissy-Swan, "Coffee Is Facing Extinction."

been touched by microbes from a patch of soil, drops of rain, caresses of sun that will *never happen again.*

And it was very good.

Our crowded technological world has aided us in avoiding many losses. This has come with great cost and has resulted in a myriad of ramifications, among which is that we've lost a large degree of resilience. We just aren't that resilient (in the Global North at least) to pain or loss, particularly in ways that our not-so-distant ancestors were. As a culture, especially in America, we don't sit with or face our pain as much as fixate on ways to mitigate it. The pain of "hitting our ceiling" is just a waiting room before the next "breakthrough."

One of the shows that my oldest daughter is surprisingly into is *Shark Tank*. She has always had an inventive spirit with a capacity toward engineering, so I guess it's not too surprising. I can hardly watch the show because of the compulsory eye roll, which is my bodily reaction to many of these "inventions." We live in such an age of technological progress that we've now got kitty litter that changes colors to tell us about the health of our cats! Or like a curved snack bowl that is specially molded to nestle over our leg while sitting on the couch watching television so that our chips don't spill. We're solving problems we didn't even know we had! If there is a pain point out there in the world, someone somewhere is working on some techy solution for it right this very second and hoping to make a buck off of it.

One such "product" on the show is called Beulr (cleverly named after the movie *Ferris Bueller's Day Off*). The original Beulr product attended online meetings for you while making it seem like you are there. The idea is that there are online classes or meetings that you have to attend but you simply don't want to. You record a simple clip of yourself looking like you're paying attention, upload it, put in your meeting information and schedule, and an automatic bot takes it from there. Voilà! It looks like you're there, but in fact you're still in bed! So, you know that one guy who never seems to talk in your meetings? He may not actually be there!

CHAPTER 4 | COFFEE, CURTAINS, AND THE HUMAN CONDITION

The business eventually flopped, but the company pivoted with AI integrations. Their new idea creates an AI version of you. Now if you're somewhere and cannot join your online meeting but can still use your voice, Beulr overlays an AI generated version of you with your voice, just so you that you can be "seen" on the video call.[2]

To be blunt, this may be a classic case of a dumb idea getting dumber. Rather than simply joining a meeting with your voice, this program will use an incredible number of resources to just achieve something that could be as simple as talking on the phone.

It's important to pause and reemphasize the importance of the creative spirit that we all have as humans created in the likeness of the Creator. Being creative is inseparably a part of who we are and what we are made to do; yet, that doesn't mean that we're always doing it well or that we need another new and improved fidget spinner. What might it be like to actually resist the urge to outsource all our problems to technology? To resist the fidget? This is important especially as we understand that these advancements are invariably intertwined with issues of equality. Further, one might argue that taking time to sit within our natural pain and limitations is the necessary space prior to healthy creative birth.

When I was a kid, *Willy Wonka and the Chocolate Factory* literally scared my pants off. Now as an adult, it hasn't gotten much better. (Some things you just don't recover from!) I think Willy Wonka bears to us some deep-seated truths if we have ears to hear.

It's a story about children who get what they want. Rivers of chocolate. Entire meals in a stick of gum. Willy Wonka's candy-tech is the stuff of legend.

If there's one thing children don't come prepackaged with, it's a grasp on their limitations. If you've ever seen a kid make themselves sick after eating too much Halloween candy, you know what I'm talking about.

---

2. Poole, "Beulr Update."

One by one, lessons are learned. A girl who can't help herself is blown up into a giant blueberry. A boy is washed away in a lust for chocolate. The movie is frighteningly real. The natural consequences of getting everything we desire with no limits may look more like hell than heaven. (Even though potential death-by-chocolate could be the best possible way to go.)

Here's a question: Where exactly are we trying to get to? What end might we be striving to achieve? Is it a time in which technology does all our work for us, feeds us, accomplishes our art and creative needs, and entertains us indefinitely? Decades ago, Wendell Berry sarcastically wrote about our "industrial dream of the future-as-Paradise," saying,

> The future is the time when science will have solved all our problems, gratified all our desires; when we will all live in perfect ease in an air conditioned, fully automated womb; when all the work will be done by machines so sophisticated that they will not only clothe, house, and feed us, but think for us, play our games, paint our pictures, write our poems.[3]

We know now more than ever how close we've come to this reality in certain parts of the world.

So, have we self-actualized yet? Have we transcended our human boundaries yet? Have we reached the heavens and made a name for ourselves yet?

Wrapped into this narrative of progress is a discussion on how we are making ourselves obsolete. In fact, you could say, just as large corporations engineer their products to be "designed for the dump"[4] for the purpose of generating continual income through planned obsolescence, the wider work of our societal values does the same, except with human lives. Are we praising the ability to finally escape all work as the ultimate human goal of life? "Is the obsolescence of human beings now our social goal?" Berry inquires in his book of essays *What Are People For?* He continues by offering some stark words: "In a country that puts an absolute premium on labor saving measures, short work days, and retirement, why should there be any surprise at

---

3. Berry, *Unsettling of America*, 61.
4. Zero by Fifty, "Designed for the Dump."

CHAPTER 4 | COFFEE, CURTAINS, AND THE HUMAN CONDITION

permanence of unemployment and welfare dependency? Those are only different names for our national ambitions."[5] In our efforts of chasing reprieve from the lifelong demands of the capitalistic workforce, do we mistakenly uphold bodily obsolescence as the greatest achievable good? Berry says, "we must save ourselves from the products that we are asked to buy in order, ultimately, to replace ourselves. The danger most immediately to be feared in 'technological progress' is the degradation and obsolescence of the body."[6]

In our quest to escape the ordinary, is it possible that we miss everything that we are here for?

Is it possible that "the ordinary" is the actual goods?

Returning to that morning cup of coffee with Noah, in his tears, we have the opportunity to hear a deeper note ringing out within our limited and mortal lives. If we'll stop and look closely, listen attentively to the earth and our own hearts, I believe what we will see is not a life designed for struggle but a life intentionally limited, for beauty, enjoyment, and praise. Noah leaves us with this poem.

This is worth missing.

Perhaps not the exhaustion or lack of care,
but the joy so few will know in loving this bean.

She kisses my lips with flavors of
lemons, oranges, a handful of cashews,
sunflower seeds, and bliss when met by milk!

Touching this ground feels like the closest
I can come to dancing in the fields among her kin.

Trapped in an industry, functioning for someone else's day,
I find solidarity in holding this sacred crop.

---

5. Berry, *What Are People For?*, 125.
6. Berry, *What Are People For?*, 190.

She has journeyed for their purposes and so have I.

Meeting at the crack of dawn only to be crushed
into more than what we are, hoping to be free, hoping to be remembered.

I hope they remember her—I hope they remember me.

"Santa Maria," by Noah Starr[7]

FIRST CLASS CURTAIN

I think if we're honest, we often believe that if we put in the hours, make the bricks, stack them day after day, we'll get to a place higher than we started—heck, we'll even reach the top and just be... finished!

So many of us, at any given time, are working on "climbing the ladder." It's the effort of self-actualization as we finally have "all the things we deserve." We are running the company, driving next year's model, and sporting the latest Apple gadgets. In my book *Garbage Theology*, I write about this wheel we become stuck within, a society stuck in a *bigger-better* loop. One decision made in the effort to climb the ladder mandates the next, which over time gives way to a life enclosed within a system that promises well-being but never delivers and, ultimately, could not deliver such a thing. Instead, it keeps us just content enough with the in-flight snacks of life as we're seated on a plane fourteen thousand feet in the air.

Now, I've never flown first class but from what I can tell, it's a whole new world up there! The whole boarding process is so that you must walk *through* first class on the way back into the stables, *after* those most fortunate ones have already seated themselves. Some first class seating looks more like individual space capsules than seats. I'm not certain, but it seemed that on one flight they may have even had their own private massage therapist!

On a less glamorous flight, I once found myself so close to first class that I could reach out and touch that holy airline-blue curtain. Or rather, on this small flight I was unfortunate enough to sit directly

---

7. Find more of his work on Instagram @offeringsforthepeople.

CHAPTER 4 | COFFEE, CURTAINS, AND THE HUMAN CONDITION   69

behind the completely unnecessary privacy curtain that was drawn upon take off, which propelled back upon my body for the duration of the flight. Though they were drawn, I could still see through the crack into the inner courts, where a young boy sat with an entire row to himself. To his delight, he flopped around all three seats bouncing up and down. He was probably around age ten, and that much space could've been an entire bedroom for a kid his size.

Once he settled down, I noticed he took out his tablet, which basically captivated him for the duration of the flight. It was like watching someone speak who was fluent in another language. His small fingers masterfully slid across the sticky-streaked screen with fingertip precision, moving from this app to that app. Having a daughter of similar age, I was curious what kind of game he would settle on. He selected a game called *Solar Smash*. I thought, "This sounds interesting, what could this be like?"

You're in space. In front of you is what appears to be a planet of your choosing; then, before you are god-like choices in which you must carefully decide on and select a singular planet-destroying option. Finally, you watch as your planet gets "smashed!" Solar smash.

In that moment, something caught me off guard. I have to admit, there was something that made me feel uneasy, seeing that little boy sit and play a game in which he was *entertained* through destroying "worlds" with a swipe of his finger.

There, on the threshold between first class and economy, I glanced behind the curtain to see worlds being destroyed.

There's an absurdity to all of this. Our lives are absurd, really. At least for those of us in the Global North who have a front row seat to the cutting edge of the Anthropocene: all of this human-centric nonsense that has been created with the lure of "giving us what we want."

We are told that these are things that improve our lives, that make our lives infinitely better, that give us freedom, but what if that's just it? What if these new things, this new technology, actually doesn't make us free? What if they hold us captive? What if these new advancements aren't advancements at all? What if that's the catch to the whole ladder-climbing, tower-building game? What if the higher you get, the further away you are from the beautiful, grounded, human life you're created for?

What if, at some point, human advancement doesn't look like more or higher or bigger or better, but rather less and lower?

Here's the deal: if you wanted to hold someone as a slave and simultaneously get the most work and benefit out of that slave as you could, the best way to do it would be to convince them that they aren't a slave at all. You would offer them the illusion of control. All they have to do is pay off their debts (which just happens to increase every day). If you believe that working for your captor will eventually give you ultimate freedom and happiness, then at best, you'll live your life trying to attain more and more while eventually becoming numb as you get further and further away from being grounded and truly free. At worst, you live out your life trapped, bloody, broken, and enslaved.

Captors don't always look like devils. In fact, empires do their best work with slaves who believe in the oppressive mission of the oligarchy. You see, the curtain makes for a sly trick. *The Wizard of Oz* offers us a timeless warning to ask who is pulling the levers. Who benefits from your and my participation in all of this? Well, in this instance, it's the airline. It's the tech company. It's anyone who we pay with our money and with our attention. Meanwhile, we keep busy flying above the clouds, behind our curtains that make us feel special and playing on our screens that make us feel in control of the universe.

Our very lives have become an open-pit mining operation. Our data is mined. Our time is mined. Our resources are mined. But worse than that, our very spirits are mined, our humanity is mined. We're trapped in a slave system whose business is to keep us "content and climbing for more," so that we become clueless to our own capture, exploitation, and slavery.

What if there is a curtain . . . behind the curtain?

The first curtain is the tangible blue piece of fabric brushing my leg, letting me know I'm "back here." It's the layer that exists between you and me in coach, roughin' it, and the good life: up front, with

CHAPTER 4 | COFFEE, CURTAINS, AND THE HUMAN CONDITION

drinks in hand, leg room, three pillows, and galaxy smashing. These first curtains exist in thousands of ways for us every single day. These are the limits that we spend our days working hard to break through to "have better lives."

But the second boundary, the curtain behind the curtain, is a story as old as Scripture itself. It's the tale of those who take people captive and of those who are in captivity, just as Babylon becomes the place of captivity for the people of God later in the biblical narrative. The site for growth and development in Gen 11 becomes ground zero for exile later on. You think you're sitting in first class until you find that you're being taken somewhere you don't want to go against your will. Who is flying this plane? The systems that we were sure existed for our benefit become the very thing that keeps us from a life of well-being. What is more, these systems never had the true authority to offer well-being in the first place.

True well-being is unaffiliated with flying first class, having an air fryer on our kitchen counter, or driving an SUV across rugged terrain (like every car commercial says we'll be busy doing).

The irony about the curtains is that we spend all our time, energy, and money working to break through these boundaries and get to the other side. We want to overcome our ceiling. We do it through genetically modified food and air travel. We do it through our continual quest for the fountain of youth in every concealer we buy, Botox we inject, and hair loss product we try.

Yet, for every boundary we break, we have to mitigate our losses. There is extra energy, time, and waste that is produced in our efforts to keep climbing higher and moving further away from the earth and our own humanity. The underbelly to our "advancements" is that there are so many costs. It's the paragraph of side effects read to us at breakneck speed at the end of our life-commercial. *Warning, this lifestyle may result in bleeding, inauthenticity, a never-ending and exhausting quest for more than you have, depression, loneliness, oppressing your neighbor, planetary degradation, and a meaningless death. Consult with your doctor before taking.*

Culture attempts to flip the script on all the things that are broken by naming them "breakthroughs." But what if our breakthroughs are what is breaking the whole thing?

What if the sacred task ahead has more to do with mending what is broken instead of breaking through any more natural barriers?

What if the good life was never on the other side of the curtain? What if the grass is not greener? What if it is never boarding the flight at all?

What if you're on a flight and you want off?

SUPER OR HUMAN

Loss, pain, and death are the trio of experiences that push up against our mortality, our physical limits. No one wants to die, and we are trying really hard not to most of the time. Even if pain can be helpful in keeping us alive and growing us as humans, no one wants it. Nobody likes to lose anything. So we avoid it, naturally. We work pretty hard not to experience loss. But it's eventually coming for all of us, despite how hard we work against it. I can't help but wonder if it's our avoidance of loss, pain, and death that becomes the very thing preventing us from the work of healing?

Pain comes in all shapes and sizes. We can talk about pain in reference to the feeling we get when anything goes wrong. Theologian Norman Wirzba, in his book *This Sacred Life*, frames this by using the language of friction. Pain may be too strong of a term to really reflect the kind of life annoyances we are working to avoid today. Technology, social media, and companies like Amazon are all pushing us toward a value system of "friction-free" living.[8] It would seem true that, on the outside, it appears we all generally desire frictionless living. Can't we just have everything go smoothly all the time? Is that too much to ask?

Sometimes, I think that if I were an alien from another planet landing on Earth, at a quick glance, I might describe humans as creatures who do not like being who they are. In other words, what

---

8. Wirzba, *This Sacred Life*, 49.

CHAPTER 4 | COFFEE, CURTAINS, AND THE HUMAN CONDITION

I would see are beings attempting to live their lives in opposition to their natural limits. Beings who are in a state of perpetual pushing-against their own creatureliness. "Sleeker, stronger, higher, quick-dissolving, fast-acting, new and improved, 2.0, 3.0, 4.0...." I would be an extra-terrestrial observing beings in their own home environment who wished that they themselves were aliens.

No, I don't like pain either, and attempting to better ourselves is part of what is at the heart of being human. At this very moment, I'm on antibiotics to deal with some "bad gut bacteria" I tested positive for and just inserted some Dr. Scholl's into my soccer cleats for my plantar fasciitis. Modern technology and medicine are at work in and on my body. So, how might we assess our relationship with these systems and choices of dealing with friction and pain?

Underneath this rub of friction and limitations is a primary discussion on the things that we've named inherently bad or inherently good, necessary and nonessential. How do we know which things to try and overcome and which limitations to embrace? Should we just "hu-man up" about some of this pain? Or should we receive the good gifts of modern technology and medication?

One evening, as I was tucking in my youngest daughter, Daily, she shared with me her litany of "I wants." Unprompted, she eagerly gives a long list of all the extravagant desires of her little heart, which range from "I want a trampoline" to "I want a go-cart." Finally, at long last, the catalogue climaxed to "and I want Adam and Eve to pick the right fruit so I can fly... and be Batman."

Similarly, one morning, as I drove my kids to school, my oldest daughter, Story, asked me about pain and sickness. She recently had suffered from a stomach bug, which is notoriously the worst kind of bug!

"Daddy, I have a question."
"Yep."
"If Adam had never eaten that forbidden fruit... would there be any sickness today?"
"Hmm, that's a great question. I'm not sure, but maybe not?"
She replies, "That sneaky snake, that sneaky snakey!"

It didn't take long for this to spiral into a conversation about feeling pain. I explained how there are a few people in the world who don't feel bodily pain because of a rare genetic condition. I explain that people with this condition may inadvertently lead difficult lives because they aren't receiving the critical information that pain communicates. "Pain tells us that something is going wrong," I tell her. In other words, if you didn't know you cut your foot, you wouldn't go to the doctor and get stitches. If pain and discomfort weren't there, we probably wouldn't live long. Pain receptors are critical functions for living well. Pain reminds us that we are still growing, stretching, and becoming in the world. It reminds us of our humanity.

Pain reminds us of our limits. When something is painful, it's like a referee waving the flag: "offsides," "out of bounds!" Pain keeps us all playing by the same rules. In a way, pain is an important part of keeping the game going and, ironically, keeping things fun. Pain says, "Here are the rules, and no one gets to cheat!"

We are a people fascinated with superheroes. Movies about people who transcend their limitations are everywhere! You know, faster than a speeding bullet, stronger than a locomotive, and all that. I mean, come on, what's more entertaining than *Guardians of the Galaxy*?

I remember, back in the day, when the first *Spiderman* movie came out; I'm talking Tobey Maguire stuff. These kinds of films hadn't really happened yet for Marvel fans, and here we were at the theater, opening night, and it was packed. One of my favorite people-moments happened as the opening credits began to roll scenes of a page-turning comic book, and the gentleman sitting in the squished row behind my friend and me enthusiastically belts out in repetition, "Oh yeah, oh yeah, oh yeah!" That guy had his life changed.

The superhero movies are out of control, let's be honest. They just keep coming. We are obsessed with this idea that we can be more-than-human. What would it be like if pain weren't so oppressive? If my skin was like impenetrable steel? If I could laser eye those bank robbers and fly above the clouds? Hollywood has capitalized on our

CHAPTER 4 | COFFEE, CURTAINS, AND THE HUMAN CONDITION

trans-humanist fantasies. Admittedly, they are fun! But I wonder, do these narratives have any effect on us?

Recently, during an attempt at a "date night" out, Emily and I found ourselves inadvertently shoe shopping for our daughter. (Like you do as parents!) Walking around this shopping area, I became so struck at all the television-induced goods for sale. T-shirts, knick-knacks, toys, and even food for sale, each a reflection of some show, film, movie-saga, and so on. It stood out to me how many of us have packaged our lives around these fictional narratives.

Now, don't get me wrong, I love Ninja Turtles and Batman as much as the next millennial, but how much of these narratives are we creating, and what here is creating us? Eventually, we are shaped the most by the narratives that captivate us. What are you captivated by?

There are true heroes today you'll never hear of. They're out there doing the research, small farming, cleaning up ecosystems, and caring for their community. They are doing the modest work of restoration in places unseen. They are humble and low to the ground, changing the world under all our noses. I'm captivated by these stories, by these cape-less heroes. These people don't fly, they walk. They don't have superhuman strength but rely on the gifts of their community. These people do the hard work of pursuing a better life for their family while it's completely out of the way and countercultural.

Back to my daughter's question about the first humans eating that fruit and sickness entering into the world—right there in the beginning, a few pages into the story of humanity, we are trying to do the same thing.

Transcend our humanity.

Overcome our barrier.

Breach the boundaries.

What is the deal? Did God forget to edit that part of the human-script? Is there an error in our coding? Why has this been a pattern for us? Is this a program malfunction? I mean, think about it: sinless humans living in utopia succumb to the temptation of the forbidden fruit.

Adam and Eve, there in the beginning, were confronted with their boundaries. The tree of the knowledge of good and evil was the embodiment of their limitation. Out of bounds! Don't eat it!

We often think about limits as wrathful rules for God's unruly kids. But what if the limits are actually the gift? What if the limits are God's love language? What if there's gravity . . . and then we get the moon?

What if the limits are set there by a God who wants to see us flourish? What if certain trees are put in the garden as God's way of saying, "I love you enough to make a boundary, even though I know you're going to struggle with keeping it"? If we weren't created with enough "pain-receptors" to struggle with this boundary, could we truly experience God's love?

It's certainly a lot to consider and can make your brain hurt just thinking about it!

In the case of the garden, as with gravity, these limits are part of who God designed you to be and the setting in which we were designed to live. For you to be the best version of you, created in the image of God, these limitations are part of that design! In other words, the tree was necessary. The tree represents a choice. This God is a God who desires sincere and authentic relationship with creation, thus the tree. Without that tree, without the opportunity, the choice, there is no relationship to be had. Without the tree, we're just cogs in the wheel, preprogrammed robots, mindless caretakers in the garden of creation.

There's more though.

The tree, rooted there in the best topsoil planet Earth has ever seen, tall and beautiful and "pleasing to the eye," stands to remind us that it's not all about us. We, humanity, aren't the central actor of this drama, God is. In the beginning, there is something there in this Eden (paradise) garden that is *not for* humanity. What we know is that the fruit wasn't for Adam and Eve's consumption. The tree bears fruit, which keeps us humble—that reminds us everything is not about us. Yet, it was planted there in the garden for us to "serve and keep"[9] along

---

9. Gen 2:15.

with every other part. Imagine! God wanted us to care for something that we weren't allowed to consume? The audacity.

You know how the story went. We were tempted to eat that fruit, and we did. Since that day, we have been striving, pushing, pulling, jumping, climbing, just trying to transcend this garden gravity of being a human, being in our seemingly frail state.

I wonder if what marks our "fallenness" isn't our human condition but the lustful desire for more? Maybe it has to do with our continual discontentment and gluttony rather than our mortal limits. Consider how we think about our humanity. We often think about our humanity as a consequence of the fall rather than part of the design. Prior to Gen 3, we weren't superhumans. We had flesh and bone bodies. We didn't even wear clothes! Arguably, we were more comfortable with our humanity prior to eating that fruit. We didn't gain or lose our humanity as a consequence of the fall but entered into a series of broken relationships that included one another and nonhuman creation.

Prior to that, walking in the garden with God, we were as human as ever! As far as we know, we couldn't fly, we still gained weight if we ate too much, we didn't grow hundreds of feet tall, and we would still bleed if we scratched ourselves on a branch. Here is a key piece that is important for us to grab: our humanness, these human limitations that shape of our existence are not sinful consequences but a part of God's design for us.

THE FINAL FRONTIER

My daughter, Daily, came home from school one day with a short script in her hand. She was so excited to tell me about her part reading it in class and proceeded to read the entire paper to me from top to bottom in the moment. It was an excerpt from John F. Kennedy's "We Choose to Go to the Moon" speech.

In this 1962 speech, Kennedy memorably gives the American people "the feels" about going to the moon. Simultaneously, in the speech, we learn that we're in something known as the "space race" with other nations; but wait, somehow this moon project is to be a peace-building, collaborative effort. Either way, by the end of this eighteen-minute oration, people are geared up for this space adventure, and one would think it's in the best interest of all humanity for America to be the first ones to "land a man on the Moon."[10] Before the 1960s were over, we would do just that. We chose the moon just as Kennedy encouraged us to.

There are parts about going to the moon that I like and parts I dislike. My impressionable daughter learning about the creative spirit and ingenuity of humankind is not only a healthy thing but important. Yet, what lurks behind these stories? What are things that we might be teaching behind the lessons? What postures are we praising?

It's no secret that American pioneerism and the lingering spirit of cosmic Manifest Destiny undergirds this famous speech.[11] Kennedy orates,

> Those who came before us made certain that this country rode the first waves of the industrial revolutions, the first waves of modern invention, and the first wave of nuclear power, and this generation does not intend to founder in the backwash of the coming age of space. We mean to be a part of it—we mean to lead it.

He continues, "That challenge is one that we are willing to accept, one we are unwilling to postpone, and one which we intend to win."[12]

Looking back at that moment in history, it might be hard for us to really separate this space mission to the moon from a mission for power. It is a moment marking humanity's ultimate overcoming of our bounded place on Earth, and it offers signs to us of just how far we will go to best one another at our unbounded desires and conquests.

Hannah Arendt opens her 1958 book *The Human Condition* by reflecting on the launch of the first satellite into space, which had recently occurred. She describes it as an event "second in importance to no other." Recalling the immediate reactions of this historic moment, she notes that what she witnessed was not what you would expect. It wasn't joy, or even pride; she wrote,

---

10. Kennedy, "We Choose to Go."

11. Manifest Destiny refers to the nineteenth-century belief in American exceptionalism manifested in settler expansion in which they were "destined" to move westward across North America, resulting in the colonial displacement of native Indigenous communities.

12. Kennedy, "We Choose to Go."

CHAPTER 4 | COFFEE, CURTAINS, AND THE HUMAN CONDITION

> The immediate reaction, expressed on the spur of the moment, was relief about the first "step toward escape from men's imprisonment to the earth." And this strange statement, far from being the accidental slip of some American reporter, unwittingly echoed the extraordinary line which, more than twenty years ago, had been carved on the funeral obelisk for one of Russia's great scientists: "Mankind will not remain bound to the earth forever."[13]

What Arendt uncovers in her work, similar to thinkers such as Berry and Wirzba, is what I would describe as a fundamental "missing it" when it comes to understanding our place as humans. Earthbound humanity isn't trapped on some random planet soaring around the cosmic edges of the Milky Way, stuck here through a simple lack of interstellar car keys. No, humanity is *of* Earth. As Arendt goes on to state, "The earth is the very quintessence of the human condition." Everything from early Genesis to our microbiome points back to this "quintessence."[14]

From our first satellite to "choosing to go to the moon," now to the age of SpaceX, we've decidedly entered the age of space capitalism.[15] The US is in a brand new race to the moon in order to "claim" territory through installing nuclear power to "support a future lunar economy."[16] Other items on the docket are asteroid and moon mining, orbiting solar arrays, and attempting to colonize Mars,[17] while offering brief cruises into the upper atmosphere for a zero-gravity hit, if you have several hundred thousand dollars to burn or you are a pop-star.[18]

Recently, in one of those fun back and forth online interchanges where I am patiently attempting to explain how humanity can affect even the climate, a certain individual was, what I call, *scream-mailing* to let me know that, "God provided all natural resources for man to own and use!" What this interchange uncovers here is a primary

---

13. Arendt, *Human Condition*, 1.
14. Arendt, *Human Condition*, 2.
15. For more, check out Kearnes, "Rethinking the Final Frontier."
16. Javaid, "Race to Build."
17. Brumfiel, "SpaceX Wants to Go."
18. Malik, "Katy Perry."

biblical misconception that lies at the root of much environmental degradation for Christian people:

God does not give creation to humanity.

The cosmos are not some "gift" that God has handed over to us for our personal interest. We are not *owners* of this planet. This lesson is repeated to us over and over in Scripture. We are rather custodians, stewards, and caretakers of the garden. If you prefer to use the language of "dominion," the only way we can understand such a term is in the context of Christ and God's selfless love for creation. Anytime we return to the posture that touts creation is "ours to do with as we please," anytime we attempt to peddle a narrative that squeezes self-gaining capital out of what we have been entrusted to protect, we should be prepared to face those sobering words: "You wicked, lazy servant!"[19]

What I hope for my daughters is that they look up at the stars in wonder. I want them to see the night sky and not only understand what we can know scientifically, a moon that reflects the light of a star, but to see something deeper, to see creation reflecting back the light of God.

We return to that refrain of praise offered by St. Francis, "Praised be You, my Lord, through Sister Moon and the stars, In the heavens you have made them bright, precious and fair," or the familiar words of Ps 19:1–4,

> The heavens are telling the glory of God,
>   and the firmament proclaims his handiwork.
> Day to day pours forth speech,
>   and night to night declares knowledge.
> There is no speech, nor are there words;
>   their voice is not heard;
> yet their voice goes out through all the earth
>   and their words to the end of the world.

We are invited to worship *with* creation, to the praise of the Lord, our Creator. I want my children to expand, not across the universe, but deeper, rooted into the very place God has put them and into the

---

19. Matt 25:26.

CHAPTER 4 | COFFEE, CURTAINS, AND THE HUMAN CONDITION

very purpose God has given them! I want my children to learn what it means to be soaked in earth, one with Christ in creation, and expressing love amidst friction . . .

I want them to know what it means to be an earthbound Christian.

How might we finally debunk these false promises to our youth? These are empty words that declare progress and better lives await them far away from fields, soil, and wooded wilds. These are deceitful narratives lacking the wisdom of lives lived with toes grounded in the soil that brings nourishment, muscles brought about through participation in local ecosystems, and the knowledge earned only through the management of prairies and meadows. Flourishing is found through a close relationship to the created world. Yet, it isn't as simple as returning to "country living," but a leap forward into reintegrating all of our lives, urban and rural, into right relatedness with the earth.

It is understandable that there have been times and generations, even now, when one could easily say, "I don't want my children to have to suffer like I did." Being close to the earth has, unfortunately, become synonymous with hardship and struggle. While that is a narrative in need of much imagination, it is equally important to say "money and ease"[20] cannot be our greatest gifts to our children, but rather something real, something good, something deeper.

The movie *WALL-E* is a film set in the future when Earth has been abandoned by people due to ecological devastation. The only humans who are left live on a space station, spend all day in levitating chairs, are extremely overweight, and watch a screen inches from their face all day long. It's an entertaining yet sobering image! Ironically, the movie unfolds and we learn that Earth is habitable enough for them to return, yet artificial intelligence aboard their ship is hiding

---

20. For more on this, see Berry, *What Are People For?*, 188.

that information. Luckily, a robot from the junkyards of Earth comes to save the day! Yeah, I know, spoilers!

If we are created for the garden, this couldn't be further from it. If joy is found within closer relationships with the soil, no wonder so much depression finds its way aboard our lives when we are surrounded with indoor comforts and mindless entertainment.

I wonder if the part of "the final frontier" that we cling to can be less about a spirit of power-over creation and more of a spirit of kinship? We are a people drawn into adventure through curiosity and creativity, yet that need not be at odds with the natural world but as partners within it.

Wrestling with our limitations, our pain, and this friction, we return to some guiding questions. Does this pain or loss or friction that I'm experiencing help me become a better person? Is it necessary? Would doing all the work to mitigate this discomfort harm my community? Harm God's creation? Do I really need to overcome this boundary or can this natural limitation be something that shapes me into more of the person God would have me to be?

What here is the best way to love God, neighbor, or nonhuman creation?

> Eternal God, You created us in your likeness and placed us within a vast creation that you called very good. We confess that we've treated our humanity as if it's part of the fall rather than part of the gift.
> Forgive us for all the ways in which we've continually called your gifts curses. Forgive us for all the ways we've clamored after a successful life rather than welcome the one you've offered us. Forgive us for our obsession with what you've told us not to eat. God, we ask for the grace to follow You into the loss, pain, and friction of this world, that we may suffer with, and so be resurrected with, all that you are redeeming.
> Amen.

A BLESSING FOR HUMANS

Blessed are you, frail human,
Created in God's image,
Whose hands are calloused over from many plantings.

Blessed are you, frail human,
Who must, day in and day out, consume calories to stay alive,
Until the day, as God intends, for you to become calories
consumed.

Blessed are you, frail human,
Who lives within bounds and boundaries,
Stretching though you are, may you touch heaven on earth.

Blessed are you, frail human
Created in God's image,
As you pray ceaselessly through a life well lived,
Learning to climb only upon your earthen cross.

PART THREE

Games, Cake, and Money

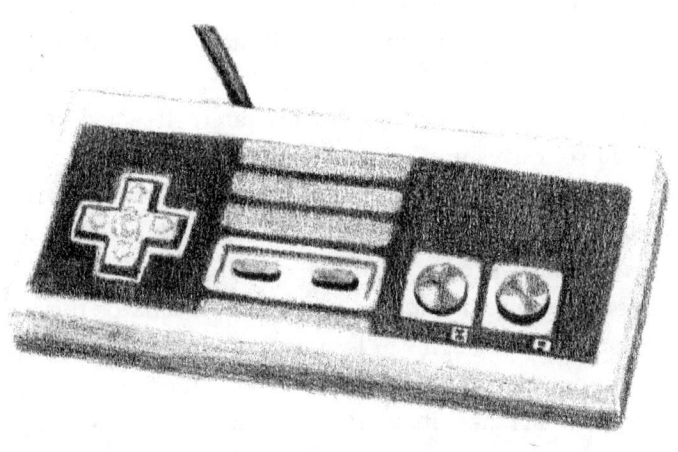

Chapter 5 | The Infinite Game

Man's unhappiness seems to have grown in proportion to his power over the exterior world.

THOMAS MERTON, DISRUPTED QUESTIONS

SOMETIMES I WONDER IF what makes anything good is the fact that it is temporary. It's why, even though I'm dog-tired, haven't had a moment to relax, I can't seem to bring myself to leave my children's bedside at night. Because I know that the next morning, this will be gone—*this* age, *this* particular day, when they are *this* height, *this* soft, *this* way, *this* moment.

I do think parents perceive time based on their children, because children act as time-barometers. They remind us, each morning, just how much time has lapsed. Marks on door trim with dates etched into them. Pants that rest higher and higher above the ankles. An Elsa and Anna coat that won't fit any longer. Car seats that barely buckle. Favorite shoes that won't fit. Games that are no longer fun. Basically, whatever it is that makes you cry whenever you watch the *Toy Story* movies!

When I was a little kid, we had first generation Mario. It was pure, regular Nintendo goodness. But I gotta be honest, I've still never beat that game! It's not that Mario was the hardest game I've ever played, or that the levels are super complicated (I mean, there are only two buttons). It's that there are no infinite lives. Once you die in Mario the game is over. These days games, are rarely designed this way. If you lose all your lives in modern versions of Mario, you can just hit "continue." You can actually choose that continue option forever.

I think it's in the moments that we are playing, what I call, *the infinite game*, that we forget just how good this *coffee bean moment* is. As soon as we believe that it goes on this way, this flavor, this day, this product, endlessly, it begins to lose its *specialness*. It no longer feels like something to *treasure* in this way. What if the temporal nature of life is part of what makes it good? What if, at the point we are playing the infinite game, we are attempting a life outside of God's created intention for us?

It's ironic that we think utopia is about freezing time. If we could just look youthful forever, enjoy this amazing dessert every single day, always live *this way*, then we would have ultimate fulfillment, right? Yet, what we learn over time, and what "the rich" often discover faster than anyone, is that attempting to live this way quickly turns into a place resembling a version of hell rather than heaven.

Recently, Daily kept begging me to take her to the trampoline park, as if she needed to do more bouncing off the walls! (Somehow, our kids are firm believers that, as parents, we are their entertainment safari guides.) I just mentioned how the trampoline park is kind of far away and pretty expensive and I'm not sure when we'll be going next. To which she responded by encouraging me to get a "real job" like "selling lemonade or something" so we could go to the trampoline park more often. So, while seriously considering a career change, I took it as an opportunity to whip out that age-old adage worth repeating. "You know, honey, 'money doesn't buy happiness.'"

It doesn't take long eating tiramisu every day to get tired of it. After about six levels of Mario played six times over, I'm cooked. We've all experienced this with some product or place. And of course, if you've ever been dangerously addicted to anything, you know where this can go and how dark and desperate it can all become. Odds are you're nodding your head to all of this in some form of agreement,

"Yep, yep, that's right." Because, deep down, there's nothing too controversial here. We've all crossed paths with this truth before.

Let's be honest, we still do it. We know it, but we still do it. We still get caught doing all the many things to try and deny, transcend, or alter our limitations. This kind of fixation on the infinite game can manifest as growing a brand; it can be as subtle as Instagram filters, chasing trends, or it can have more abrupt characteristics like long work hours, no rest, unrecognized grief, relational breakdowns, screaming at kids, and thoughts of self-harm.

We think if we can just play enough rounds, we could beat the game and finally arrive at contentment! The truth is, even if we could do such a thing, we'd soon find ourselves ultimately weary of that "perfect moment." Following that weariness would be a dullness, and we'd be back searching for the next perfect moment. Any of this sound familiar?

Why do we experience life this way? Is there divine intention here? Could it be that our struggles are meant to help us mature?

I wonder if these "unfulfillments," this inability to attain nirvana through the infinite pressing of the *continue* button, is part of God's fail-safe? It's the friction prepackaged within God's beautiful, created order that points us back on course. It leaves us still in search for the *real thing*, dissatisfied by anything less than the life God created us for.

Anything less than fulfillment within our relationship with God, the Great Ultimate Reality, the Beginning and Ending of Truth, the One Who Is, the Wonderful I Am, True Presence, will be insufficient.

We are created from this One and for this One. So much so that when we fix our gaze, set our sights, pursue anything else in creation with the effort of worshiping it, making that thing our "all in all," it will just result in self-destruct mode. (Remember what happens in Gen 3? We hold a propensity to repeat those mistakes.) This is not because God is a narcissist who needs us all to bolster God's greatness, but because anything short of this, short of us belonging with and within God, would only be a shadow of existence.

God loves us enough to invite us into losing our life inside of God's abundant, diverse, and creative life. Because that's the very place we'll find true life. We won't find it in some future moment, but in discovering the Presence, right here. Here, in the midst of imperfection, hardship, tension, pain, and starting over.

I'll attempt to restate this in a different way: We are created for eternal relationship with the One who is eternal. Deep down, we know this. We recognize that hunger for more inside of us. Yet instead of seeking the heart of God and following Jesus through the simple way that God left for us, we often try to fulfill that bond on our own, through playing the infinite game.

Many Christians have conflated the infinite game with Jesus. The gospel was reinterpreted as a successful-looking life on earth. It's a cozy version of the gospel message that became less about carrying our cross and more about some fantastical narrative where Jesus is giving us cozy lives with heated seats and weighted blankets. As author Peter Rollins points out, "Like every other product that promises us fulfilment, Christ becomes yet another object in the world that is offered to us as a way of gaining insight and ultimate satisfaction."[1] If we haven't gotten our desires met, we possibly need to pray more, do more fasting, and just get a bit holier.

We play the infinite game any and every time we strive toward fulfillment, happiness, and true well-being out of a never-ending struggle for attainment. It's an attempt to get the good life out of a harder work ethic, the continual grind, overcoming our shortcomings, transcending our mortality, pressing harder, acquiring more, and sometimes even through being more spiritual.

We get stuck hitting that continue button, hoping to eventually win the game. We believe if we just have enough endurance, push through enough sleepless nights, and finally get that raise, we'll have everything at last.

But what if instead of the infinite rat race, we did something else? What if we became less interested in the infinite and more interested in the eternal?

Norman Wirzba writes about the difference between a quantitative life and a qualitative life. He describes the quantitative life as

---

1. Rollins, *Idolatry of God*, 2.

having been reduced to the flow of various functions, its primary point, when viewed from a quantitative perspective is to extend and increase the flow: do more, have more, and live longer. A person is thus forever wanting and disconnected because there is little ability to imagine what a complete or whole life might be, a life that respected limits and could be satisfied with enough.[2]

Infinity is about quantity. Infinity is about us doubling over our efforts to achieve production that never ends. It's about pushing that "continue game" button over and over, even if the game is no longer bringing any joy or well-being. It's about digging in the earth for minerals that we believe are just there for the taking. It's about attempting to stretch our topsoil, our skin, our time, our energy, and every resource we have until we are unrecognizable as human beings and Earth is unrecognizable as our home.

An eternal posture is the opposite of that.

An eternal posture acknowledges finitude. Scratch that. It *loves* finitude. It's qualitative. It embraces boundaries and celebrates wrinkles. It is represented in someone whose life is "hidden with God in Christ." It's when your center is with the One rather than attempting to make your own center the one. Someone with an eternal posture is comfortable within her own boundaries, within her own finitude, in loving embrace of the sacred gift of being a frail human. This eternal person is unafraid of the friction because she sees holistically, and in that, pain gives way to joy.

The eternal person isn't playing some game. She has no VR headset over her eyes. She is not seeking fulfillment in reaching the next level. She "can't lose" because she has clear eyes and a full heart, experiencing oxygen in real time, tasting all flavor notes and hearing the lyrics of creation. The eternal person is aware. She is here. Are you here?

Some things do go on and on and on into eternity. Those things are love, creativity, and inward growth . . . and perhaps the universe itself.

---

2. Wirzba, *This Sacred Life*, 54.

STACKING BLOCKS

There is something deeply therapeutic about playing with Lego bricks. The work of creating something with our hands is innate. Snapping these little blocks together resonates with something primal inside of us! The possibilities are endless.

Imagine you lived on a planet made of these little bricks. Sounds pretty epic, doesn't it? I know more than a few people whose vision of heaven goes something like that! So, imagine you live on this planet of building blocks and you spend every day and every night building. You build cities, and cars, and airplanes, and anything that might entertain you. Eventually, everyone got *really* good at this, but even more, we began collaborating across this Lego planet to go even further than we ever have. Years, decades, and centuries come and go; meanwhile, we build, build, and build. Until one day, we notice something horrific: the number of building blocks available have dramatically dwindled.

We'd never really thought before about having a finite number of blocks. We'd never noticed before that every time we built something, our planet of blocks gets a little bit smaller. We never noticed before that every time we build something "on top," everything that makes up what's "beneath" is reduced. In fact, we never noticed that we could actually build ourselves *out of* a home. We could build until there was nothing left to continue building with. Our Lego brick planet is in big trouble if it continues like this.

How can we continue to build endlessly when our blocks are not endless? If our entire system is dependent on having an infinite number of blocks, it will fail.

As I write this, people around the world are building. Our worldwide web language has fast-tracked the progress more than we could ever dream. We are playing the infinite game with all of God's creation. We're building that tower of Babel, and ironically, it is costing us everything we have loved to do it.

Just because we can doesn't mean that we should.
Just because there are blocks doesn't mean that we should stack them.
Just because it grows doesn't mean we should consume it.

At this juncture, we should all have a healthy grasp on climate change and the ongoing global environmental degradation occurring around us. It should be regular discussion at churches, schools, workplaces, and street corners! Yet, we don't, and it isn't. This is the greatest threat humanity has ever faced. Where is all the chatter?

The reason for so much of the silence is not because people don't want to know what's happening with our planetary environment, it's because that, by and large, those who make the most profit from "the building of blocks" control much of the way we see the world. Much of the information about how our "building block" emissions, pollution, and overconsumption are affecting the planet have been around for decades. But when the truth about something threatens the deep corporate pockets of the brick empire, history reminds us of who gets put on a cross, and it's not the brick masters. When a certain few elites start taking all the bricks for their own use, not only is it not very fun for the rest of us, but the ugly by-products begin showing their heads.

How many times can the experts warn us that we have a very short window left to prevent runaway, irreversible climate change and ecological disaster?[3] How many natural consequences do we need to shrug our shoulders at before things get changed?

Floods.
Fires.
Hurricanes.
Drought.
Desertification.
Ice caps.
Sea levels.
Insects.
Extinctions.

Here's what I believe:

Deep down, living in harmony with the planet sounds like a good plan to everyone; we just don't know how or what that will look like anymore. I believe the news often leaves us paralyzed rather than empowered. I believe we are created in the image of a God who is in the business of restoration and reconciliation, and the tools to heal a

---

3. IPCC, "AR6 Synthesis Report."

breaking world are in our hands. The thing is though, they may not be the tools we think they are.

The story of Lego began in the woodshop of an early twentieth-century Danish carpenter named Ole Kirk Christiansen. "Lego" is from the Danish phrase *leg godt* meaning "play well." I wonder what it would look like for our brick economies to play well in the world today?

I remember many years ago when I was a kid, our parents bought my sister and me one of those original Lego buckets. The side of the bucket showed how many of each piece you received and some ideas of what you could build. Each block was precious as it held so many possibilities!

At the time, my grandfather, Pop, drove this 1985 Ford van for his work, and my sister decided she was going to build a block replica of the van and give it to him. In the end, she did a pretty good job; and after her crowning achievement, the Lego van, much to my despair, went up on a shelf. I was so upset—I wanted to play with those bricks! But they were strictly off limits. Why? Because that would have meant destroying the van.

My own children do this today every time we play with those colorful bricks. They'll spend hours constructing their towers and palaces, complete with bathrooms, bedrooms, and balconies with slides. Impressive stuff. At the end of each play time, I am the bad guy who says, "Time to clean up." Sometimes we'll allow the structure to sit in the kid's bedroom for an extra day or so, like a monument to the weekend. In the end though, what we built, we must tear down in order to build again tomorrow. *If we want to be able to play well later, we've got to be willing to properly deconstruct and clean up today.*

To date, we've built some epic things. We've got city centers that are the stuff of dreams. Urban growth seems bigger than ever before as the train of development attempts to squish as many souls as possible into metropolitan areas. We've got every form of transportation you can think of, every restaurant you can imagine, hundreds of different industries and businesses, along with tiny and giant-sized boxes to live in. All this just within a ten-minute drive from Taco Bell. We've built a lot of things.

It's not just *the things*; it's *the thing that built the things*. We haven't just built buildings and structures but *systems*. We've built a certain way of life that also builds in particular ways. So, as society, are we building the kind of lives we want to have? Or are we busy building something else?

AIMING AND ARCING

There's something about a bow and arrow that really draws me in. It represents some of the earliest equipment humanity could create out of wood and string. It was a tool for survival in earlier times. More than simply pulling a trigger, there is an earthen craft to the bow and arrow. With great strength, you pull against the pressure, arc for distance, acknowledge the gust of the wind, and correct arc for the distance. Precision aiming with a bow and arrow is next level.

I always recall that scene when Robin Hood (Kevin Costner movie reference again, keep up!) saves a boy who is hanging by a noose. He shoots an arrow over the crowd from a great distance to cut the rope in two! Or when he pulls feathers off of two arrows with his teeth and releases them both at once! (Needless to say, as a kid, getting a bow and arrow was pretty high up on the wish list in order to free the world from the tyranny of corrupt empires! I guess a pencil will have to do.)

A famous line by Henry David Thoreau says, "In the long run, we only hit what we aim at." Thoreau was a remarkable human. He was a brilliant writer of the nineteenth century; he graduated from Harvard, refused to pay taxes as a means of protest, and may have been the original minimalist. He became friends with Ralph Waldo Emerson, who allowed him to build a small homestead in the wilderness of Emerson's property. So, Thoreau did and lived alone there encapsulated by the wilderness. He wrote, "I went to the woods because I wished to live deliberately, to front only the essential facts of life, and see if I could not learn what it had to teach, and not, when I came to die, discover that I had not lived."[4] There is some serious mileage to be

---

4. Thoreau, *Walden and Other Writings*, 100–101.

found in this quote. Thoreau sought simplicity in his small lifestyle deep within the natural environment and wrote about it at length. It's fascinating to consider that this person, hundreds of years ago, felt to be in conflict with a cultural posture of progress and consumerism. In the mid-1800s, he was critical of any promise of contentment or happiness through the gain of more material improvement. He criticized any mechanical advancement that touted gifts of control and freedom as new forms of potential enslavement.

What in the world would Thoreau think about our Western lives today? How about those little screens in our pockets that we couldn't imagine going an hour without? He said that rather than turning to more technological advances, we should return and look to the natural world, which holds important lessons and spiritual significance.

Today, as I'm writing this, it is Martin Luther King Jr. Day. I think if we're going to make any day a recognized American holiday, this is one of the best. King was a man who reshaped history, and his work continues changing the world as the ripples of his life move outward. It happened that Thoreau was one of the influential thinkers that King admired. Thoreau had famously spent a night in jail for not paying taxes as he refused to support slavery and the American–Mexican war. With fire in his belly, he wrote his famous work *Civil Disobedience*, which truly never caught its stride until it landed in the hands of MLK and the civil rights movements of the twentieth century.

It would be naïve of us to think that these threads of technology, nature, and justice are coincidental or circumstantial. These threads are woven into the tapestry of history. As we looked at in the last chapter, "violence and dispossession and enslavement" are how we arrived in the kind of economy and world we live in today. But getting here also "required crafting a new story about nature . . . getting people to see nature, for the first time, as something . . . inferior and subordinate," as pointed out by economic anthropologist Jason Hickel.[5]

Thoreau saw some of the trap that was ahead that most of us are neck-deep in today. It is a society that has all but spoiled nature in ways that we never suspected could occur, all under the disguise of creating a better world. These pollutions hide under the big blanket

---

5. Hickel, *Less Is More*, 254.

of deep-seated beliefs that what betters our economy betters our lives. Yet, this blanket statement has inflicted much harm for human and nonhuman creation, especially the fence line communities and those who have been historically marginalized.

Years ago, newly married, I was desperately searching for a job. Just about anything would do. It was 2009, and jobs were very scarce. You'll likely recall in 2008, we experienced a global financial crisis, which was the inevitable outcome of our broken economic system. Amidst the naïve belief that free market economies will self-regulate along with the highest praise for highest profit ideology, banks were offering home lending like it was Monopoly money! The capitalistic prioritization of short-term gains coupled with risky deals all in the name of ever-increasing profit eventually popped that big bubble. So, we all got a little taste of just how fragile this system is; but did we use the time to look deeper at the problem, or work harder to get it back, new and improved, with eight cylinders this time?

I pulled up to an interview. It was a chiropractic office. Not my ideal setting, but at least it would be income, I thought. There was a room full of applicants, and I appeared to be the youngest person in the room. At last, the chiropractor himself came out, greeting us and giving us papers to fill out. As the moment unfolded, I slowly understood what was happening: a group interview. But not just any group interview; it was a competition. We were being pitted against each other. It was the chiropractic-office-job Hunger Games.

We were each given a stack of surveys. We were told they were "health surveys." We had one hour to go "out there" into the world and get as many of these surveys filled out as we could manage. That was basically the interview. It was a test to see how we could handle this proselytizing work.

I already hated it, but I knew if it meant a paying job, I could do it. "You have one hour, go!" Grown adults basically jogged out of the lobby, clipboards in hand, frantic. I had already thought about our proximity to the nearby shopping centers. Shamelessly, I pulled up at one. First stop: Starbucks. Fortunately, I was already dressed-to-impress because of the interview, so with my matching clipboard and pen, I jumped in the deep end. Way out of my comfort zone, I approached person after person. I harangued people out of sheer desperation wherever I found them for the next hour. The thing was, I really needed a job and was unashamed to use my desperation. My opening line became, "I'm sorry to bother you, I am applying for this job, and I'm in need of a few people to fill out a survey for me, would you please help me?"

I don't think there is a more accurate example of the spirit of our "grab life by the horns" and "pull up your boots" economy than this. Me, thinking about my new rental agreement, my newly married wife, my empty cupboards, my electric bill, the gas I needed to put in my car—all of it was pushing me to "do whatever it takes." But anyone whose been there knows that you can't function under the whatever-it-takes pressure for long before it takes *you*. Operating out of that spirit leaves you empty on the inside while offering false future promises of giving back. It's a kind of life that offers no rest, no nutrition, and little hope.

I pushed, bugged people, ran down sidewalks, pleaded, and came back at the end of the hour with a stack full of surveys. I thought I had done well, especially as I saw another man returning with maybe seven. The chiropractor looked at my stack of surveys and said, "Wow! I can see you don't mind this kind of work!" Inside I was thinking, "Um, that was horrible." I was called back for a real interview, but there was a problem. He had looked intently at the information I collected. None of the surveys were fully completed. Some information was plugged in here and there. People offered a few details, but hardly anyone took enough care to include helpful data or their contact information. So, for chiropractic purposes, they were useless. Apparently, I had gotten quantity over quality in my proselytizing. Instead of aiming at acquiring informative health information out of people, I had, in transparency, asked people to fill out those forms so I could land a job!

By some miracle, my giant stack of surveys got me the gig. We had to celebrate. That evening, Emily and I went to the swankiest Italian restaurant we knew of: Maggiano's! "To the future!" we said. Little did we know that a mere two weeks later, I would find myself in the parking lot of a mall, having just been kicked out of another establishment for pestering people, in tears. No one wanted to be bothered, everyone just wanted to be left alone, and ultimately, soliciting people for chiropractic care outside of Target was my idea of hell on earth. I soon left that job behind.

There are a number of things I learned from that experience. The first is to wait at least a month after you get the new job before you spend all your money at Maggiano's. The second is about aiming at the wrong target. Not only did I aim at the wrong kind of work for me, but even the way I went about it revealed someone working toward the wrong end. If money was the greatest achievable outcome possible, then maybe I should have kept that job. But as I found, it wasn't.

What if our greatest achievable outcome isn't something that always comes with more money? This is a micro-example of our whole economic problem. We've made money our highest aim. In the end, this is a *get what you give* scenario. If, as Thoreau said, we hit what we aim at, we better aim well.

What kind of society do we want? What sort of lives are we working toward and getting out of bed for every morning? The capitalistic operating systems that we're stuck in are ones that don't promote human health and well-being but rather promote more of the same life-extracting systems perpetually. It doesn't aim at ecological or human health but aims at selling more products to the masses. Success, as we have defined it economically, is having more money today than you did yesterday—more things, more toys, more home, newer models, more access, and first class seats. It's a race to the cornucopia in the attempt to hoard what we can. It's a battle to the top of the ladder. It's a system that pits us against one another. Its markers are scarcity and violence.

So, if we want to win that game, if we want all that, we're going to have to pay for it. But money isn't our most valuable currency. No, we are paying with our very lives, which we won't get back.

CHALUPA SUPREME

Years ago, I had a friend with whom I went on a quest for a "chalupa supreme beef" from Taco Bell whenever he visited America. Since he was coming from Europe, I recognized the novelty of such a thing, and we had a laugh over it. But let's be honest, the chalupa supreme may be the embodiment of everything gone wrong with creation today! Looking back, friends don't let friends "chalupa supreme beef."

I have to confess, though, that back in my professional trash-hauling days, if I hadn't had the bandwidth to pack lunch for the day, I'd set out to find $2.19 in some property I was cleaning out. If I scrounged up enough change in some random couch cushions, I could swing through Taco Bell and get one bean burrito and a spicy potato soft taco for that exact amount. It's the approved lunch of garbage people everywhere.

It still strikes me to this day—how it is that they can sell multiple food items for little to nothing? The answer goes all the way back to our discussion on the airplane, to that propensity to throw gravity the middle finger and launch ourselves higher.

Here is what I mean: a place like Taco Bell is a top-tier example of what a couple centuries of "overcoming" our natural limitations can get us (cheap food, very fast). Back to those tractors that help us manage more fields faster than ever before—chemicals repel other forms of life that we may not want eating our crops of onions and beans. Container ships transport loads of food halfway across the globe. Refrigeration allows us to stock up on ingredients for weeks at a time. Capitalism affords Taco Bells everywhere to have the same menu and lunch for around $2.19. Additionally, people are somehow getting paid, leases are kept, lights are turned on, and bathrooms are cleaned (well, sometimes). You can begin to see that $2.19 is not the *true cost* of that meal.

The reasons some things are so cheap is that we are not paying the true costs. Somebody else is paying that cost. The true cost is underpaid labor, non-nutritional food, factory farms, animals stacked on top of other animals, ecologically-bankrupt fields squeezing out another bean or tomato, increased carbon emissions through the global distribution of these temperature-controlled commodities, and don't forget your and my healthcare bill. In other words, because we live in an age when we've transcended so many of our natural limitations, we can have something like Taco Bell.

But does it take more than it gives?

Every road trip I've taken with Emily, at some point, as a semi-truck nearly grazes our car side mirror, she states, "I wish truckers just had their own highways!" As in, I wish there were no semitrucks on the road with us.

Admittedly, no offense to those in that occupation, but traveling would be a lot more enjoyable without all those eighteen-wheel giants on the road swerving around us. Some folks may be taken aback at just the thought though. An affront against truckers feels like an affront against America, doesn't it?

Can we be against the rights of production and distribution? Isn't that an affront to freedom itself?

Can we set our knee-jerk reactions aside for a moment and dream?

A world without so many large loads of goods being moved across the world, what would that mean? It would mean the return to locally oriented economies. It would mean truer levels of independence. Yes, it would mean work, it would mean genuine effort, but it would also mean sustainability.

Ironically, the parts of America that many look back on with nostalgia is one of small towns that look nothing like the small towns of today. Walmart offers no nostalgia. Costco affords no feelings except the promises of individualized leisure, the high of getting a good deal, and the famous $1.50 hot dog. Money will give us what we want, even if what we want are big box stores of temporary pleasure with long-term planetary devastation.

The thing is, putting all the onus on government and big corporations is just as faulty as putting it all on the consumer. It isn't a "this or that" conversation. Environmental degradation has never been a binary problem with those kinds of solutions. Its relational and interconnected, the web of life, as God created it to be. Yes, these industry giants and those "at the top" must make those critical changes, but the problems are deeper than we often care to look. It's the curtain behind the curtain.

I sometimes wonder, if we are plugged into the *Matrix*. (Yes, the nineties film that just keeps on giving; thank you, Keanu, for everything.) We may as well be secretly run by the machines that we created. Isn't that a great irony? Consider all the Hollywood media that has generated millions of dollars by playing off our fears of artificial intelligence becoming sentient and taking over. Hasn't this already occurred? We wake up in the morning and everything from our quick lunch, to our fast fashion, to our frictionless communication simply feeds the capitalistic machine. It keeps us efficient, cozy, docile, well dressed, and well fed. Where else would we want to go? Why would anyone want to be unplugged from it?

In Spain, there is a geese farmer who's famous for his foie gras. Foie gras is a sought out culinary delicacy by many food enthusiasts. The hitch is, getting foie gras isn't as easy as it sounds. Foie gras is produced when a goose is intentionally fattened, typically through a kind of force-feeding called *gavage*, in the effort to serve up its enlarged liver on a platter. If you're uneasy about this, you're not the only one. Serving foie gras may be already unlawful depending on where you live. It is an ethical anomaly considering the horrific means in which all other livestock are treated in most concentrated feeding operations.

The situation is different with farmer Eduardo Sousa. On his farm in Extremadura, he doesn't force feed his geese. In fact, he doesn't even fence them in because he senses that the geese are not as content if they feel like they are captives. They can fly away if they chose to at any time. Yet, the opposite occurs here. Geese arrive at his farm all on their own! They fly down to see what's going on, find goose paradise, and never leave again. Eduardo has created a utopia for geese. This goose garden is dripping with olives, figs, and seeds, and in that environment, the geese gorge themselves, unknowingly preparing themselves for dinner. Within their unfenced curated paradise, they fatten themselves until they are just right for slaughter.[6] What looks like heaven ends up being hell.

Casinos operate on the very same principles. In those artificially lit arenas, there's no windows to let you know how long you've been there, buffets of food to eat, and just enough lure to keep you rolling the dice. You are free to go whenever you like, if you can.

---

6. For a great synopsis, see Barber, "Surprising Parable."

This is precisely how capitalism functions. The systems of capitalism are the farm; we are the geese.

We believe that this place is for our benefit, but it's not. It's a trap. This is not freedom; this is farming. We're being farmed.

In the dominating economic system of today, what may appear like the opportunity to pursue the good life to some offers suffering and oppression for many others, and eventually consumes us all. Wealthy food enthusiasts eat foie gras and our current economic system eats the earth.

How did we get here? Is this what we really want? Is this really what we're aiming for?

To be honest, I think that there are some people who are aiming for this exact thing. They are aiming for a life of ease and comfort, and the last thing they want to do is look around and discover that the system is broken. These people are content playing the infinite game, pulling the slot machine lever, and hitting continue as long as they can if it means they get to stay in artificial paradise and gorge themselves on olives, figs, and chalupas. They don't dare peek behind the curtain as long as they've got a good enough seat on the plane.

Can we pursue our own personalized well-being apart from the well-being of the rest of God's creation, apart from the well-being of our human siblings? Can we love our neighbors and stay in goose paradise? Can we follow Christ and continue to blindly participate in systems that aren't Christlike? Can we continue attempting to spread the message of the Creator while participating in the devouring of creation?

All that's left now is to think on all of this over some cake and doughnuts.

> *Creator God, remind us, we pray, of who we are in you. Remind us that our worth is not contingent upon our production, but rooted in your love. Remind us that we are your children. God, give us the patience and grace to aim for your kingdom. Help us to seek your face with our whole hearts and your kingdom above all else. Jog our memory that we may reorient our entire lives around the economy of your kingdom, as it is the only place in which flourishing occurs.*
> *Amen.*

Chapter 6 | American Doughnuts

ONCE UPON A TIME, on Constitution Avenue, I found myself inside the National Archives—a place of democratic sacred ground. It's a place where no photographs are allowed (which, if I'm honest, is kind of refreshing for some reason). It is a place where our special American texts are kept and where there are endless references to the movie *National Treasure* (the Nicolas Cage hit from 2004 where the Declaration of Independence is stolen). Inside, one could easily spend an entire day looking at all the documents that compile the history of our young nation. But honestly, I didn't spend much time wandering the secondary halls of information; I was there to see the goods.

Entering the low-lit rotunda where they keep the large documents that forged American democracy has some gravity to it. I have to admit that the experience caught me off guard. Not because I'm someone who cries red, white, and blue tears, but in the way that one becomes slightly more aware of being a part of something larger than oneself. Before stepping up and into the main area where the Declaration of

Independence, Constitution, and Bill of Rights are kept, there is an officer and an enormous gate. She lines up everyone who is waiting to go in shoulder to shoulder, as if there's about to be a troop inspection. I could barely hear because of the echo, but I think the instructions were something like, "Don't try to pull a Nicholas Cage."

What struck me as I approached the Declaration was how aged it seemed, tucked away behind the layers of bulletproof glass. Many of the actual words were faded, written in elaborate calligraphy to boot, making it pretty difficult to read. I scanned the document, finally catching the bottom of the parchment and perhaps the most powerful part. There, I saw the signatures. I remember thinking, "That is Benjamin Franklin's signature, right there. Bro put his hand right there and signed it. Absolutely nuts."

I glanced upward in the document and saw the famous refrain, "Life, Liberty and the pursuit of Happiness." Before it was on a baggy T-shirt, a magnet to stick on your freezer door, or a pair of DC jogging pants, it was here on this parchment forming a new government and forging a new future.

> We hold these truths to be self-evident, that all men are created equal, that they are endowed by their Creator with certain unalienable Rights, that among these are Life, Liberty and the pursuit of Happiness.[1]

The Declaration, couched within history, in its own way represents a leap forward in consciousness. Even so, we can look back and see all the ways this "new world" fell short.

It states that "all men are created equal." Without a doubt, Americans today are still struggling with what a radical "created equal" statement would entail. Ironically, even with declaring large ideas about equality, our forefathers were still stuck in the world of patriarchy, racism, and white masculine-centered freedoms. In some ways, this pursuit appeared to be a leap forward, but as we know, this notion of "liberty" somehow continued to coexist with the colonization and genocide of many Indigenous peoples, the enslavement of black Africans, and the suppression of all women's rights.

Attempting to put ourselves in the mind of these "forefathers," we might ask, what does it mean to have the right to life, liberty, and

---

1. Declaration of Independence, para. 2.

the pursuit of happiness? There is doubtlessly an eighteenth-century interpretation of "independence" at play in these words. I can't help but think that these radical notions of our indivisibility from British colonial overreaching fingers defined a certain altitude that is less accessible for us Americans today who might venture to define these terms.[2]

What sort of life is a "life"?
What does it mean to have "liberty"?
And how do we define a "pursuit of happiness"?

After my stroll through history, I had lunch at a café across the street pondering the questions: What would our forefathers think of America today? Did they have any idea of how this would play out centuries later? Are we living the sort of lives they were hoping for? Did we attain the kind of liberty they wanted? Did we pursue happiness altruistically? Would they be amazed to find that you can get a bean burrito for a couple of papers and coins bearing their image?

Could they have ever imagined what would happen when we took those values, hit "super-size me," and plugged them into an industrial revolution? Did they ever consider what might happen when *life, liberty and the pursuit of happiness* slowly became a synonym for the individual right to have as much as one can get?

Could these great minds of the past ever have guessed that we would then turn to create an economic machine that would redefine prosperity as product? Could they have considered that we would "use" that liberty to consume however we wanted to consume, despite the ramifications of inequality in the world? That we would use that freedom to defend whatever industrial rights we felt that we should have? That a wave of individualism would be born and grow up to be thoroughly religious in its idolatry?

No, they probably didn't see that coming.

---

2. It's hard to miss the Christian threads in these early American documents. It is important to clearly state that one of our greatest shortcomings has been an attempt to conflate the governments of this world (namely here, America) and the kingdom of God. Christian nationalism is a spreading disease that seeks to syncretize America with Christianity. Living as Christians in America is not synonymous with Americanized Christianity or Christian nationalism. We are left to address American values as Christians who live within certain times and spaces, particularly as these values have drastic impacts upon God's good creation, human and nonhuman.

DEATH BY CAKE

What is the point of an economy? It doesn't take long reflecting on this question to come up with some answers that we generally agree on. I think that what we truly desire out of an economy is that it serves us, improves all our lives, increases our well-being, makes us healthier, is sustainable, and is ultimately life giving for everyone involved (this includes the planet)!

But we live within an economy that doesn't do these things. We live within an economy that suppresses the least of these. As it stands, only certain groups "come out on top," and even those who are on top, as they accumulate more possessions, may find that they are also accumulating an impoverished spirit, void of true flourishing.

Currently, much of the global economy operates out of the principle that more sales, factories, industries, mines, extraction, and more market growth is an unquestionable good. The economy produced by capitalism touts that success looks like ever-increasing GDP (Gross Domestic Product). But what if infinitely increasing GDP doesn't create universal well-being? What if the "bottom line" isn't the best indicator of how well any of us are doing? What if this ever-increasing consumption doesn't offer the good life at all? What if it takes it?

GDP is the metric used to tell of the "monetary value of the goods and services that are being produced and consumed within a given nation or region."[3] More than that, this measurement has today become synonymous with prosperity, happiness, and life satisfaction. Sure, we can easily admit that we all want enough financial growth to avoid poverty, have food to eat, clothing, and a roof over our heads.

That's a far cry from equating this economic metric with what it means to be a flourishing human being. Jason Hickel cites that "in the United States, happiness rates peaked in the 1950s when GDP per capital was only about $15,000 (in today's dollars). Since then the average real income of Americans has quadrupled, and yet happiness has plateaued and even declined for the past half-century."[4]

Despite what good it may have done for some certain American and Western families of the past, this measurement of "success"

---

3. Jackson, *Prosperity Without Growth*, 3.
4. Hickel, *Less Is More*, 180.

now sits distinctly separate from the kind of flourishing we need as a society. It is a system that's busy making deeper pockets out of a few deep pockets, deeper mines out of already gaping world wounds, and celebrating the growth of a stock market without taking any stock of what truly creates a good and meaningful life.

Deep down, we all know this on some level. We know that more stuff doesn't equal more joy, contentment, health, or a life well lived. We know that at some point, we don't need more or advanced things, bigger homes, or more money . . . in fact, we might even need *less of it* to be whole. Maybe that's why one of the secrets of the kingdom of God is that in losing your life you are able to find it.

> The growth is actually in the way.
> It is growth for growth's sake.
>
> Some call this *growthism* . . .

and growthism may be the greatest idol humans have ever created.

Hickel names growthism as "the pursuit of growth for its own sake, or for the sake of capital accumulation, rather than to meet concrete human needs and social objectives."[5]

The idea of growth for many has become a synonym for "good," but they are not the same. Generally, when we think that someone or something is growing, we interpret that to mean something positive (and often, it is). We want our children to grow, our gardens to grow; we want to grow spiritually, intellectually, and so on. In nature, nothing grows infinitely. Trees grow to certain heights before gravity ceases their journey upward. Kids grow to five or six feet tall. Can you imagine someone growing taller infinitely? No one wants that. It would be misery. It would be unnatural.

As a culture, we've become so fixated on growth that we stopped considering what maturity looks like. What does it mean to be fully grown? To be someone or something that has matured?

If discovering a place where human well-being is within reach, was the original goal of boarding the train of capitalism, researchers

---

5. Hickel, *Less Is More*, 101.

Katherine Trebeck and Jeremy Williams argue that, for many wealthy countries, we arrived at that station a long time ago. In their book *The Economics of Arrival: Ideas for a Grown-Up Economy*, they discuss the importance of shifting our understanding and language from the need to grow to "arrival and the notion of making ourselves at home."[6] As our societies' pursuit of unchecked growth harms the environment, perpetuates inequality, and generates an abundance of waste, they assert that there is already enough wealth and resources to meet our needs. Can we work on improvement rather than enlargement? Rather than deboarding at the right time, at the correct destination, society has remained on that GDP-powered train. How far will it take us, we wonder? (Spoiler alert: it's the same plot to every other train film—the bridge is out up ahead.)

Professor of sustainable development, Tim Jackson, frames this discussion noting that there are harsh realities we must face, which include

> the swiftly diminishing returns on growth beyond a certain income; the huge advantages of income growth below that point; and the remarkable performance of some poorer countries who are able to enjoy levels of human well-being on a par with the richest nations on earth on a fraction of the income: all of these lessons are vital in our ability to understand the complex relationship between GDP growth and prosperity.[7]

Jackson examines the data. We attempt to attain "the good life" through an endless quarterly number that is pointing up and to the right. Here's the deal, the math just doesn't add up. Jackson highlights studies that reveal how longevity, education, and our ability to participate in a society are all factors of a life of prosperity, yet these things are not directly tethered with economic growth. There is a point of financial growth that simply doesn't yield returns of wellness for us. Higher incomes aren't synonymous with prosperity. At a certain point, our health, our happiness, our life, doesn't improve any further no matter how much money we throw at it. We know this, but how do we get out of the hamster wheel?

---

6. Trebeck, *Economics of Arrival*, 197.
7. Jackson, *Prosperity Without Growth*, 79.

Hundreds of years into capitalism and we are not only still witnessing extreme poverty in the world but also the largest conceivable gap between the wealthy elite and those experiencing socioeconomic oppression, meanwhile rates of global environmental destruction are beyond what we ever dreamed possible.

As a human, I like cake. By "cake," I mean cakes plural! Particularly, Little Debbie Snack Cakes. Growing up, my Pop sold Little Debbie cakes to backwoods country stores all over southern middle Tennessee, and whenever possible, I was in the passenger seat of that van. The way it worked was if a store had cakes that didn't sell and were expired, we'd switch them out for new ones—which meant that there was often a nice little pile of expired, but still delicious, cakes just waiting for some young, chubby, growing boy to come along. *Don't mind if I do!*

The result was that I had copious amounts of cavities. Quite literally, my mom eventually went to work for a dentist for the rest of her career, which may have just been to get the discount on dental work.

Capitalism wants you to have cake. It wants you to have lots of cake. It wants you . . . to want . . . to have cake. It wants you to have your cake . . . and to eat it, too. Our economy doesn't just want you to have cake and eat it, too, but to have your cake, share with no one, and eat the whole thing alone. Even if it makes you sick. Even if it's painful. Even if it kills you—more cake.

At some point, it's no longer about any semblance of bettering society (though we still believe it is); it is about making bigger cakes and larger profits for those who sell them. It's about keeping all the "cake factories" open. It makes kings and queens of all the cake-makers. Then they use their money and influence to make society . . . even more about cake production! What can we say? They have a right to turn the whole country into cake if it's something they can pull off, right? Because ultimately, we're free and have the right to climb that capitalism ladder as high as we can. We're free to be our own demise.

We often talk in this language of "rights." My right to carry a gun, my right to do whatever I want with my body, or my right to say whatever I want, when I want. For Americans, this has been our blessing-curse, to be a society fixated on our "rights." If you've never read through the list of human rights listed within the United Nations Declaration on Human Rights, it's worth spending time with. These rights are about dignity, equality, freedom from slavery, asylum, work, rest, culture, education, and health.[8]

In America, we mostly talk about our rights in reference to "I should receive what I've sweated for," or "I deserve," or "I have earned." But that's not what these rights are about. These rights are about what we receive because *we are*. These rights are reflections of human dignity within every person born. These rights are about universal equality. These rights are about justice. If you are a part of the few who haven't personally experienced the violation of these within your life, they may not mean as much for you; but if you live in the global majority who are marginalized by the lack of one or many of these rights, you understand how great they are.

What if, as Christians in the world participating in economies, pursuing well-being in our lives and community, we became less interested in the kind of rights that added to our comfort and more interested in the kind of rights that validate whole personhood for all humans? What if we became less interested in kingdoms of cake and more interested in the kingdom of God?

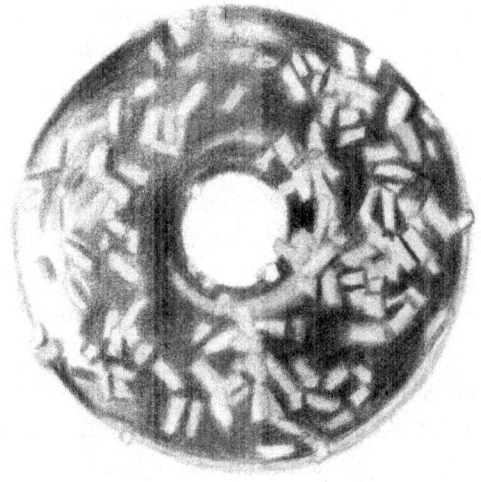

8. United Nations, "Universal Declaration of Human Rights."

CHAPTER 6 | AMERICAN DOUGHNUTS

Despair is the too little . . . As pride is the too much. The shoddy work of despair, the pointless work of pride, equally betray creation. They are wastes of life . . . Good work finds the way between pride and despair. It graces with health. It heals with grace. It preserves the given so that it remains a gift.

WENDELL BERRY[9]

The problem with infinite growth economics is that we live on a finite planet. Economist Kate Raworth expounds on this further in her book *Doughnut Economics*. Raworth uses a familiar image of the doughnut for all of us who have, at some point, eaten more of these sugary circles than we ought.

Imagine with me two circles forming a doughnut. (Feel free to draw it out yourself in the space below.) First, draw or imagine a small inner circle. This smaller circle represents "the social foundation." Next, draw an exterior larger circle around it and label this larger ring "the planet's ecological ceiling." (You should be looking at a doughnut shape now.) Between those two circles in the empty space, write, "the safe and just space for humanity."[10] Staying within the frame of these two circles is everything. Our lives depend on it.

---

9. Berry, *What Are People For?*, 10.
10. If you're just not seeing it, try a quick internet search for "doughnut economics."

What you have drawn is a fundamental understanding of our human boundaries for existence. If we fall too far in toward the middle, past the inner smaller circle, we are faced with "critical human deprivation," yet climbing outward past the larger outer circle, we are confronted with "critical planetary degradation."[11] In other words, if we don't have enough to live on, we are in trouble. But if we overconsume, if we take our gravity-defying rockets even higher, the issues will become greater as we undo the safe boundaries for humanity's existence on this planet. What Raworth understands is that if we reorient ourselves around our known limitations rather than our posture of infinite growth economics, we can find a new and healthy way forward.

Raworth explains that, for most of history, humans have struggled and worked diligently to simply stay within the smaller circle, to have just enough to live their lives. We're familiar with life too far inside the doughnut: it's a shortage of water, food, health, education, work, justice, political voice, social equity, gender equality, housing, networks, and energy. But today, for many of us, especially in the Global North, we are among the first humans to ever live who are witnessing the outcomes of a large mass of people breaking through our ecological ceiling. Never did we imagine that we might climb so high as to shatter the very barriers that keep us safe and whole.

Among these visible outcomes of overreach are climate change, ocean acidification, chemical pollution, nitrogen and phosphorus loading, freshwater withdrawals, land degradation, biodiversity loss, air pollution, and ozone layer depletion. In other words, our extractive practices have so reshaped this place we call home that it is becoming uninhabitable for us. Within the Anthropocene, we've so attempted to reshape the earth in our own image only to discover that our actions are making it unfit for human life.

According to a study released in 2024, "between 2016 and 2021, the global economy has consumed 582 billion tonnes of materials—nearly as many materials as the 740 billion consumed in the entire 20th century."[12] In other words, in only six years, we have globally

---

11. Raworth, *Doughnut Economics*, 43–45.
12. Circle Economy Foundation, "Circularity Gap Report 2024."

consumed 75 percent of what it previously took us an entire century to consume! Yes, there are also six billion more people in the world than there were a hundred years ago, longevity has increased for certain people groups, and we have alleviated poverty in some world areas. So, it would be an easy out to look at that and say, "OK, this is natural." Except what is clearly unnatural is the current state of the natural world! At current consumption rates, humans are eating the world alive, and us with it. The rate at which we are consuming today is busting through our ecological ceiling, and it's all happening in the blink of an eye. The good news is that living in a sustainable relationship with creation, alongside over eight billion people globally (and counting), is completely achievable.

While the language of the Anthropocene is helpful in understanding our current setting, many economists, sociologists, anthropologists, and even theologians argue that more precision is needed—building on the reality that it isn't all of humanity who are responsible for this ecological overshoot but rather largely the systems and structures of capitalism and those who are at the top of that tower.

To recap, capitalism is a global economic system and its primary goal is not the flourishing of humanity, the promotion of well-being, or the prosperity of creation. Its ultimate goal is the production of more gross domestic product. Remember, for capitalism to function, it doesn't just need a *certain amount*, it needs an *infinite supply* of goods. And where does that infinite supply come from?

The earth.

And who brings it? Who supplies that endless clamor for more?

Humans.

When will it stop?

When either humans die or the earth is no more.

The time and place that we live isn't reshaped by all humanity but by this system. Out of this understanding, a new term has been adopted by many to better frame the present issues and age we live within: the *Capitalocene*. This Capitalocene is primarily driven by wealthy individuals and companies who are the main actors in this endless supply and demand loop.

Norman Wirzba borrows well from author Jason W. Moore[13] for an apt description of the Capitalocene,

> specifying that "capitalism was built on excluding most humans from Humanity—indigenous peoples, enslaved Africans, nearly all women, and even many white-skinned men (Slavs, Jews, the Irish) . . . They were regarded as part of Nature, along with trees and soil and rivers—and treated accordingly." To observe that just ninety corporations are responsible for 63 percent of cumulative emissions of carbon dioxide and methane from 1850 to the present means that our focus should not be on human beings in general but on that very small group of men that created, often through violent means, systems of production that are highly destructive in their effects.[14]

The language of the Capitalocene helps us realize that this isn't just greed but violence. One often comes with the other, like the situations we've already discussed taking place, from Egypt to Babylon and from colonial cotton fields to the taking of indigenous lands.

In the world, there exists "islands of prosperity" amidst "oceans of poverty" as the wealthy consume more than their share, Jackson points out.[15] The wealthy few consume the vast majority of Earth's resources. We know that if everyone consumed at the rate as America does, it would take several Earths to sustain us. We've already overdrawn our account. Meanwhile, our brothers and sisters who live in the Global South face the more immediate brunt of climate change through the outputs of waste and issues such as sea level rise and extreme weather shifts. They also live in world areas that need more infrastructure and resources, yet often are left with less than leftovers

---

13. Moore, "The Rise of Cheap Nature," in *Anthropocene or Capitalocene?*
14. Wirzba, *This Sacred Life*, 10.
15. Jackson, *Prosperity Without Growth*, 4.

in the global distribution. Further, many are left without the buffers that others benefit from, such as access to clean water, grocery stores, air conditioning, insurance, healthcare, and technology, making these communities severely vulnerable.

The level of abuse that human bodies and the earth's lands are suffering due to the onslaught of gluttonous wealth mixed with the worship of growth is the stuff of dystopian novels. Any time human or nonhuman creation simply becomes a unit of production, objectified for usefulness and profit, the sacred becomes desecrated.[16]

So, maybe we need to do some confessing. Can we confess that this system is clearly not working?

What questions are we not asking? Like, what actually is well-being? What does human flourishing really look like? What would tangible prosperity be like for our community, for our spirit, for our health, for our home? Are our current economic systems making any of this better or worse? Should I really eat any more of this cake?

If our social and economic systems are taking more life than they give, should we just keep going with business as usual? If we wake up and find that we are now participants in a Babylonian economy that worships growthism and enslaves the least of these to make more bricks for production, shouldn't we be praying for God to part the Red Sea? If this system that we've pledged ourselves to isn't giving our children better futures, promoting healthier lifestyles, creating equality, increasing our happiness, decreasing our anxiety, and making us better communities . . . should we keep it? As the people of God on earth, how are we called out for moments such as these?

MOMENT OF PAINE

We have it in our power to begin the world over again. A situation, similar to the present, hath not happened since the days of Noah until now.

THOMAS PAINE

---

16. In "How to Be a Poet," Berry writes, "There are no unsacred places; there are only sacred places and desecrated places." Berry, *New Collected Poems*.

At the American History Museum, I have about an hour and a half to spare. There is simply too much to see and take in. There sits the thirty-by-four-two-foot American flag that was sewn by Mary Pickersgill and her daughter, nieces, and African American indentured servant, Grace Wisher, in 1813. The flag waved over Fort McHenry the morning after the Battle of Baltimore bombardment, inspiring Francis Scott Key to write *The Star-Spangled Banner*. Out of all the things to take in down those halls, one phrase made out in large letters amidst a sea of American history stopped me. It was a quote from Thomas Paine: "We have it in our power to begin the world over again."[17] Paine, whose use of words is known to have inspired the revolution, were still doing their work today.

Tom Paine, though his name may be less familiar, was a central actor in the oncoming of the American colonies and the separation from Britain. Through his writings, especially in his booklet "Common Sense," he did the faithful work of explaining the environment, the situation that colonists found themselves in, and what he believed was the necessary way forward for independence. In the end, the American Revolution hinged open largely because of Paine's poetic fervor and passionate words.

We are in a global Thomas Paine moment.

The American revolution was born out of an attempt to escape tyranny and oppression. It was a search for new beginnings. History has a way of always bringing us back here again . . . to attempt to ask the question of how to "begin the world over again." We can see now that while early Americans fled the tyranny of England, they did not escape the tyranny inside themselves. What landed on the shores of "New England" was just that, the reconfigured version of the old thing as we took native lands and built our industry on the backs of enslaved people.

Now, centuries later, are we still living the same story and finding our lives entangled in the same sins of our ancestors?

What do we do when the systems and structures that were created for such occasions of freedom aren't making people free?

What's next when everything, from our neighbors to our soil to our atmosphere, has been colonized?

---

17. Paine, *Common Sense*.

What's next when these "structures of freedom" are producing groups of rich elites who hoard wealth while others are stuck in systematic oppression?

Is it freedom when those with power use it to devastate and pollute the water, land, and food that we all rely upon?

Is it still a pursuit of well-being when companies can dig, mine, and extract endlessly from the earth, until the earth is no more?

It's not freedom when there are no limits or boundaries to mitigate our gluttonous appetite. Our efforts today cannot be called the work of a flourishing society if it is our children who pay for our progress.

I wonder, do we have it within our power to begin over again? What kind of power is needed for that? What do we do when all this growth causes all this oppression?

It's said that "justice is the antidote to growth."[18] If we're going to do the meaningful work of deboarding this plane, unplugging from the Matrix, going behind all the curtains (pick your metaphor!), and healing the world . . . equality is the way forward.

Jackson highlights data from countries around the world in reference to health, social problems, and equality. He writes, "Life expectancy, child wellbeing, literacy, social mobility and trust are all better in more equal societies. Infant mortality, obesity, teenage pregnancy, homicide rates and incidence of mental illness are all lower . . . Society as a whole suffers from the face of inequality."[19] Is it really any wonder that places where justice and equality thrive, people flourish?

World altering justice is to "Love your neighbor as yourself."[20]
This is still the most revolutionary phrase you'll ever hear.

Loving our neighbors must win out every time over against growthism. If our neighbors in Memphis suffer under the tyranny of Colossus in the wake of our addiction to AI, if our siblings in Indonesia are working in sweatshops to make our fast fashion, if we're losing

---

18. Hickel, *Less Is More*, 198.
19. Jackson, *Prosperity Without Growth*, 206.
20. Matt 22:39.

prairies, rainforest, and freshwater to keep eating copious amounts of beef, that's not progress. We've traded off the abundant life for the artificially flavored version. You think it tastes good, until you finally try the real thing.

Is it possible that many of us are missing the kind of work God is about in the world because we're stuck in old narratives? We've been told that the opposite to capitalism is socialism or communism . . . or some other "ism." No one wants to trade off Egypt for Babylon or Babylon for Rome.

As people created in the image of God, we've got all the creativity inside of us right now to imagine and embody something new! We can build arks for a new tomorrow.

Ark-building is an invitation to practice hospitality. In the storms of the Anthropocene, hospitality is not merely the offering of a bed or a meal; it is the reordering of our lives to make space for the flourishing of those who are endangered. It is a posture of humility and attentiveness—a posture of listening closely enough to the world's wounds that they become our own, responding with the deliberate shaping of spaces where life can take root again.

AVERY DAVIS LAMB[21]

Although not much is said about it, Paine was clearly moved by the Noah narrative. In Genesis, the story of Noah reflects the tones of the creation story. A close read reveals this in Gen 8:15–18:

> Then God said to Noah, "Go out of the ark, you and your wife and your sons and your sons' wives with you. Bring out with you every living thing that is with you of all flesh—birds and animals and every creeping thing that creeps on the earth—so that they may abound on the earth and be fruitful and multiply on the earth."

These few verses are repetitions of the sixth day of creation.

We are quick to recall the story of Noah, the giant ark, animals lined up two by two, and the unforgettable rainbow. It makes for a

---

21. Lamb, "EPA Has Abandoned Reason."

great coloring page and cute pop-up book. And have you been to Kentucky? You can now visit an actual scaled replica of that ancient ark in Williamstown for just $59.99! (Which may be why no one boarded but Noah's family; they just couldn't afford it!)

While this story continues to captivate us today, there are a number of things going on in this text that are worth wrestling with. It holds a narrative about a faithful family following God's call on their lives, even when it didn't make sense, for the well-being of the world. After that desperate season of storms and floods, it is a rainbow in the sky that remains as a reminder for us today. After the rains ceased and the clouds cleared, God placed that bow in the sky as part of a covenant. But what we often miss is that it wasn't just a covenant between us and God. After the flood, God said to Noah, "This is the sign of the covenant that I make between me and you and every living creature that is with you, for all future generations: I have set my bow in the clouds, and it shall be a sign of the covenant between me and the earth."[22]

Of this covenant moment, theologian Howard Snyder notes, "God delights in his creatures and wills their protection as part of the well-being of the created order. Given creation's complex earth-heaven ecology, human destruction of species violates the covenant in respect to all three parties. The creation groans."[23] The three parties in this covenant are God, humans, and creation. Our failure to be faithful covenant partners in this coming together is unfolding in dire ways today. What this Scripture reminds us of, through God's covenant making with us and the earth, is that what is required is relational. For too long, and still now, we attempt to "fix" the earth rather than enter into right-relatedness with it.

There is a reason God's covenant extends from humanity to also include the earth and all living things. Healing can happen no other way. Even later, the covenant God makes with Abram, highlighted in Gen 17 (that typically we read anthropocentrically), reveals that this covenant is also about Abram and Sarai's belonging to a *land*. Later in Exodus, the people of Israel are brought out of Egypt with their sights on this *promised land*.

---

22. Gen 9:12–13.
23. Snyder, *Salvation Means Creation Healed*, 91.

We have forgotten that land is land. We try so hard to make "land" mean something other than land in the Bible. Our temptation is to spiritualize everything in Scripture.

Our covenantal relationship, that eventually finds ultimate accomplishment in the person of Jesus Christ, is wrapped up in land. Jesus' coming doesn't make God's people land-less. Jesus' coming brings about the further fulfillment of our covenant-faithful God! Our God is about the "reconciliation of all things," as Paul writes in Col 1:20. This includes the land.

The only power we have to "begin the world over again" is through a covenant relationship with God and God's good earth. It is as God intends it to be, and it is a power that is unlike the powers of the world, as it is one marked by humility, grace, meekness, patience, and suffering love. It is an upside-down power that isn't afraid to draw close to the ground. And if something here is worth holding on to in these halls of American history, it is a reinvented, deeper search for new "life, liberty and happiness," for equality and well-being for all, which must include the flourishing of all God's creation.

> *God of all things, set our gaze on the holy reconciliatory work you are calling us to participate in as your people. Help us to be a people more interested in your kingdom coming to earth and less interested in growing the kingdoms of this world. Soak us with your love so that it may then spill out of us for the flourishing of all creation, in which you have graciously included us. Open our eyes so that we may see the deeper good work before us left to do. Help us engage in the ark-making and covenant-keeping work before us as we seek a new balance between human and nonhuman creation in a flooding world.*
>
> *Amen.*

PART FOUR
The Boundary Layer

Lord, you alone are my portion and my cup;
you make my lot secure.
The boundary lines have fallen for me in pleasant places;
surely I have a delightful inheritance.

PSALM 16:5–6, NIV

Chapter 7 | Deeper Than the Holler

Truly embracing the fragility and tensions of life . . .
brings with it the possibility of true joy.

PETER ROLLINS[1]

ALBERT EINSTEIN IS ANECDOTALLY known to have said that "you can't blame gravity for falling in love."[2] While there is a truth found in this whimsical quote, I wonder if there's more to unearth here. Don't get me wrong, I've got nothing on Einstein! I'd love to have had a conversation with him about this one because I believe gravity certainly has "blame" in the love-game!

Gravity is the line drawn, the skin worn, the sexual silhouette, the parameters in which something can be known and thus eventually loved. Without gravity, what would we be loving? What would our aim be upon? Poetically, we consider true love to be boundless; yet, what if true love can only be revealed through that which expresses

1. Rollins, *Idolatry of God*, 85.
2. Einstein, "Albert Einstein Quote."

boundaries? What we love in life is not ethereal, formless, or void. What we love has form, figure, and foundation. It is some thing, it has a name, it has a place, and to love it is to know it.

When we speak of having limits, we usually contemplate it in the negative sense. We think of being trapped, stuck, or leashed rather than liberated, free, and happy. However, everything we know within creation has boundaries. God created the world with these boundaries and called it very good. In fact, what unfolds in the Genesis days of the creation narrative is God's boundary making. God separates sky from sea, land from water.[3] Within these boundaries are found all plants, rocks, creatures, and places. So, in an age when we've extracted so much of God's creation in our pursuit to be unleashed, unbounded, unlocked (and pretty much any number of catchy self-help titles you can think of!), might we consider what it means to be earthbound?

I freaking love the ocean. I'm one of those "salt life" humans. Recently, I asked Emily what she thought about me having a midlife career change and becoming a marine biologist, but I was reminded that we live nowhere near the ocean and I'd just watched *Free Willy* too many times.

Once a summer, our little family makes the commute down from Nashville to the Gulf to eat snow cones, put our toes in the sand, and get a little burnt. I love opening the car door and smelling saltwater wash up under my senses. It feels sacred.

I don't think there's any coincidence that humans are so often drawn toward water, especially the ocean. Coming to the ocean after being away for so long is like returning to the world's end. For as far as the eye can see, water, deep blue, far and wide, *tohu* and *bohu*;[4] it's as far as we go. The ocean tells you exactly where your boundary is: *right here and no further!* What lies beyond this shore is over our heads.

So, we take our pilgrimage when the sun is hot in the sky and long days call us out to play. My girls and I jump, splash, and build in

---

3. Gen 1:9: "And God said, 'Let the waters under the sky be gathered together into one place, and let the dry land appear.' And it was so."

4. Reference to the Hebrew words for "chaos" and "void" found in Gen 1. They're the conditions prior to God's speaking creation into being in the ancient Genesis poem.

the sand right there at our boundary layer ... at the thin place that is a shore. Even though we cannot cross it, we are embraced by it, splashed as we dance in this liminal space and as our lips eventually shrivel with salt, its waves push us to shore again.

When families want to get away and take a vacation, they often go in search of somewhere that they can be closer to the earth. They're in search of some place where the layers between them and creation are slim. This is because deep down we realize that, in order to catch our breath, to take a break from the grind and rest, we need to reconnect with the more-than-human world. We crave to venture out there and live on the edges again. To be bodily present in wild places where we are surrounded not by steel towers but by towering clouds and trees. Whether that's submerging ourselves in the mountains with a hike down the Appalachian Trail or venturing into the deserts of Canyon Lands National Park, we're hungry for it. We journey outward to these places in order to release and reconnect to something inward. In the end, we return with maybe a few bites and burns, yet somehow, our spirits have received the gifts of rejuvenation and clarity.

No one told us to do this. There was no point at which someone sat you down and said, "Go get you some waterfalls and snowy peaks!" No, something inside us craves it, needs it, knows that these places—this earth—is an irremovable part of our flourishing.

If you want to see a perfect example of what living close to the earth looks like, see if you can spot some moss. In *Gathering Moss*, Robin Wall Kimmerer writes about the secrets found within the life cycles of this humble plant community.[5] She writes about how moss lives and thrives at the boundary layer. Moss hugs the surface in a wondrous embrace of existence. Mossy communities live down at the bottom edge between earth and atmosphere, where they thrive in their closely earthbound life. Down low below friction, rough winds, and turbulence, moss offers us glimpses of the beauty and benefits of smallness. Underneath and often unnoticed, moss lives its best life

---

5. Kimmerer, *Gathering Moss*.

within its small moist ecosystem as it clothes its host in blankets of green fluff—no doubt the stuff of Dr. Seuss textile legend.

What struck me in this mossy exploration is Kimmerer's insistence that if moss grows beyond its natural boundaries, it does so at its own peril. "Up there," in the dry wind and heat and light, moss wouldn't survive.

Nonhuman creation inherently knows how to thrive like that. These creatures embrace their place-ness and create beautiful scenes and scents and songs as they easily fit within the frame of their home.

Jesus pointed this out:

> Look at the birds of the air; they do not sow or reap or store away in barns, and yet your heavenly Father feeds them. Are you not much more valuable than they? Can any one of you by worrying add a single hour to your life? And why do you worry about clothes? See how the flowers of the field grow. They do not labor or spin. Yet I tell you that not even Solomon in all his splendor was dressed like one of these.[6]

What if we looked out our door one morning to see a group of birds that had started stacking sticks together to build a Lincoln Log-style bird tower reaching stories into the air? Like a bird penthouse. Like a blue jay Trump Tower situation. I'm imagining a big pigeon who's the bouncer at the door while all these birds are just up there dining and laughing like its the flippin' flying Great Gatsby.

Of course, this is ridiculous for multiple reasons! Even if birds had opposable thumbs with tiny little hammers and nails, they still wouldn't waste their time doing this because they already have everything they need; they're called trees. Birds have nothing to worry about! Well, except for human towers, that is. (In North America alone, more than one billion birds die every year due to colliding with buildings.)[7]

Why can't we be more like birds? (Just watch out for windows!)

Why can't we hug the earth like moss?

Why can't we grow like a flower? Blooming where we're planted?

---

6. Matt 6:26–29, NIV.
7. Kornreich, "Rehabilitation Outcomes."

Well, let's stop and consider those flowers. You see, those lilies Jesus pointed out—they're dead now. Those birds fluttering around Jesus and his disciples—they're long gone. Did they grow without care? Yes. Did they flourish under God's nourishment? Yes. Are they now dead and gone? Yes, they are.

Here is the point: when Jesus invites us into a life marked by reliance upon our Creator, carrying the easy yoke of his life, he isn't inviting us into a life that seeks to defy its own mortality or limitations. Rather, it is an invitation to welcome them. It is about discovering that the most beautiful life one can live is one that *moves into and through* our mortal boundaries. You see, the bird and the lily are clothed, fed, and live magnificent lives within their limitations. The reason Jesus turns to the birds of the sky and lilies of the field as our teachers is because they're earthbound and loving it.

How did we ever turn the gospel message into one of escape when Jesus, God incarnate, comes *here* and spends all his time teaching us how to also be *here* better?

Knowing that you are mortal doesn't mean that you live a life worrying about death. Because who can add one minute onto their life by worrying? Jesus says you can't. But I know a lot of people who certainly try. Jesus seemed to know just how much we would worry about everything. I wonder if Jesus knew that worry might become obsession, and that obsession might become greed, and that greed might become a destructive enterprise. I wonder if Jesus knew that worry itself might become a hidden gateway leading us all the way back into the captivity of Babylon?

If unbounded worry is a way into captivity, could trust, love, and presence be a way out?

PRESENCE

Being fully present, at any given time, is something that our culture hasn't made easy. It requires a different pace and a level of vulnerability that many avoid. You can usually tell by how uncomfortable someone gets with just the least bit of silence. In fact, we don't call it silence anymore; it's always "awkward silence." We've scrolled, binge-watched, and lived within the frictionless arena of high-speed internet for so long that standing still for a moment has become, well, weird. Even if you go somewhere and you don't have you're phone with you, people would think you might be *a little off*.

If you want an oversimplification of what it means to be Christian today *and* heal this broken creation, here it is: loving presence.

Once, at a local justice conference, we participated in an exercise of presence. We were required to turn to the person next to us, stare into their eyes for three minutes straight without looking away and without talking. While looking back at us, the other person answered a few questions about their life. It sounds so simple, but wow, it was hard. Eye contact can feel intimate, can't it?

Have you ever had someone give you their full attention before? It's something that is unfortunately rare. Presence is a ministry in and of itself. Being fully present with one another is an act of care that cracks us open in ways that ministers to our souls.

When was the last time you were fully present with someone? What about with the environment around you? What about with yourself?

It's why the mystics are always returning to talk about presence. It's the real gift behind the gift. It's about a way of living in the world that offers meaning. It's the being rather than the doing.

When you live primarily in the world as a doer, you're always going to be focused on the next item you're consuming, the next thing you can check off your list, or the next event you're planning for—which likely becomes one step away from potential anxiousness or worry, and then we're back in the cycle.

But being a human being . . . well, that's different. Being present, right here, is about receiving something deeper that says, "Hey, you; you belong here. You're loved, and there's nothing you can do about it!" This is what my old youth pastor used to say every single Wednesday night, and I loved it.

> Being present—that can feel
> vulnerable,
> naked,
> mortal,

weak,
temporal,
and fragile.

We don't always like those feelings. Those feelings make us feel powerless. They make us feel exposed. They make us feel too . . . human.

But that's exactly who we are and who we need to be! What's more, once you finally succumb to it, it becomes the next level of joy! It's the kind of enjoyment you find when you finally let go of trying "to win" because you realize that you've already "one." (Bit of a mysticism pun there, you're welcome.)

We've set the bar for fun pretty high these days. Literally. Just consider theme parks, giant roller-coasters, virtual reality, zip lines, video games, bungee jumping, or as previously mentioned, rolling out of airplanes. Now, I love a summer trip to Holiday World as much as the next guy, but personally, I mostly just like to be under a blanket on my couch with a book or in my garden. That's what I "do for fun." This very idea of doing "for fun" has been captured and harnessed for capitalist gains. We often associate fun with doing or buying something new. I think, though, that if most of us were pressed on it, we'd agree that sort of fun is more of a fleeting high. Just like a drug, you've got to get a bit more and climb a bit higher each time you do it. We need more likes, more hearts, more Tiks on our Toks. This can be translated into getting the newest model phone, vehicle, or designer clothing. For many of us, we've coalesced fun with purchasing something or attaining some new experience. We've created endorphin driven fun rather than lifestyles of deep and eternal, yet temporal, enjoyment.

When we are able to reframe this idea of "doing fun" to lifestyles of enjoyment, of treasuring the "this-ness" of now, then just waking up and getting to be a human on earth again today becomes the greatest of gifts. Sure, there's plenty of pain and trouble to go around, and that's real. As we've already discussed, finding a way into our pain and loss is an important part of the kind of life Jesus calls us into. What if there is no such thing as joy without the willingness to sit with and move through our pain? What would it look like to allow the friction points of our lives to slow us down and limit how we behave in the world? Friction is not the antonym of flourishing. What if, in those present spaces, we find some real joy? What would it look like not to just tolerate your earthly boundaries but to actually love them?

It's fascinating that in the Babel story, God says, "Let us go down and confuse their language there, so that they will not understand one another's speech."[8] Thus, the tower building ceased as they could not understand one another and the people became scattered.

The tower of Babel was an effort to surpass our limitations and creatureliness, but we find that God's solution was to bring us back down to our appropriate good and earthly place through the gift of a diversity of languages. Fast forward, what occurs in a world full of humans who continue being fruitful and multiplying into the billions now comes a variety of languages, places, and cultures—which, again, was part of the original plan that God had already reminded us of after the flood. And at the tower of Babel, it seemed God was going to give us a little nudge in the right direction.

Language is certainly one of our most undervalued gifts. To be able to communicate affection with precision and nuance is the pleasure of being human. Additionally, the gift of celebrating the food, craft, and color of cultures around the world is a feast for our senses. Our diversity is a blessing for us and creation.

Unfortunately, America has a track record of suppressing diversity. In fact, most of our ecological (and other) problems today could be summarized through forced homogenization. From racist practices to monoethnic rhetoric, patriarchal policies to monocropping . . . it seems that every time we attempt to squelch God's diverse intentions for the world, we find ourselves as practitioners of injustice.

As early Americans journeyed west across the plains, having decided the world was up for grabs, we forcefully displaced any Indigenous peoples who got in our way. After taking their land from them, we worked to make them as much like us as possible.

---

8. Gen 11:7.

Now, as scientists, ecologists, policymakers, and activists search for ways to repair the planet, research around the world has fittingly shown how the earth flourishes in the care of Indigenous hands. While Indigenous peoples make up less than 5 percent of the population, 80 percent of global biodiversity is in their care.[9] What has been uncovered is a measurable link between high rates of cultural diversity and ecological diversity. We now realize that concentrations of biodiversity frequently overlap with places of Indigenous cultural richness. Local community and culture play a crucial role for environmental flourishing. Preserving one is preserving the other.[10]

Project Drawdown cites that securing land tenure with Indigenous peoples "addresses long-standing Indigenous rights issues, protects carbon stocks equal to hundreds of gigatons of carbon dioxide, and provides a basis for sustainable rural livelihoods."[11] Further, studies have now discovered that conservation efforts are far more effective when Indigenous peoples and local communities are given real autonomy and power for the work. Too often, we simply acknowledge this need for more Indigenous wisdom, ending our quest at lip-service and consultations. After analyzing hundreds of conservation cases, 85 percent of the places that offered Indigenous communities autonomous involvement in the care of the land had much greater ecological benefits than those where Indigenous peoples were simply stakeholders (18 percent).[12]

Cultural freedom and wealth correlate to ecological freedom and wealth! How cool is that?

A massive part of the work ahead for us to heal the broken parts of God's creation is directly connected to reconciling relationships between ethnicities and people groups. A diversity of cultures, alive and thriving in the world, are the secret keys to unlocking ecological restoration! Of course, this is true! Restorative and relational healing is also remedial good news for rivers, otters, fish, and all wild places.

How might we rediscover the gifts of cultural precision and care as a people in close relationship with the earth? I like to imagine this

9. Garnett, "Spatial Overview."
10. Levis, "Contributions of Human Cultures."
11. Project Drawdown, "Indigenous Peoples' Forest Tenure," 19.
12. Dawson, "Is It Just Conservation?"

ancient Babel narrative, which warns us of great heights, greed, and taking ourselves too seriously, comes with a divine course-correction that says, "Come down before you hurt yourself, diversify, grow roots, enjoy creation, create culture, and make some really yummy food."

SONGS AT BEDTIME

We could never have loved the earth so well if we had had no childhood in it, if it were not the earth where the same flowers come up again every spring that we used to gather with our tiny fingers as we sat lisping to ourselves on the grass, the same hips and haws on the autumn hedgerows, the same redbreasts that we used to call "God's birds" because they did no harm to the precious crops. What novelty is worth that sweet monotony where everything is known and loved because it is known?

George Eliot (Mary Ann Evans), *The Mill on the Floss*

There is no time quite as special as bedtime. When it comes to roles and putting children to bed, I am the tucker-inner and song-singer. Bedtime at our house is no joke though. I'm certain that children have an internal alarm that goes off close to bedtime that aids in creating chaos and general insanity. When it comes to bedtime, after teeth have been brushed, books read, and pajamas put on, I typically get the job of "the closer." I corral my girls into their beds as they beg me to "do a puppet show tonight!"—doing everything within their power to delay the inevitable sleep part of going to bed.

One of the best parts is when I ask them, "What are you thankful for today?" Story quickly begins reciting a litany of things she is grateful for, almost as an act of recalling the entire day by memory. "I'm thankful for waffles for breakfast, watching *Bluey*, playing with my friends, jumping on Jubilee's trampoline, doing art with mommy, and eating Popsicles!" Occasionally, this dips into a brief list of things she's also *not* thankful for: "and I'm not thankful for lasagna! Yuck!"

Daily, rather than recalling a timeline-ordered list of gratitude for the day, flutters about structureless in her gratitude. "I'm thank-you for . . . ," she pauses to think, "ice cream!" "I'm thank-you for playing with Audrey, and for going to Poppy's house," which is something that happened last weekend, "and Fred and George!" She has named her socks today after the Weasley brothers.

But our girls know that just saying "everything!" when asked what they're thankful for won't fly. (Although, admittedly, I've had to cut Story off a few times as we breach the eight-minute mark of saying what we're thankful for!)

True gratitude has to be specific. If you're generically grateful for "everything," you may get caught not truly being grateful for anything. Just saying "I'm thankful for all of it" doesn't *really* say anything at all, does it? At the end of the day, what we actually love and cherish about a person, place, or thing are the features. It's the particulars that draw us in. I love the way she crinkles her nose when she laughs. I love the way the grass feels under my feet when I run barefoot. I love the way mom's hair smells when I jump on her lap. I love the way dad's buttermilk biscuits taste right out of the oven, especially on Saturday mornings. I love the way she sings at the top of her lungs to *Frozen* and dances with her underwear on her head. (You know, the usual.)

What we really treasure are the endless particulars. The touches, glances, and smirks of our loved ones. We love the feel of bark on a birch tree, the fur coat of a fluffy cat, the scent of a summer's cool breeze, the way our childhood home's kitchen makes us feel, and how every time we hear that song, we cry a little.

That's what we're thankful for.

You could say what we love are the boundaries. The parameters. The body, the container, the specs, the curves, the shapes, the outlines, the silhouettes, the rules, the sizes, the colors, the place-ness of the place, the colors of the culture, and the peculiar-ness of the people. Love is anything but generic. We're not thankful for the generic; we're thankful for the uniqueness, which is really, funny enough, all of it!

Every thing and every one is unique. Everything has that which makes whatever it is . . . whatever it is. Anytime we simply lump a part of God's creation into a generic category of "them," we are in danger of othering instead of loving. Love recognizes that she has a name. Love sees the mole on her cheek and the person that she is. Love is intimate like that.

Which brings me to the other item on my bedtime résumé, the singer-of-bedtime-songs. In the dark, lying there, we've sung a lot of songs over the years. Music is another way that we can convey what is meaningful to our children and express the love and gratitude that comes with living life. Being a country boy deep inside, I've been known to infiltrate some good country music into my kids' lives at bedtime. (And I'm proud to say that I've now even caught my wife occasionally humming some Tim McGraw.) One of our nighttime go-tos is "Deeper Than the Holler" by Randy Travis. The song tells of those "city singers" who try and sing about love being big as the seas and higher than the stars. Yet, these descriptions are too lofty and grand for country people. Travis lyrically confesses that such things would be insufficient in communicating his love. His love is about hollers, rivers, pine trees, and whippoorwills.

While country music has more than its share of bad tunes, it also is known to champion the beautiful limitations of "country life." It is precisely those things that make it meaningful and worth singing about.

Until we are willing to fold our life here on earth into the joy that is a good bedtime routine, we're going to miss the whole thing. There are people, organizations, and political efforts all working to save the earth today. But without love, as the apostle Paul spoke, we are just a clanging cymbal. This is the kind of love that names names. It's the love language of calling out what we've come to know and cherish in the world. Love is that which will draw us down into the necessary particulars of creation care. Until we open the door to grateful hearts, until we write the notes that make the songs, until we sing the names of lakes, rivers, streams and watersheds, we won't get far. Because we save what we love.

So y'all, may we learn them, say them, love them, save them.

In this space below, or in your heart, write some names of what you love that is part of God's creation (human or nonhuman).

SWEET WATER

Zero traffic lights, one K-12 school, and one gas station/restaurant—that's how I describe to people where in Tennessee I grew up. It's called Culleoka, a Native American name meaning "sweet water."

There is something sweet about Culleoka, and it's not just in the water. In the early twentieth century, our small community sourced cantaloupes for all over the Southeast—or, as my dad occasionally says, "We were the cantaloupe capital of the world!" Local farmers tag-teamed with a couple of brothers, Erastus J. and Hardie Park, to make the Culleoka Produce Company, and for a time, it was the stuff of local legend.[13] Nowadays though, Maury County's agricultural claim to fame tends to be mules rather than melons, due to our annual "Mule Day" celebration.[14] You gotta love small towns.

Sometimes, really seeing what makes your hometown so sweet requires another level of curiosity. The "sweet water" we grew up on came flowing to us out of "The Duck." The Duck River, running from Waverly to Manchester is the longest single river in the state, offering life to small rural communities. Yet, it wasn't until my late thirties that I discovered the real secrets of this river. The Duck River is reported to be "the number one most biodiverse river in the nation," and "in the

---

13. Historic Maury County, "Lost Cantaloupe Capital."
14. You can't make this stuff up, people. Check out Maury County Bridle and Saddle Club's "Mule Day," https://muleday.com/.

top 5 most biodiverse rivers in the world."[15] Flowing over 280 miles through the green hills of Tennessee, guided by farmland, caves, cliffs and waterfalls, this river is home to 151 species of fish, more than twenty species of snails, and over fifty species of freshwater mussels![16]

When I learned how amazing this body of water around me is, I couldn't believe it. "We're talking about the same muddy Duck River here?" I thought. It makes one wonder, what sweet secrets are hidden right in plain sight for us as people who each inhabit particular places alongside a variety of species within God's creation? The richness is not in undeveloped property valued for its production capacity but in the land and water, as they are already "developed" habitats for the last remaining natives around us. In this case, they're mussels.

It was precisely some of these endangered mussels that played their part in stopping the development and, eventually, the dismantling of what was left of a local dam.

Beautifully, this area in Columbia, Tennessee, is now the Yanahli Park. A Chickasaw name meaning "to flow through," Yanahali offers sanctuary to a section of the Duck River. Here many amphibians, mammals, waterfowl, and others find protection in this Wildlife Management Area.[17]

The cultural history here along the river is very special. Thousands of significant indigenous sites and many artifacts have been recovered here around what's called Cheek's Bend. The cave here is known to have been used by Indigenous peoples dating back ten thousand years.

The lessons I'm learning today have to do with being a part of something larger and older than myself. The land and water that I grew up barefoot on is the same land and water that other little children ran barefoot on before me, my parents, and the generations before them, going back for thousands and thousands of years.

My mom grew up in a part of Columbia called Riverside. It's right there near downtown where the Duck River was closest and would occasionally flood. My dad, also born and raised sharing these waters, has spent the majority of his adult life as a general contractor digging

---

15. Duck River Conservancy, "No. 1 Most Biodiverse River."
16. Duck River Conservancy, "No. 1 Most Biodiverse River."
17. Maury County, "Yanahli Park."

waterlines for rural communities to access fresh water from rivers like the Duck. This watershed has shaped our whole lives. Even the day I asked Emily to marry me, I took her out to spend an afternoon splashing in one of the Duck's tributaries and afterward found a nice spot for a premeditated picnic.

Today, on the heels of drought mixed with mega-development and growth sprawling out of Nashville into these quiet corners of Tennessee, the Duck River has reached its water supply capacity. Organizations like the Southern Environmental Law Center have worked hard to continue protecting this special place. So, rather than placing any more straws into the river, new plans are in place to dig giant pipelines either all the way down from the Cumberland River in Nashville or up the Tennessee River (ironically in Alabama) for development to be able to continue.[18]

Here is a story, my story, which is all too familiar for all too many communities. It's some continued version of growth and development versus ecological well-being.

Which one will we choose?

The question itself reveals a false binary between our efforts to live better lives and protecting the earth. When we create a dichotomy like this, it forms an "us versus them" narrative with everything that offers us life. In truth, there is no such thing as ecological well-being apart from human well-being. There is no such thing as the thriving of humans in middle Tennessee apart and segregated from the thriving of fifty species of mussels in the Duck River. Fostering this dualism is what fuels any and every ecological crisis of our time: fragmentation.

Biologists confirmed long ago that all life is supported through groups of organisms of many species together making a living network. It is a "dynamic equilibrium."[19] We live within a web of encompassing relationships. Therefore, any time we attempt to go about our lives in the world, create policies, do business, and pursue a good life

---

18. Nolan, "Water Pipeline Proposed."
19. Botkin, *Discordant Harmonies*.

without acknowledging the *withness* that we have with the rest of the created world, we'll only create more brokenness.

Fragmentation occurs every time we try and separate that which God has placed together, and there will always be consequences for that. The way God has created is through the gifts of mutuality and co-flourishing.

There is a familiar spiritual term for when we talk about fragmentation and separation: sin. When we speak of being disconnected and separated from God and God's intention for our lives, we call that a life of sin.

For generations, we identified sin as something that says our material lives are separating us from our spiritual salvation. The problem with that is it creates the very narrative that the good news of the gospel is working to repair. It creates more separation and more fragmentation. God never divorces the spiritual from the material like we attempt to do. No, God is the One who placed them together by design! To separate the spiritual from the material is to miss the whole thing! To do so would make one blind to fully seeing God's creation.

How might we resist the capitalistic temptation to see the "natural world" through fragmenting eyes? We are a part of creation, not over it. Exploitation requires fragmentation. But for us, as Christians placed on earth, we recall the sacredness of the ground on which we reside, just as God reminds Moses at the burning bush. God was already present here; you just didn't realize it before. The bush was already burning. God's presence has been here the whole time—take off your sandals and let your feet touch the earth.

Just as God calls Moses by name, God also calls us by name with the invitation that we might look up and listen . . . that we might become aware of holy ground. Just as in Exod 3, we might also then be ready to receive God's name in return, "I am whoever I am." Once again, presence.

Then, and only then, will we be ready to do the work of ministering to our sisters and brothers enslaved by the brick masters and lead them out toward the promised land.

CHAPTER 7 | DEEPER THAN THE HOLLER

I believe we live in a time when many people are absolutely starving to draw closer to the earth. Although we may not be able to name those desires, nevertheless, there is something that whispers to us, "Dive deeper." No doubt our legs are tired from treading so much water here on the surface.

Here are some simple practices to go deeper.

Learn what tree species are close to where you live. Take a walk; see if you can come to name each tree on your street. What do they look like? Do you know them? Study their leaves. Let that knowledge of leaf, bark, and color seep into you. Introduce yourself.

Take off your shoes and socks and physically put your feet on the ground. Research is uncovering all the benefits of what's called "grounding." Over twenty studies have given us data on just how putting your bare feet on the ground can aid in your physical health. From inflammation, blood pressure, sleep, or dealing with pain, it's been shown that simply reconnecting your body to the soil around you works to bring healing.[20] Lay on the ground. No blanket. Just you and the field.

Research native plants in your area. Invest in planting native plants near and around you.

Examine what the invasive species are around you. Remove them.

For one singular meal, discover where every element of your food comes from. What farm? Who grew it and where?

Make your own bread. This is a skill, no doubt, that many of us may fail in our first attempt, yet the attempt itself is important. There is something deeply human about bread-making that goes back to deep ancestral roots, so give it a try! If you are gluten free or want to do something other than bread, explore another meaningful option, but try to keep it basic (as in a fundamental food).

When was the last time you got muddy? Next time it rains, jump in a puddle and get mud on your face. Sing in the rain.

Download an app! Merlin Bird ID is a wonderful app that uses your phone's microphone to identify singing birds around you.

---

20. Ultimate Longevity, "Grounding Research."

Similarly, there are many apps to help you identify the plants growing around you.

> *God, this boundary layer in which you have placed us is beautiful. Bring us into your presence so that we may not miss it. Offer us patience in order that we may take our time and discover a more meaningful relationship with your creation. Help us to be vulnerable enough to live close enough to the earth, that we may understand our place within it. Give us courage to be part of the freeing of your creation amidst systems that want to devour it.*
> *Help us to embody love in your world.*
> *Amen.*

Chapter 8 | Subatomic Salvation

Human beings ... are soil that has been fashioned to have the forms and powers that define a human life ... It is by studying the life of soil, its vulnerabilities and possibilities, and by attending to the life and death that comes in and out of it, that human beings come to know who they are, where they are, and how they should live.

Norman Wirzba, *This Sacred Life*

No one really likes to use the term "dirt." Scientists and farmers know "soil" is the preferred and more respectable term for speaking about the ground underneath our feet. To simply say "dirt" feels like a dirty word! Soil indicates a deeper awareness of something. To speak of soil is to recognize that there is an intimacy here between us and the ground. All life as we know it is utterly dependent upon the top several inches of ground called topsoil. In just a few inches of soil comes all food and vegetation on planet Earth.

I've spent years combing through books, scientific research, podcasts, and webinars, and I've discovered that when it comes to solving almost every single global environmental issue today, from climate change to desertification, nothing speaks like healthy topsoil. Our topsoil is literally the issue underneath so many other issues, connected to the food that we eat and the lives we live. No singular human-generated technology comes anywhere close to doing the kind of healing work that healthy topsoil can do. For being a substance that all life hinges on, it couldn't be more underrated and underappreciated in society.

As the future of agriculture is threatened due to soil mistreatment and erosion, some are finally taking a closer look at soil health like never before. So, what is a healthy topsoil? What is soil at all?

To be honest, until later in life, I never really thought about what comprises the dirt under my feet, which I think is probably a familiar story for some of us. The stuff that is always present—we must physically walk over it to go anywhere, all life is dependent upon it . . . and who knows what it is?! How is it that soil health isn't one of the very first lessons we learn in grade school? What could be more important?

The secret of the sauce is that soil is not just *one thing*. Healthy soil is made up of a variety of different parts. (The beauty of diversity once again showing itself within God's creation!) First are minerals (think rocks that have weathered into tiny pieces over thousands of years) that take the shape of silt, clay, sand, pebbles, and so on. There are many kinds of minerals that can make up our soil, but that's not all that's down there. Water occupies about a quarter of the soil territory, and about another quarter is empty space that is between the particles themselves. Air is a key ingredient in the health of the soil. In fact, one reason that many soils struggle to "do what they need to do" is that it's been compacted by humans (which is why you should avoid walking on the places you're growing plants). After the minerals, water, and air is all the organic matter and our little microbial friends. Finally, roots, humus, vegetation, and animal excrement, along with all the wonderful little microorganisms and creatures create their own economy of goods beneath us! Therein lies all the special parts that comprise healthy topsoil.

CHAPTER 8 | SUBATOMIC SALVATION

To describe what is occurring here is like trying to imagine an entirely new universe full of matter, energy, and life. It's the very place where everything that dies becomes part of something living again, as organic material decomposes and becomes food for the next thing.

The soil is where resurrection happens in real time. At the very core level of all life on earth, it isn't just one singular thing called "soil" but a network of nature in relationship with itself. Imagine microorganisms who are in community with one another, growing, eating, dying, and rising again.

It shouldn't be too surprising; this cycle is one of our God's favorite maneuvers.

Microbial life is continually "mining and recycling" nutrients, as David Montgomery, author of *Growing a Revolution*, describes it.[1] One way to think about this is that these tiny little microbes, along with mycorrhizal fungi, are nature's little farmers.

The work that this microbial life accomplishes cannot be overstated. Imagine being a little plant, ready to grow and live your life as a healthy, growing, sumptuous plant. Just a mile down the street is a grocery store with everything you could ever want! Except there's a problem. You have no way to get the food! (You are a plant after all, so no walking around!) In the end, you live a short, scraggly life, eventually starving for nutrition and die an early death with delicious food in eyesight.[2]

Microbial life down in the soil are the Uber Eats delivery drivers for all thriving plant life, and thus for you and me. Without them doing their part, we're finished. These little life forms break down the organic matter and minerals so that plants can actually eat and drink from their roots in the ground. Without these little farmers or delivery drivers doing their part, the plants don't get the nutrients they need and neither, then, do we.

Meanwhile, in the greater micro-economy, the plants are also giving back. In an epic ongoing exchange, plants are capturing more carbonaceous molecules, which translate as yummy proteins and

1. Montgomery, *Growing a Revolution*.
2. Both our soil and our neighbors have experienced the same marginalization through food deserts and food apartheid. How we've oppressed the earth often reflects how we've oppressed our neighbors, and vice versa.

sugars, as food for microbial life. Let's just say that plants are great at tipping their Uber driver! Then, it's basically like a night out on the town after payday with dinner and dessert for these little "fun-guys"! (Sorry, couldn't help it!)

There is a reason that entire books have been written on what the relationship is between minerals, water, microbial life, and humans. This sacred exchange stretches on and on, meanwhile, going deeper than we even fully understand. It has been said that we may know more about what goes on within our galaxy than we do of the crust of the earth.

Consider McDonald's: it may frequently "pass" for food, but is it? And at what cost do we create it? It's just cheaper and easier, right? We want to better control the when, how, what, and even the visual appeal of the foods we grow. We're told that in order to grow food, we've got to have all the specialty equipment, patented seeds, and appropriate synthetics. Plus, it's just your lucky day because all these things just happen to be on sale at a dealer near you.

Instead of having nature's microbial life available to bring plants healthy and nutritious goodies, we have simply decided to spray our fields with a host of products, imposing upon soil that which is unnatural. We've been told that to continue to feed the world, we need a hard dose of these chemicals. It is estimated that over a third of the planet's agricultural land has degraded in just decades due to heavy use of fertilizers and pesticides coupled with ongoing monoculture. The delicate balance that God created to occur in the soil, that amazing micro-economy has been subjected to chemical warfare.

After World War II, when we were finally finished making weapons, it forced the economy to shift focus. It was just a quick minute later that we turned the chemicals used to make weapons and explosives into nitrogen-based products to "feed" our plants. Yesterday's weapons became today's fertilizer and pesticides.

Civil war has now ensued between bombs of pesticides and fertilizers used to battle what we call "pests" and nature's process. If humanity chooses to continually battle against the earth's natural processes, we will decidedly lose that fight. We will lose by making enemies with nature, and then, in turn, destroy ourselves through this battle. Rachel Carson highlighted this over sixty years ago in her formative work *Silent Spring*, which catalyzed an entire environmental movement.[3] Unfortunately, decades later, we still haven't learned the real lesson. The moment we, in our pride, believe we can dominate the earth, as if we were completely separate from it, that is when we will truly lose.

It isn't just our soil that has paid the price but our health. Because, as we know, we are soil. Everything that makes up our bodies comes from that wondrous world beneath our feet, and when we die, our bodies return to it (ideally). (I imagine if soil could talk, it would speak of a thousand lives.) When we then abuse the soil, pollute it, and mistreat it, we are mistreated. Our well-being is greatly affected by exposure to chemicals in our food, and even our clothing and home goods.

If we reshape the earth, we reshape ourselves.

The link between cancer (along with other negative health outcomes) and chemically-induced agriculture is no stranger to the research community. For many decades now, we've had the opportunity to study these carcinogenic correlations.[4] The results confirm it; the link between fertilizers, pesticides, and cancer have been replicated time and again. But the system keeps pushing and extracting for more products, despite the cost.

After spraying foreign substances on our soil, we then turn around to take foreign substances, in the form of pills, to try and fix our bodies. This is our story. Bayer, one of the largest pharmaceutical companies in the world, is simultaneously producing your prescription drugs *and* the Glyphosate-based herbicides (such as Round Up) that are being sprayed on your food. Take some time to think about that! What sort of beast has been created by the systems of exploitation that prey on human and soil health for profit?

---

3. Carson, *Silent Spring*.

4. Gatto, "Farming, Pesticides, and Brain Cancer"; Manuel, "DDT and Breast Cancer"; Peñalver-Piñol et al., "Occupational Exposure to Pesticides"; Perkins, "Exposure to Combination."

God's gift of soil, doing what it naturally does, offers us everything we need. Nature just wants to do its thing. When we draw close to the land, it affects everything else. It's all connected. Even when it comes to the deadly influxes of greenhouse gas emissions rising into the atmosphere, healthy soil easily holds within it the capability of drawing down and offsetting these extra gases. This happens as that underground economy, described earlier, gets the chance to thrive.

Given the opportunity and a little space to prosper, soil is a miracle worker just by its own little self, and we get the opportunity to steward that relationship. The created order has a way of balancing itself out.

Even as you and I become conscious consumers around the food we buy, the farmers we support, the bills we advocate for, the local garden-education clubs we get involved in, and the soil in our own backyard, things can change! If you're in an urban setting, begin advocating for changes in local code regulations so that you're able to grow more food right where you live. In many cities, we've made it illegal to have chickens clucking around, tall grass, a compost, or a goat on our property. Building momentum around these small local changes toward a land-economy is critical work for us to engage in.

How might we shift our thinking away from massive chemically induced monocropping operations? The lie we've been told is that we need these big farming systems to sustain planetary food production. Around the world, the perhaps surprising reality is the majority of the world's food is produced by smaller, often family operated, farms. We should be protecting healthy soil, not big corporations.

What are we aiming for? What advances here are improving our lives? The skills that sustainably minded farmers are practicing, and that research has shown to be regenerative for our land, doesn't involve anything new, shiny, or sold on a shelf. The simple practices, such as no till-farming, crop rotation, and cover-cropping, have the potential to sequester loads of global carbon, produce healthy and hefty harvests, and stop soil erosion.

This is "technology" that works with nature. It is relational, between human and soil. It's about listening to the land, not feeding the machine, holding the lives of our children above even our own; it is God-ordered right-relatedness with the humans and the humus.

Until we find more ways to work with the natural order rather than against it, we'll be rolling a boulder uphill until our imminent crushing when we run out of energy. The good news is that the earth is radically forgiving, crazy regenerative, and humans have the special opportunity to help the natural world to flourish while having more than enough to feed everyone, stop climate change from worsening, and get home for dinner! Just changing our everyday eating habits around what kind of agriculture we support can change the world.

Understanding and caring for this soil is about caring for ourselves. Any way we slice it, we are made of this soil, and this soil is made of us. So, what kind of place do you want to belong to?

IMPOSTOR SYNDROME

Anytime I get to hang with my friend J. T., it brings me joy. We've had more than a few good laughs together! One particular time, I brought him along with me to DC for a National Faith and Climate Forum. You know, the kind of stuff you do when you're way down the rabbit hole of earth care. Getting ready in the hotel room, so many things go through your head. It should be stated that wearing ties, while occasionally appropriate, is *not* my thing, but I came all the way to DC with a suit and a tie in my bag, so my plan was to dress the part! After getting ready and taming my ever-imposing cowlick, I look at J. T., who was wearing jeans and a polo, and say, "Is it too much?" He said, "Well, you are looking spiffy!" and we laughed. The truth is, when we are afraid that we already don't belong here, we enter into a spiral of decisions in the effort of "fitting in" that, in turn, make us feel more weird and out of place. As it happened, I was the only one wearing a tie that day.

Impostor syndrome is a phrase we hear more and more. What does it mean that so many people consider themselves as someone who doesn't belong? We all want to belong. Like many, I've experienced those feelings of unbelonging at times in my life. Whether it was the soccer team, the church friend group, or at school, a fear occasionally raises its ugly head whispering things like, *you don't really belong here.* (This is the kind of therapy stuff that you unpack in your thirties!) I like to think that when you know you belong somewhere, it gives you a feeling of safety. It's about being comfortable where you are. It's about being with people who know they belong there, too. It's about presence. And maybe, most importantly, it's about you being authentically you . . . the real, honest, open, vulnerable, truth of you.

When we don't feel like we belong, it is a fracture that seeps all the way down into our bones. That is a fragmentation on the inside. We are made to belong, and when we feel that we don't, it throws everything off.

I firmly believe that God wants to hold every single person and creature on earth, wrap them in a deep hug, look them in the eye, and say, "You belong." One of the greatest mistakes the church has made is spreading a narrative of unbelonging. As the church, we've done our share of pointing out every way in which a person doesn't belong, which seems to be the very opposite of what Jesus was consistently doing in his ministry. Maybe this is why so many people have latched onto the show *The Chosen*. I'll admit that the producers have done a good job at depicting the kind of people Jesus initially chooses. Jesus' first followers were all the "don't-belongs" and had no business following a rabbi.

Here is another reason I love gravity. Gravity is the force that keeps us here and reminds us of where we belong. It pushes and pulls us back to the ground again and again, reminding us of where we are meant to be. It grieves me to consider how many believe that we don't belong here. The "here" I'm referring to is "within God's creation," on Earth (you know, the only actual place humans are born and live). We are *chosen* for here, and the force is with us.

Try this on:
God creates creation, heaven, and earth.
God creates sky, water, and land, and all creation is filled with life.
God creates humanity *within* creation, in the *image* of God, and trusts humanity with *tending* creation.

Fast forward to today when a main narrative promoted by Christians is that humans do *not belong with or in* creation but that what awaits creation is its burning. This "gospel" is quite difficult to reconcile with the image of our God who creates and loves creation. Nevertheless, many have done the work to create and jump through vast theological hoops in order to justify their positions of unbelonging. It's just easier that way. When we fundamentally choose to believe that we don't belong here, we can treat "here" however we like.

Every now and then, I'll come across someone's Facebook profile description that makes me stop and think. You know, it's those four or five words people put under their photo, like "Mother of two, lover of Chihuahuas and pancakes, and Frisbee golf fanatic." Then there are the Christian-ese ones: "saved by grace; Jesus freak; in the world, not of the world," and so on. One that I recently saw caught my eye; it just said "Exile."

> Exile.
> As in, I'm not supposed to be here.
> As in, this is not where I belong.
> As in, I've been taken captive against my will in a foreign land.
> What are the ramifications that one of the primary ways we describe ourselves is "in exile"?

The stories of exile for the people of God within Scripture are key for us to understand, receive, and be shaped by (as we explored earlier). Yet, we can surely say that we are not "in exile" as humans living on Earth! Earth is the only place in which God has placed us. There are no impostors on Earth. It's the only place we can belong, as we live and breathe.

So, take a moment, inhale in, and exhale out. Maybe this is the needed contemplative mantra for our time. Clear your mind and consider: *I belong here.*

DUAL CITIZENSHIP

Recently, from the backseat, Daily asks, "Where is heaven?"

It's a question that you've always known is coming, yet despite the foreknowledge, you are no less prepared to answer it. Because, contrary to popular belief, it's not "up there." We've been to space—didn't find it. "Up there" has always been a human-generated placeholder for a heaven that slips past our visible line of sight. According to Jesus, heaven is increasingly getting closer to earth.

In Scripture, heaven and earth are almost always held together. They seem to have their own gravitational attraction. Just look at the very first line of the Bible: "In the beginning, God created the heavens and the earth."[5] In the Pentateuch, through Old Testament writings, in the Psalms and the prophets, even the words of Jesus and all the way into Revelation, "heaven and earth" are there sitting together. We find in the prophets that heaven and earth even co-suffer together.[6] Finally, heaven and earth are within the same breath for Jesus. "I thank you, Father, Lord of heaven and earth."[7]

Early in the Gospels, Jesus declares that "the Kingdom of heaven has come near"[8] (near to what? . . . earth). He teaches us how to pray and he says, "your will be done on earth as it is in heaven."[9] My personal favorite is in Matthew when Jesus is sending out his disciples to heal and do good work in the towns, saying, "As you go announce: the kingdom of heaven has come near."[10]

The apostle Paul writes about God's plan for the fullness of time, "to sum up all things in Christ, in heaven and on earth."[11]

Heaven and earth are two kids from the same parent. They live under the same roof! They share a bedroom. They're both in every goofy family photo. Grandma knits them both sweaters they don't want to wear. Where you find one, you find the other somehow.

Once, while staying in a hotel, I flipped on the TV and there is this Matt Damon movie playing that I've never seen before. Damon was playing a conjoined twin alongside actor Greg Kinnear. They

---

5. Gen 1:1.
6. Isa 24:4–5.
7. Matt 11:25.
8. Mark 1:15.
9. Matt 6:10.
10. Matt 10:7.
11. Eph 1:10.

were short-order cooks working in Martha's Vineyard, but they head to Hollywood because one of them wants to be an actor. As the story progresses (spoiler alert!), they eventually have a special surgery and become separated in order to have their own individual lives. But does this work out like they wanted? (I legitimately don't know because I didn't finish the movie!)

I wonder, is this so different than what we've done in our conversations and theology around heaven and earth? We've surgically removed them and perhaps even forgotten that they were born from the same womb.

Where you believe you belong matters. We used to think that people had to behave certain ways before they could belong. Now we know it's the opposite. Belonging precedes behavior.

We get so stuck promoting a leave-behind gospel in order to board our first class seats on the 737 to heaven, when all we actually need to do is continue being Jesus' disciples right here:

amidst these streets,
in these homes,
and in these fields.

The secret is no secret at all: everything is the Lord's!

Jesus never says, "Make sure you pray a prayer, invite me into your heart, and spread a message for everyone else to do that so that your spirit can leave this place after you die; and don't worry about caring for this place here because it's temporary." No, of course not!

What did Jesus do? Heal, wash dirty feet, bleed, spit, carve wood, eat a lot of bread and fish, pray, fast, drink water and wine, feast again, sink his entire body into a river, live his entire life, and eventually die under Roman occupation. Finally, Jesus rose again and began gathering, touching, and eating all over again! Jesus occupied a space that was heaven and earth. Jesus lived his life here on earth and it was and is eternal.

It was about *something else*, yet also about *all of this right here*. Jesus is Lord of heaven and earth, and that heaven–earth kingdom is where we belong, too.

We Christians have trouble with the earth care conversation because it can feel so contrary to everything we've been taught, which, if were honest, centers around escaping to heaven. But if we are closely reading our Bibles, we'll see that heaven and earth are not competitors but collaborators. It's not against our "Christian nature" to speak of being citizens of the coming-together heaven and earth. On the contrary, I believe it is the great missing piece to the salvific sweep of Scripture and the gospel message today!

We're generally familiar with the story of how in the beginning, God created humanity in God's own image. "Let us make humankind in our own image," it reads.[12] Often though, when we consider what the "likeness" of the image of God is, we imagine heavenly and ethereal characteristics that comprise the One who is God. While this is a theologically and biblically grounded thing to do, it is also significant to consider God as the One who is of heaven and also of earth. If you're reading the Bible through page by page, it's the earth part that offers some captivating divine characteristics. In some of the very first appearances, God is found walking in the garden and scooping up fistfuls of earth to create beings.

Theologian Norman Habel, in his commentary work on early Genesis, explores this idea further. Habel draws out a different perspective of the earth as a central character in the narrative of creation, pointing out in the text how the earth itself is gifted with the ability to spring forth life (the "creationivity" from earlier). There is a partnership between God and earth in this creative process. Ultimately, Habel suggests that if we are indeed created in the image of God, we are people who creatively partner with the earth.[13]

Consider in this ancient poetic narrative as God creates, saying, "Let us make humankind in our image," and what immediately follows those very words are human beings who are made in the divine image, yet are within and for earthly purposes. The very next words

---

12. Gen 1:26.
13. Habel, *Greening of Earth*.

spoken are about humanity's relationship with fish, birds, livestock, and "every creature that moves along the ground."[14]

Next consider the creation narrative of Gen 2: it highlights even more clearly how God places fingers in the dirt, pulls some up, and breathes divine life-Spirit into it.[15]

Now, here is where I think we should all get a little more curious. What we know up to this point is that God creates humanity in God's likeness. Humans are created out of the ground and with a special caretaking relationship with all creatures. So, what about any of this is "like" God? If humans are so "earthy" and also created in the image of God, could we conclude that there must be some earthy characteristics of God?

Remember, *earthy* is not *worldly*. We so easily conflate those today.

Look around you at how magnificent creation is. Pods of whales convening in ways we know so little of, fungal ecosystems that stretch across forest floors, the water that moves from mountains to seas and back again. The beauty of the earth has struck our hearts, and that only happens because earth is capable of pointing out divine qualities.

Neil deGrasse Tyson writes, "That which is objectively true or honestly authentic—especially on Earth or in the heavens—tends to possess a beauty of its own that transcends time, place, and culture."[16] While Tyson isn't a professing Christian, I'm all onboard with the philosophy within this quote. I believe as we discover that transcendent beauty within creation, it points right back to the One who is present within it all.

To be clear, the earth is not God, nor is God earth. It's not that God is reflective of the created, but that the created reflects aspects its Creator. It is important as humans, as Christians, as those seeking to be biblically faithful, not to fall prey to only identifying how the heavenly reflects the glory of God but to also name that "the earth is full of the steadfast love of the LORD."[17] To focus solely on the heavens would

---

14. Gen 1:24.
15. "*Ruach*" in Hebrew, translated as breath or spirit.
16. Tyson, *Starry Messenger*, 12.
17. Ps 33:5.

be to create a narrative that only admires or acknowledges God by transcending the very setting God created, placed us in, and blessed as very good![18]

Some call creation the first incarnation, as in the original means by which we come to know more about our Creator. As John writes, "All things came into being through him, and without him not one thing came into being."[19] Even Paul declares that "for since the creation of the world God's invisible qualities—his eternal power and divine nature—have been clearly seen, being understood from what has been made."[20] Could it be that creation looks the way that it does because God looks the way God does? Are we created from the "dirt" because God also has some dirt under God's fingernails? Orthodoxy reminds us, after all, that Jesus is fully divine *and* fully human.

So, what if the soil itself is a beautiful reflection of who God is?

These are deep mysteries that are mostly above our pay grade.
But here is some solid good news that I am certain of: you belong.
You, dear friend, belong. You belong right here, right now, on this planet, created in the image of God, within this gravity, and on this ground called earth. You belong in this space and in this time. If you didn't, you wouldn't be here.

Can we fully know what belonging will look like after we surrender our breath back to God? No.

Can we fully comprehend what the eschatological coming together of heaven and earth will unfold like in the end? No way.

But here's what we absolutely do know. Right now, we belong here. Why?
Because God designed it that way, and you are here. And honestly, *it's what's up*.

---

18. Believing that only the spiritual things of life are good, we quickly find ourselves knocking on the door of Gnosticism, a Christian heresy. And speaking of core beliefs, we believe Jesus to be fully divine *and* fully human!

19. John 1:3.

20. Rom 1:20, NIV.

YOUR SINS ARE FORGIVEN

That Christ came out of the earth, that the Hebrew prophets, that Paul, that all the saints and poets and philosophers of the world came out of the earth; that our planet, and the system of which it forms a part, should hold the elements of such men; that they should be struck from it as the spark is evoked from the flint—such facts as these should open our eyes to the marvels in which we live.

THE COMPLETE NATURE WRITINGS OF
JOHN BURROUGHS—1871

One time, when Jesus was teaching inside a house, a group courageously and compassionately attempted to get their paralyzed friend to Jesus. Eventually, desperate, they hoisted their friend up on the roof, ripped it apart, and lowered him down into the home, stretcher and all. (I guess, sometimes ministry looks like bringing down the house and disrupting the status quo!) Jesus looks at the friends and the paralyzed man and says, "Son, your sins are forgiven." Then Mark writes,

> Now some of the scribes were sitting there questioning in their hearts, "Why does this fellow speak in this way? It is blasphemy! Who can forgive sins but God alone?" At once Jesus perceived in his spirit that they were discussing these questions among themselves, and he said to them, "Why do you raise such questions in your hearts? Which is easier: to say to the paralytic, 'Your sins are forgiven,' or to say, 'Stand up and take your mat and walk'?"[21]

There Jesus goes blurring the lines again! We struggle with this text because it doesn't fit the way we are used to speaking of "sins." What's striking here is that, for Jesus, this man's body is bound up in a larger narrative. It's not that the man was a sinful human, thus he suffered as a paralytic. If that were the case, we'd all be immobile because of our sins. The story becomes more sobering as we understand that sin and salvation are far more sweeping than we often suspect. It is wrapped up with our bodies and creation itself.[22]

---

21. Mark 2:6–9.
22. It's important to say that whether this man was healed or not, he was already

Sometimes, we make the mistake of "dealing with sin" in the church like something akin to how conventional farming attempts to deal with weeds or pests. We give a good spiritual douse of herbicidal thoughts and prayers and a spray of healing ointments rather than dealing with the underlying cause, an impoverished soil. The reason Jesus is so quick to mix sin and this man's broken body together in one healing mic drop is because God's all-encompassing salvation has to do with repairing the whole.

Should we be surprised to find that salvation through Jesus is the healing of right-relatedness between the microbes in the soil, in the food, in the body, in the legs, in the blood, and yes, in the heart and spirit of our human existence?

John Wesley wrote many books and sermons, but what many may not know is that Wesley's bestselling book was *Primitive Physick*, a practical guide to health and medicine. He didn't just preach ethereal words to those in need but knew that true good news involved healthcare, that the gospel was a holistic concern. In fact, Wesley didn't just carry with him a Bible but also a medical bag in which he would have had simple remedies and tools for dealing with common ailments. Why would he do this except that he knew that the gospel he preached extended from hearts into actual hands, from soul into actual soil? Why would he do this? I think he was just following Jesus' lead!

In *Salvation Means Creation Healed*, Howard Snyder unpacks how this current gospel disembodiment began to occur. He points out the early Greek influence within the church and how we began substituting creed for story. "When the larger narrative is eclipsed by creed, mission easily becomes the defense of doctrine rather than proclaiming and living the good news of Jesus in the world," he writes.[23] Doctrinal statements have their place, but they are meant to be buttresses of the story about the outpouring of salvation, not in place of the mission and certainly not where all our bandwidth goes. What is captivating is the story of Jesus. What is world changing is

---

a whole person, worthy of the human dignity and freedoms often denied people with disabilities. That being said, physical healing, if available, might be something that a person with a disability would welcome, pray for, or pursue as a positive change, especially in less accommodating times and cultures.

23. Snyder, *Salvation Means Creation Healed*, 8.

the expansive narrative of a people's journey with God found within Scripture.

When we reduce this salvific current to a formulated and systematic set of creedal streams, we no longer have enough wave and motion to take our boats anywhere! There is not enough excitement or white water to enjoy the ride. The mission of the church in the world is so much more involved than we hardly ever give it permission to be! It is so much more joyous, so much more loving, and there is so much more good news to share.

As the paralytic man rises to his feet, Jesus' question should stir all our hearts. "Which is easier, to say to the paralyzed man, 'Your sins are forgiven'; or to say, 'Stand up, and take your mat and walk'?"[24] The gospel is not about a set of prayers we pray, creeds we recite, or even articles of faith. The gospel, the work of God throughout history into today, has been and is always about healing.

Healing our spirit.
Healing our body.
Healing this planet.
Healing these wounds.
Healing these broken relationships between God, you, me, and all creation.
That's salvation.

How many are your works, Lord!
In wisdom you made them all.

PSALM 104:24, NIV

You and I are made from particles. Everything you've ever seen or known are made from these subatomic particles that comprise our being. If we could actually zoom in that immense distance with our naked eye to see the subatomic-ness of the world around us, we wouldn't recognize anything! It would appear microscopically

---

24. Mark 2:9.

galactic. (Think *Ant-Man and the Wasp*: Quantumania level of weird.) We would witness firsthand how everything is just magnificently connected to everything else on an atomic level. As these tiny particles join to create atoms, and these atoms join to create molecules (like H_2O), eventually, you would zoom out enough to see a recognizable substance (like water).

In an interview, Astrophysicist Neil deGrasse Tyson stated that

> there are more molecules of water, in a glass of water, than there are glasses of water in all the world's oceans. Which means that after you drink that water and it comes back out of you ... there's enough molecules that pass through your kidney to populate every other glass of water drawn from the world's water supply.[25]

You may have to read that twice! He goes on to explain how that means the water from your glass definitely passed through any and every historical figure you can think of, which includes Jesus.

Let's recap. The molecules of water that you've been drinking today would have passed through the incarnation, God embodied on earth, Jesus the Christ, thousands of years ago.

The salvific implications of this are gargantuan.

We know the importance of the incarnation of Jesus, as God taking on human form and experiencing life in a body ... living, dying, and rising again. However, we must further consider that this sanctifying work extends to the very molecules and subatomic parts of creation, as they are part of the whole!

Salvation, as the Creator intends it to be, is subatomic.

In our hearts, most of us know that salvation has never been about performing the correct liturgy, reciting the formulaic creeds and articles, but about the transformative grace of God with and within all things. It's about healing us, all creation, and even our broken sense of belonging.

To think for a minute that the redeeming activity of the Lord of heaven and earth, who is the holy Creator of all things, who is the Alpha and Omega, is simply about getting our disembodied spirits a free ticket into the resurrection is not only unbiblical but is the most narrow and self-centered version of the gospel out there. The grace of

---

25. Holmes, "Neil deGrasse Tyson," 1:09:48; Also found in Tyson, *Astrophysics*.

our Lord Jesus Christ is mighty, deep, and wide. The reason that Jesus could calm storms, multiply bread, heal blindness with mud, walk on water, and resurrect the body of Lazarus was because the great and arching work of salvation reflects the created scope of the cosmos in which God wonderfully made! Just try on our most-quoted Bible verse, John 3:16. What we so often translate as "world" is the Greek term "cosmos." Cosmos really means . . . cosmos![26]

The salvation of the Lord our God through Jesus on the cross covers and permeates all life and every single element on the periodic table, as it must, if it is to do the work of reconciling all things. The salvific work of Jesus within creation spreads wider and saturates into deeper levels of our being and of the earth than we can comprehend. It echoes what Paul writes in the Greek, πάντα, "all things":

> He is the image of the invisible God, the firstborn of all creation, for in him all things in heaven and on earth were created, things visible and invisible, whether thrones or dominions or rulers or powers—all things have been created through him and for him. He himself is before all things, and in him all things hold together. He is the head of the body, the church; he is the beginning, the firstborn from the dead, so that he might come to have first place in everything. For in him all the fullness of God was pleased to dwell, and through him God was pleased to reconcile to himself all things, whether on earth or in heaven, by making peace through the blood of his cross. (Col 1:15–20)

RESURRECTED BODIES

Why are you troubled, and why do doubts rise in your minds? Look at my hands and my feet. It is I myself! Touch me and see; a ghost does not have flesh and bones, as you see I have.

LUKE 24:38–39, NIV

It might be fair to conclude that resurrection is *not* characterized as finite. I think in our dreams of what heaven will be like, it's easy to assume some sort of limitlessness in it. We jump to all sorts of conclusions about what heaven will be like anytime we talk about it. In the

---

26. "For God so loved *the cosmos* that he gave his only Son, so that everyone who believes in him may not perish but may have eternal life" (John 3:16).

face of some impasse, of some moment when we are confronted with our limits, we say, "Heaven will be like never running out of Cheetos!" You know what I'm talking about.

"In heaven, we'll be able to fly!" "In heaven, you'll be able to eat forever, never have a tummy ache, and never have to go potty!" "In heaven, you'll be able to ride on the back of a tiger, eating your favorite candy while listening to Taylor Swift endlessly!" (I guess it depends on which middle schoolers you're talking to on a Sunday morning!)

It's funny that our wildest imaginations about heaven all seem to coalesce in a kind of place where we can consume indefinitely without ramification.

No limits.
No borders.
Infinitude in the presence of God.

Now, of course, at the great and final coming of Jesus, we may all launch into the air like Captain Marvel breaking through all of our human barriers, but here is where I'm stuck. Every single thing that I love, every single thing that I would name as coming close to heaven while here on earth, is wonderfully earthbound. It has parameters, complexity, and skin, as highlighted in the previous chapter.

Yet, when anything has inherent limitation, it will necessarily come with a degree of conflict, if we are to be in relationship with it. What this means is that any person, place, or thing that we are to be in loving relationship with will inevitably require of us a resilience to living with friction. There will be occasions when these particulars of what you love will be in conflict with your own boundaries and limits.

Love is shared in the relationship, the movement, the giving way, and working through these difficulties together. Love isn't ignoring them, pretending they aren't there, or attempting to create an artificial reality in which such struggles don't exist. At that point, we wouldn't be able to love one another holistically because our true selves would be hidden or unapproved. But it's the engagement within . . .

the lines,
the edges,
the frames,

that we will discover the particulars of that whom we love *and also* the friction, rub, pain, and struggle that naturally comes with it.

What we know about resurrected bodies is that Jesus came back, resurrected, with a body. Jesus stood in rooms with people he loved; he was touched, hugged, cooked, ate, hollered, and even breathed. Jesus' resurrected body bore scars. His body seemed to have limits of some nature. Yet, he also appeared, disappeared, and ascended into heaven.

The bodily resurrection of Jesus may be the most powerfully missed part of our gospel. Today, Jesus' body, the flesh, blood, hair, hands, stomach, teeth, and nitrogen are critical reminders for us that Jesus is resurrected and it's atomic. Cells are living, veins are pumping. You can put your hand on his side and touch him, even though he can somehow evaporate in a moment. Jesus is living in two spaces, in both heaven and earth. Jesus resurrected body is inaugurating this new kingdom, pulling these realities together.

Jesus' bodily resurrection has implications for all creation. If God's resurrecting work is tethered to our bodies, it must be tethered to the ground that grew the trees, made the coal, started the fire, cooked the fish from the lake, and fed the disciples on that sandy shore in Galilee.[27] Our bodily resurrection will not, nor could not, be separated from God's work of universal restoration. Just as we believe we will physically embrace our loved ones who have passed away, that the home being prepared for us will be the heaven-earth, true reality—the renewal of all creation is wrapped into God's cosmic redemptive action.

God made us earthy for a reason. Jesus was born, lived in, died in, and was resurrected in a body for a reason. The Bible's last pages tell of the renewing of heaven and earth for a reason.

You and I, we are *heaven and earth* bound.

God is bringing all things good together. Right here. It is a great belonging.

---

27. See John 21.

Lord, we are tattered from our quest to be tatter-less. Our hands and feet are sore from building and climbing to put our name in the heavens. God, help us to stop and to hear your Spirit whisper, "Descend." Lord, you are always teaching us about the descending path! We pray for courage to follow you back down to the ground.
We aren't trapped in a body, we are saved in one!
We aren't chained by limits but set free within their generosity!
We aren't ignorant in our lack but wise enough to know we aren't gods.
God, you have loved us well through your creation,
Lead us along better ways that we may also love you through our caretaking of it,
And may we be surprised by your mercy on the way.
Amen.

PART FIVE

Jesus Drives a Station Wagon

But God is my King from long ago;
he brings salvation on the earth.
The day is yours, and yours also the night;
you established the sun and moon.
It was you who set all the boundaries of the earth;
you made both summer and winter.

Psalm 74:12, 16–17, NIV

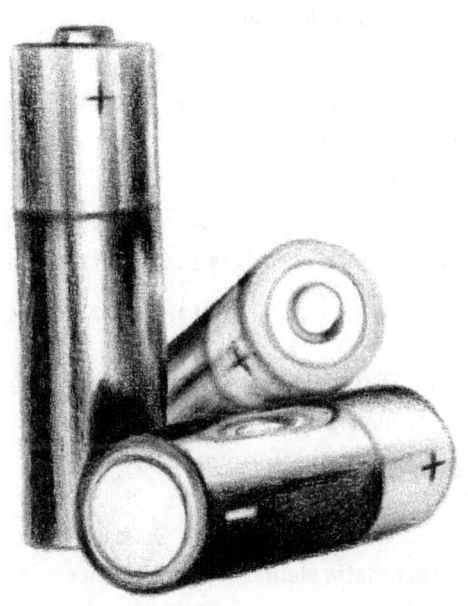

Chapter 9 | Humble Power

*Their land is filled with silver and gold,
   and there is no end to their treasures;
their land is filled with horses,
   and there is no end to their chariots.
Their land is filled with idols;
   they bow down to the work of their hands,
   to what their own fingers have made.
And so people are humbled,
   and everyone is brought low . . .*

*The haughty eyes of people shall be brought low,
   and the pride of everyone shall be humbled,
and the Lord alone will be exalted on that day.
For the Lord of hosts has a day
   against all that is proud and lofty,
   against all that is lifted up and high . . .*

> *Against every high tower*
> *and against every fortified wall;*
> *against all the ships of Tarshish*
> *and against all the highly prized vessels.*
> *The haughtiness of people shall be humbled,*
> *and the pride of everyone shall be brought low,*
> *and the Lord alone will be exalted on that day.*
>
> ISAIAH 2:7–9, 11–12, 15–17

LATELY, IN OUR HOME, we've been leaning into medicinal herbs. Wrapping our swollen ankles in comfrey, putting yarrow over our cuts, chewing on yellow root for our upset tummies, bee balm for our stings, and basil for our rashes. Herbs are one of my favorite ways of living closer to the ground. I love walking out of my back door to harvest these aromatic elements that enhance my well-being. Even though this practice is more ancient than civilization itself, it has become foreign to most and is a threat to a kind of system that wants you to consume an increasing amount of pharmaceutical goods. I wonder if herbs, with their attractive scents and medicinal properties, aren't God's humble reminders that our flourishing isn't found somewhere higher up but lower down.

Being God's people has always been about being a people who are humble. Humility is close to the heart of God. Being an earthbound Christian is about living a humble life. It's an exploration into the simplicity and goodness of being human created within a place. Hannah Anderson, in her book *Humble Roots*, describes humility as a correct sense of self, understanding where you come from and where you belong.[1] True humility is about being the very creatures God has created us to be. Made in the image of the Triune God, we are a diverse body of beautifully earthed people with God-intended, humble roots.

Our story is one of humility. Our God is the God who brings the mighty low and sets the captive free. Our God is the God who says the last will be first, those who lose their life will find it, and on the day of the Lord, the high places will be made low and the valleys raised.

---

1. Anderson, *Humble Roots*.

God has made creation humble. Soil is humble. Stars are humble. Owls are humble. Otters are humble. Trees are humble. Streams are humble. Surely, this must be the reason we return to wild places to find our center again and to remember our humble place.

Humans are the ones lured by pride. We are tempted to outstretch limits, reach for forbidden fruit, and consume beyond ourselves toward that which harms us. Of course, the consequences of this pride spill out over all the rest of creation; how could it not?

Both the words "human" and "humus" have roots in the word "humble." It's all connected. So, how do we become humble humans with the earth once again?

We discover that the life we were created for, the life that offers wholeness to all of God's creation, is one close to the ground, lowly, meek, generous, openhanded, trusting, vulnerable, and selfless.

What I hope is becoming clear is that what we define as "prosperity" is most often not prosperity. The good life, a life of true flourishing will not and cannot be found at the altar of false gods. Worshiping the gods of growthism perpetuate Babylonian economies that take life and all creation into captivity.

OUR FRIEND, FAILURE

Pass on what you have learned. Strength. Mastery. But weakness, folly, failure also. Yes, failure most of all. The greatest teacher, failure is.
YODA, *THE LAST JEDI*

Listening to the radio, some lyrics leapt out at me recently. It was a familiar phrase: "I don't believe in failure." We've heard that saying so frequently, it has become part of the cultural furniture. Aside from the fact that failure isn't something to believe in or not, it's no surprise that over time we've done everything we can to avoid it. We take up the language of waging war on failure. We want failure to fail!

At the heart of the growthism mindset lies our fear of failure. It's similar to the kind of attitude that we take when referring to death and dying. We don't like it, we don't want it, we refuse to look at it, and if we lace up our work boots tightly enough, we think we can avoid it. I believe we all know that, just like death, failure is inevitable.

What if failure is not only inevitable but necessary? What if failure isn't just necessary but can be one of the best things that could happen to you? As Franciscan Richard Rohr shares,

> Any talk of growth, achievement, climbing, improving, and progress highly appeals to the ego. But the only way we stay on the path with any authenticity is to constantly experience our incapacity to do it, our failure at doing it. That's what makes us, to use my language, fall upward. Otherwise, we're really not climbing; we're just thinking we're climbing by saying to ourselves, "Look, I'm better today. Look, I'm holier than I was last week. Look, my prayer is improving." That really doesn't teach us anything or lead us anywhere new.[2]

In life, no one would improve at anything if we did not fail at it. It is through these crucibles that we are formed into who we are. It is the way in which we fall short that we learn, in the end, how to better love and become better humans. Gravity stumbles and humbles us as we learn to walk with more and deeper awareness over time.

Failure is the most natural thing in the world, even if it's a pain in the butt! I don't know about your kids, but my tween daughter isn't going to wake up one day and magically be a responsible adult. Rather, it will be her repeated failings at being responsible that ultimately bring her into maturity. Her failure drives her development.

Galadriel: Why the Halfling?

Gandalf: . . . I don't know. Saruman believes it is only great power that can hold evil in check. But that is not what I have found. I've found it is the small things, everyday deeds of ordinary folk that keeps the darkness at bay. Simple acts of kindness and love.

THE HOBBIT: AN UNEXPECTED JOURNEY

---

2. Rohr, "We Learn by Doing It Wrong," 3.

We may not spend our lives physically building great towers in Babylon, pyramids in Egypt, or monolith for Sauron, yet our pursuits today aren't that different. From early on, we are taught to climb ladders. We give ample effort, education, money, and time figuring out which ladder we are going to climb. Onward and upward. More and higher.

But where are we climbing to?

Is climbing the ladder what it looks like to pursue well-being? Do we all just need to get to the top of our individual ladders and stand on the highest rung?

If you've ever tried to stand on the top of a ladder, you know how that ends! There's nothing and no one to hold to.

Are we all building and ascending this great tower together? If we ever finish, I wonder if we will find that there's only room for a very few on that top step. Maybe just 1 percent?

When Jesus came to the Jewish people in the first century under the occupation of the Roman empire, he was highly misunderstood. If there was one area of the faith that everyone agreed on, it was that the Messiah was going to come and help the Jews climb back up the ladder. Yet, in the Gospels, we come face to face with the descending Jesus. Disciples ask Jesus to reign down fire from heaven upon sinners and want to sit at his right and left hand in the coming kingdom. People rally around him expecting war horses and the strong arm of divine justice. Jesus will have none of it. He just keeps eating with sinners, touching lepers, healing on the Sabbath, loving all people in all ways, reattaching a bleeding ear, and saying things like "Blessed are the meek." But to say that Jesus did no climbing would be missing a big part of the story.

The one time Jesus did climb was up on a cross.

I imagine Jesus standing at the bottom of all our ladders, gazing up at us and gently saying, "You can come down now, it's OK."

Life is not meant to be a series of endless ladders.

Life does not have to be an unceasing climb. It's not about finding the correct wall or the sturdiest blocks.

Life lived well is about learning to descend. It's about becoming friends with gravity. Failure is not when you hit your limits in life but when you refuse to respect them. Jesus knew that the abundant life is not one of extravagance, like we often want to translate it. No, a life well lived is a life that knows how to flourish within its own bounds.

The idea of "hitting our ceiling" might sound like the worst thing that could happen to us, but what if it's the gift that keeps on giving? Jesus continually compares the kingdom of God to hidden seeds and treasure. The whole point of the mustard seed is that it is ridiculously small yet matures to become a means of God's loving kingdom in the world, offering refuge for those around.

Is it any coincidence that the introduction of Jesus' opening message offers us this road map?

Blessed are the poor.
Blessed are those who mourn.
Blessed are the meek.
Blessed are those who hunger and thirst.
Blessed are the merciful.
Blessed are the pure in heart.
Blessed are the peacemakers.
Blessed are the persecuted.[3]

Jesus names the kind of people who have easy access to the kingdom of God. Why? Because they have already descended. There is little to nothing in the way.

They aren't busy growing their GDP or making sure all the balls are in the air. These people are already on the ground ready to plant kingdom seeds. These are the pure in heart who are ready to see God.

We climb these ladders assuming that we'll see God up there, yet instead we fall prey to that old temptation of just trying to become a god ourselves.

---

3. Matt 5:1–12.

Finally, in Matt 25, Jesus stuns those around him as he reveals the kind of people that the Messiah is associated with when the "Son of Man comes in his glory." Jesus tells us that we have served God when we have served the hungry, the thirsty, the naked, the lonely, the prisoner, and the sick. So many still miss this teaching of Jesus today. The only kind of "growth" the church is meant to be about in the world is increasing our love, care, respect, and the dignity of the lowest, lost, and least of these.

Boundaries are the distance at which I can love you and me simultaneously.
PRENTIS HEMPHILL

Living within limits is as much good news for us as it is for all other parts of creation. As Robin Wall Kimmerer states, "All flourishing is mutual."[4] This book is not a call to sacrifice our well-being for the comfort or betterment of others. Rather, it is about the tangible pursuit of true well-being for you, me, and all of the created world.

When we find the reclamation of our own boundaries, limits, space, humanity, and right to exist without harm, we will be participating in the gospel embodied in all places! This is our Christian journey: discovering that care for others is care for ourselves, and care for ourselves is care for others. Honoring our boundaries builds capacity to show up for others in rooted, just, and holistic ways.

What does that mean for those of us who live within oppressive systems that hoard power or wealth? What does it mean for those of us who are held captive by these Babylonian systems? We know that financial wealth, under the current structure, mostly rewards those who are already close to the top of the tower. The US Congressional Budget Office released a report that studied wealth distribution from 1989 to 2022, revealing that "America's top 10% own the majority of wealth in the country, but the top 1% control nearly a third."[5] After many decades, we can safely say that rising tides do not raise all ships. In fact, it's more likely to sink them (at least all but the 1 percent).

4. Kimmerer, *Serviceberry*.
5. Pringle, "Over the Past 30," 1. Karamcheva, "Trends in the Distribution."

These great waves of wealth have become tsunamis, wreaking havoc on all public well-being and the natural world.

Recently, here in Tennessee, some lawmakers pushed to pass a bill that will remove pivotal state protections for our vital wetlands. This came from lawmakers who are highly motivated by developers and their lobbyists. What lies underneath this legislation is the same old song and dance. Money talks, and the idea is that people *ought to* be able to treat *their land* however they see fit. In their eyes, freedom is understood as limitlessness. What is short-sighted are the myriad of ways in which these wetlands are protecting us, preventing future floods, drawing down carbon, and fostering essential biodiversity for all generations to come. (This is not even to speak of the posture of partnership rather than dominance or the posture of care over colonization.)

The point isn't to create villains but to seek just economic practices within our lives and world that benefit all creation. My wish is that those lawmakers would see this as a deeper issue involving their faith and what it means to follow Christ in the world. We need to channel our imagination, invest with sweat equity, and love our neighbors. We need to see the work before us as an exploration into holy living.

What will it take for us to wake up from what is easy and pray, "Not my will but yours be done"? Will we learn from the disciples' mistakes in the garden of Gethsemane? Will we sleep or will we wake up, pray, and walk with Jesus toward the healing work of bringing God's kingdom to earth?

To the world, this will look like foolishness . . . maybe even like death. It may mean not building that new house or keeping up with the Joneses. It will mean repairing rather than replacing. It will mean a life that is rich with meaning and wealth that is communal rather than the ghostly existence of individualism and the lifestyle of having the world delivered to your doorstep. It will look like inconvenience but will be the true first steps of efficiency.

In a board meeting, you will sound more like John the Baptist, who was called a madman as he declared something different and paved the way for the Messiah. It will look like calling company values into question and looking for deeper meanings beyond quarterly growth. It will require reframing and standing against that which will consume any corner of the planet left unprotected.

Further still, we have to actively advocate, protest, rally, and divest from harmful industries. This is the way.

As it currently stands, the systems of destruction are in place, holding back healing. It requires nothing of us to keep things going as they are. The only way to change the world is through repentance ... literally turning around and going the other way. Repentance gives way to resistance, which gives way to reimagination, which gives way to re-creation. Remember, recreation is a synonym for joy and pleasure!

TECHNOLOGICAL KINSHIP

The first step is to stop believing in bright green fairy tales that technology will save the planet. Instead, put your belief in soils, grasses, forests, seaweeds, and the billions of living beings who every moment are working to regenerate the conditions that support life and beauty on this planet.

BRIGHT GREEN LIES[6]

Advancing technology isn't the solution we think it is. While the tower of Babel is a story that reminds us of technology used in the wrong ways, it also tells us about the creative potential inside us. Our urge to create can bring us together in ways that nothing else can; this is what is most hopeful in this ancient story. If we can have such synergy, drive, and creative energy to produce self-glorifying towers, imagine what we might create if we came together for good in a posture of humility?

What we learn from Gen 11 isn't that bricks are bad. Bricks are bricks. Can you eventually produce too many of them? Yes. Can you use them for wrong purposes? Absolutely. Can we pull them down and build something new and beautiful out of the rubble? One hundred percent, yes!

As creative beings, we will always be shaping, reshaping, tweaking designs, and perfecting our work, but that cannot come at the

---

6. Jensen, *Bright Green Lies*, 442.

expense of the planet. The irony is, we may in reality lay waste to the earth in the wake of glorifying technology as something we hope will save the earth and launch humanity into a new age.

My daughters are a couple of math whizzes. I'm always so impressed by how fast they seem to churn out their math homework. The apple has fallen and rolled far from this tree! Yet, of the little I understand of math, I know that to get the right answer, you've got to solve the right problem. Or, to put it differently, if your truck breaks down because of problems with the transmission (big problem!), you'll never solve that issue by changing out the battery and replacing the alternator. It will never happen; you're working to solve the wrong problem.

My farmer friend Jason and I have had many good-yet-despairingly-nervous laughs at the ways in which society usually talks about solving the environmental issues of our day. The pitch usually goes something like if we could just switch from "this form of energy" to "that form of energy," we could solve climate change. Sounds simple, right? If we could just unplug from this dirty outlet over here and plug our devices into this clean outlet over there, we'll solve this existential planetary crisis. In a nutshell, this is most often how many, even in the green movement, "sell it." Most unfortunately, this is solving the wrong equation.

Our problem isn't that we need a new energy source; the problem is our *continuous* desire for *more* energy.

Let that soak in. That's a big one.

To be honest, this is where many fall off the wagon. Energy . . . well, that's life, right? We have to have energy! Yes, of course we need energy, but our *desire* for more energy far outweighs our *need* for energy.

There is no shortage of green tech solutions out there. Solar, wind, biofuel, hydropower, and more. Each of these are attempts to "techno" our way out of our collective carbon crisis. At the end of the day, these can be helpful things to engage in as we stumble forward in the relationship between earth and human science. Yet, none of these things will be helpful in the end if we don't deal with the issue underneath. The heart of our calamity is our gluttonous economy and postures of growthism.

The amount of infrastructure required for the world to "go green" would mean unholy amounts of new carbon to be put into the atmosphere, new levels of mining for raw materials, and further destruction of prairies, grasslands, marshes, and forests just to connect it all together, as unpacked in the almost-five-hundred-page book *Bright Green Lies: How the Environmental Movement Lost Its Way and What We Can Do About It*.[7] Any solution, any grid, any battery, charger, or screen comes from the earth, and much of this tech will need replaced in only a few decades, leaving us needing an upgrade.

Even if we could somehow achieve this goal of 100 percent clean energy in the world and do it in a way that required almost no major ecological footprint, we likely would be in deeper trouble than ever. The reason comes down to what we would do with an unlimited source of energy. The world's production would become more consumptive than we could ever imagine. In fact, from what we know, any energy we've already "saved" through wind and solar is simply getting spent through increasing demand. Green energy is not actually displacing fossil fuels, only expanding our energy consumption.[8]

Let's be clear, green energy infrastructures are important pieces toward solving some of the ecological problems, but the solutions are much more complex than "switching plugs."

What if, instead of existing like hamsters on a wheel, trying to carbon our way out of carbon, the real work is still waiting to be engaged in? What if the answers are right under our noses? What if it's right under our toes?

The best kind of technology will work in harmony with creation and lift up nature-based solutions. The earth wants to heal; how might we humbly remove everything in the way of that while also bolstering natural efforts?

---

7. Jensen, *Bright Green Lies*.
8. Thombs, "Does Renewable Energy Production."

Imagine a technology that requires no energy input from us. Imagine that this tech could capture carbon and give back oxygen. It grows its own nitrogen to recharge itself and prevents soil erosion. It catches rainwater and transforms it into food and medicine for us. It can create water vapor cooling the air, meanwhile cleaning up airborne pollutants. This technology can also provide habitats for wildlife. This revolutionary technology can duplicate itself, and when it eventually wears out, we are still using its parts hundreds of years later. What if I told you this technology already exists? It does, after all. What I have described is a tree.

I once heard someone say that photosynthesis is where heaven and earth come together. Sure, we could pause to have a biology lesson on this special endothermic reaction where sunlight is used to convert carbon dioxide and water into glucose and oxygen. Although, it may carry more weight to say that this chemical process offers us the gift of food to eat and air to breathe. Without photosynthesis, there would be no life. It's an amazing gift embedded within creation, constantly working for our good.

As far as these technological gifts of nature go, the ocean is a rock star. Around the world, oceanic life absorbs copious amounts of carbon dioxide and produces somewhere between 50 to 80 percent of the oxygen we breathe.[9] Seagrass, which is essential for marine life and even life on land, while constituting only 0.1 percent of the ocean floor, draws in 18 percent of the world's oceanic carbon. However, seagrass is under threat due to dredging, agricultural runoff, and illegal boating activities.[10]

Nature is actively working toward repair; the most important work we can do is support that process. The technology we so desperately need God has already created. It is the wetlands, the wild prairies, the forest floors, and the urban canopies. These natural systems are incredibly powerful. Simply moving toward systems that care for the life of the soil has the capability of drawing down carbon, catching flood waters, and growing food in the smallest corners of the world. It's a solution that is as old as Gen 2:15; it is "serving and keeping" this garden we call home.

---

9. National Ocean Service "How Much Oxygen."
10. United Nations, "Seagrass."

If we are going to flourish here in this garden, finding ways back into lifestyles that are in closer relationship with God's animal kingdom is a big part of that repair. We know that grazing cycles are a large piece of the puzzle with our domestic livestock, but beyond that, how can we support wildlife? A study from 1970 to 2020 found that we've lost 74 percent of global wildlife.[11] Another study evaluating insects found that populations globally have declined by about 45 percent in just the past forty years.[12] A survey between June 2024 and the following February reported over a 60 percent decline in American commercial honeybees.[13] Meanwhile, we know that the majority of our food relies on these humble creatures to do their part.

We know that removing dams offers a cascade of restorative activity by allowing water flow and fish migrations.[14] Creating land bridges over roads and highways for wildlife and special tunnels for amphibians to access areas without harm decrease road accidents and increase critical habitats. Planting native plants instead of lawns around our homes and churches can foster places of refuge for pollinators. Reintroducing keystone species also play a critical role.

After Yellowstone returned grey wolves to the park in 1995, it had what scientist call a trophic cascade of effects. The wolves impacted the number of elk, then allowing for foliage to return; following this, the river banks began to firm up, new habitats for rabbits and mice were created, snakes and birds of prey had new sources of food, berries grew in number, songbirds returned, bear populations increased, beavers made more dams, and fish populations grew. All this occurred through reintroducing wolves, a beautiful animal that we thought the land was better off without.[15]

Not only do we have great power to change these larger systems by the way we choose to advocate, eat, purchase, and consume in the world but we hold incredible power simply within the micro-economy of our own life. The world around our individual lives, homes, and work cannot be underestimated. Just today, I looked out my bathroom window to see six turkeys grazing in my backyard. While

11. Fallah, "Catastrophic 73% Decline."
12. Rice, "North America"; Wagner, "Insect Decline."
13. American Bee Journal, "Survey Estimates."
14. NOAA Fisheries, "Successful Fish Passage Efforts."
15. National Geographic, "Wolves of Yellowstone."

not everyone may appreciate the long grass, native wildflowers, and host of other things growing around our small half of an acre, the animals do. In metropolitan Nashville, where it's mostly a food desert for these woodland creatures, they don't have to dumpster dive to find food at my house. In our yard, we regularly see coyotes, deer, rabbits, snakes, bees, bats, hummingbirds, butterflies, and dragonflies. And, of course, the raccoon family gets snacks out of my compost buffet-style. It's all good though, because as omnivores, they play a key role out there consuming insects and rodents while helping disperse my native plant seeds. This small biodiverse micro-economy offers life to God's creation for miles around us. Imagine all our homes creating these spaces of refuge and repair.

Creation is miraculously forgiving if we foster its recovery; just look at Chernobyl, a place ravaged by nuclear blasts, just forty years later is teeming with new life and called a haven for wildlife![16]

How can we integrate these protections and places of refuge as prerequisites to all new efforts of advancement? It really isn't "rocket science," as we like to say! In fact, there are no rockets required!

Let's stop attempting to overcome *here* in order to save *here*. Let's stop attempting to save our limits through transcending them. Our limits really do have to be saved. To save them, they must be valued. We can't continue making every decision based on finance and GDP growth. Corporations and governments will tout "green growth." In reality, it's what we call "greenwashing," which is, to be blunt, just lies to sell more product. The systems that eat the world to survive can't and won't save the world, which is why we return to those gentle, divine hands that call out to get us down from that tower. God knows that if we climb that ladder to try and get to the top, we will climb forever, only to lose our soul in the process. Here's my unpopular opinion: you can't get to heaven that way, and heaven won't get to earth that way either.

The important takeaway is not doom and gloom but understanding the complexities herein. The way forward is advocating for energy innovations *while* dramatically lowering our footprint *and* drawing into a closer relationship with the earth.

---

16. UN Environment Programme, "How Chernobyl Has Become."

CHAPTER 9 | HUMBLE POWER   181

The way forward is less about mining for new technology and more about kinship and rediscovering Indigenous wisdom. Relationships can be messy, and what lies ahead for us is very relational.

How fitting that the new technological advancements we need to embrace in order to participate in planetary healing are found in the very ways of life eradicated by America's founding. Real progress doesn't leave behind a trail of tears. Authentic advancements aren't based on extractive "leaps forward" on the backs of enslaved people, systems of hierarchy, the superiority of certain classes or genders, and certainly not from stolen land.

As previously mentioned, a large majority of the world's biodiversity lies under Indigenous care.[17] These caretakers are people such as the Sápara, who live in Ecuador as guardians of the Amazon, the Maasai in Tanzania, or the Sengwer and Ogiek peoples in Kenya.[18] Even so, there is hardly an Indigenous culture that is not under continual threat of losing their land rights to development, tourism, and pressure from the government. All in the name of the false god, growthism.

Indigenous conservation methods are so effective because what is understood, at the core, is that within nature's own systems lies the greatest solutions to the environmental problems and climate crises of today.[19] Indigenous wisdom knows that when we care for the earth, we care for ourselves. Indigenous wisdom listens to the needs of the earth and responds as a friend. What is a prerequisite for us all is that we strive for deeper and more intimate understanding of the ecology surrounding us and our place within it.

Lifting up stories of Indigenous wisdom is essential to understanding the posture and work required of us ahead. What would it be like for us all to behave like native earthlings? What would it look like for us all to enter into Indigenous relationships with God's creation today?

17. Garnett, "Spatial Overview."
18. National Geographic, "Indigenous Peoples Defend"; Ndasi, "Protecting Ancestral Lands"; Dahir, "Ecotourism Is Being Used."
19. Bastida, "Indigenous Wisdom Can Heal."

What will it look like for us to allow Indigenous cultures to lead the way toward proper stewardship and fellowship with the land?

One example is the 125 acres in California that has been returned to the Yurok Tribe. This land was ravaged by gold miners and loggers, and it was stolen from the Yurok people almost two hundred years ago. Now, in recognition that there is no one who knows how to heal and care for this land better, it is at long last being returned to the care of its original dwellers. By careful management, the Yurok people are healing the ground through controlled burns, a process that works closely to mimic nature and seed new growth. Streams that have been void of life are seeing salmon return in numbers, and the Yurok people are also reintroducing the California condor back to the land. As salmon spawn and die, and as the condors hunt, nutrients return to the land and ecosystems find new balance.[20]

Indigenous stories of ecological kinship may feel quite distant from our lives. We're busy running kids to soccer practice and gymnastics, getting to the grocery store after work, or preparing for that Sunday small group lesson. Yet, that is the very temptation we must resist: seeing our everyday normal human lives as something different or separate from the rest of creation. We are a people who are entangled and interwoven within creation. Everything we do, not do, eat, buy, or touch is affecting God's world at each interval! *We are close to the earth already.*

Even as I say such things, my heart knows to proceed with caution. Because, behind a conversation involving Indigenous peoples, the nation of America, and a religion called Christianity . . . is not a pretty story. As Kaitlin Curtice, in her book *Native: Identity, Belonging, and Rediscovering God*, writes, "What does it mean to be Indigenous and to have ties to the person of Jesus without being tied to the destructive, colonizing institution of the church? It is a constant decolonizing."[21] All those values stated earlier about life, liberty, and the pursuit of happiness occurred under the premise of taking the freedom, land, and all facets of well-being from the original peoples of this continent. Therefore, pursuing solutions, even ecologically, that

---

20. Vigliotti, "More Than a Century."
21. Curtice, *Native*, 206.

aren't also about truth, healing, and repair in all relations fall short.[22] We must be about the decolonization of all things, as it is a prerequisite for reconciliation.

We have so much to learn from our Indigenous siblings, what it means to belong here and live lives closer to the ground.

HUMBLE TEACHERS

Ian Malcolm: "God creates dinosaurs, God destroys dinosaurs. God creates man, man destroys God. Man creates dinosaurs."

Ellie Sattler: "Dinosaurs eat man. Woman inherits the earth."

JURASSIC PARK

As I'm sure you've noticed, I love sneaking in a few good movie quotes. From Hobbits in the Shire to Jedi Masters in a galaxy far, far away, what lingers underneath culture and is baked into the very fabric of society are our humble origins. There is a reason we root for the underdog. There is a reason we are moved by stories of small characters overcoming great empires. Secretly, we know humility is the key ingredient for the whole recipe. God has hidden this message not just within the natural world but also within our hearts.

Even in the fantastical stories we tell about the rebirth of extinct dinosaurs or some future when humanlike AI occupies our world, over and over, the narrative we create is some version of this *Jurassic Park* quote. These sci-fi scenarios unfold where "man" plays god one too many times and it eventually catches up with them. Perhaps my favorite part of this quote is the gender-specificity: "Dinosaurs eat man. Woman inherits the earth."[23] While we can't blame a single gender for our modern ecological overshoot . . . by and large, men have been more than a significant part of the problem.

The research is conclusive; empowering women within culture and society is one of the topmost means of creating ecological healing today. Female empowerment in development, conservation,

---

22. For more on this topic, see this downloadable resource for your faith community from Creation Justice Ministries: https://www.creationjustice.org/truthhealingrepair.html.

23. Spielberg, *Jurassic Park*.

agricultural efforts, education, and family planning can be catalysts for ecological care and societal transformation. Further, we are more disembodied, disconnected, and less innovative without women fully present, everywhere and in all things. Anywhere women are not empowered to be fully who God created them to be, humanity is disempowered, and thus creation suffers.[24] There will be no way forward to heal God's creation that doesn't involve full participation of women, who, through centuries of gender oppression, have been driven closer to the earth and humbled in ways that many men cannot understand.

As climate change worsens, we are finding that it is not "gender neutral."[25] Women, particularly in the Global South, carry the brunt of this inequality due to their roles of acquiring of food, water, and fuel for their homes.

Women in India, who themselves own little more than 10 percent of the land, comprise around 80 percent of the agricultural workforce. Being so close to the land, they have witnessed firsthand the bankrupt farming practices and depleted soils left behind by corporate agriculture. They are "nurturing a regenerative food system that challenges both ecological degradation and entrenched patriarchy."[26] Women like this are standing up and leading the way into healing the land through composting, polyculture, and working to transform India's farmlands through a blend of traditional knowledge and ecological innovation.

There are so many stories like this![27] What's beneath the surface here is, again, our Christian call to work toward justice and equality and following the footsteps of Jesus' most faithful disciples: women!

I'm continually struck by Jesus' audacious statements about children. Jesus just went around saying things like, "Unless you change and become like little children, you will never enter the kingdom of heaven,"[28] and, "Whoever then humbles himself as this child, he is the

---

24. Wilkinson, "How Empowering Women"; Madeira, "Want to Save the Planet?"; Ellis, "Link Between Female Empowerment."

25. UN Women, "How Gender Inequality."

26. Earth5R, "Women of the Soil," 1.

27. Johnson, *All We Can Save*.

28. Matt 18:3.

greatest in the kingdom of heaven,"[29] and, "Let the children alone, and do not hinder them from coming to me; for the kingdom of heaven belongs to such as these,"[30] and, "Whoever receives one child like this in my name receives me; and whoever receives me does not receive me, but him who sent me."[31] Children are the secret-keepers of the kingdom of God. Their innocent questions about how the world functions, about money, pain, and love, are our mirrors for finding a better world.

My friend Zach and I have had many conversations over the years about how we hope that we haven't already "messed our kids up too badly!" Inevitably, in ultimate parent failure, our own brokenness breaks through and we briefly allow our shadows to also shadow our children. Our wounds burst out with screams and balled fists into our children's lives uninvited but not completely unexpected. What neuroscience is now teaching us is that what's most important is not doubling down as parents who know everything but confessing our wrongs to our children.[32] Honestly, we're human and we will all make big mistakes and say and do wrong things as parents. It's going to happen, but what's most important is that when it happens, we model correctly what to do next. We embody the repair. That is, we model to them how to say, "I'm wrong, I should never have screamed at you like that. Daddy had a bad day at work and I'm so sorry that I took that out on you. Will you forgive me for doing that?" Confession then becomes the real lesson, rather than "dad is always right."

Our children are inheriting this world. These streets are where they are going to live. These fields are how they are going to eat and feed their families. This water is what they will drink. This air is how they breathe. How ironic that we, as Christians, would be so absolutely focused on helping children in the womb enter this world, and when they become little children, we become hyper-focused on teaching them about an escapist, the earth-doesn't-matter faith? We have the opportunity to pour just as much protection and care over every moment of this child's life, and as they mature, show them love by taking care of this planet in which God has placed us.

29. Matt 18:5.
30. Matt 19:13–14.
31. Mark 9:37.
32. Thompson, *Anatomy of the Soul*, 202.

You can believe whatever you want about "the end times," but that doesn't change a single word about how we are to live today as followers of Jesus called out to be like little children in the world. I know if I were a little child in today's world, with climate change and all that is unfolding, I'd like to know there were some grown-ups confessing their sins and showing me the way forward.

Confession and forgiveness are the tools that help us descend our ladders. If we are going to be a part of mending God's broken creation, it will involve seeking a closer relationship to the earth, advocating for healthy soil and animal habitats; it will do the work of lifting up our Indigenous siblings, empowering the women around us, and following our children's lead.

The work of decolonizing ourselves, of coming out of exile, will be about the same kind of work that Jesus was about in his day—deep renovation rather than conquering power and intellect. Can we see so clearly how Jesus' first hearers missed this entirely, and yet, we still miss this today?

I think if Jesus had a car, it would be an old station wagon. It's a family car, but it's humble. Unlike tall SUVs, station wagons are close to the ground. It requires a level of unpretentiousness just to climb into that backseat. Yet, if you're willing to get low, you'd be surprised how many disciples you can fit! The reality is, Jesus pulled up in God's humble station wagon and said, "Y'all who can, get on in!" But as it happened, most expected Lamborghini Jesus. Thus, the Messiah came and went, and they failed to see. Jesus really did take that wheel . . . but maybe, the truth was, and is, that we don't like what or where Jesus is driving.

Descending the ladder,
carrying your cross,
decolonizing your consciousness,
being born again,
failing,
being humbled,
confessing,
forgiving,
empowering women,

becoming like little children,
preferencing Indigenous wisdom and nature's technology,
these are the lights lighting the way if we're vulnerable enough to find it and brave enough to follow it through.

In hiding from God, the man and woman augment their sense of being alone. They move against the relational gravity of creation that led God to declare that it was not good for the man to be alone (Genesis 2:18). But God is not willing to leave them in their isolation.

CURT THOMPSON[33]

Back in the garden, in Gen 3:9, we are given one singular Hebrew word, *ayeka*, that we translate as "Where are you?" We are there, having climbed some branches and eaten from the wrong tree, and now we're hiding and naked in the bush. God's question, *ayeka*, comes to us searching, locating, and probing us. Where are you?

The way forward is to come out of hiding.

This is a self-check moment. *Ayeka*, God wants to know. Where are you?

Inversely, this book is also about pride. Pride is what's continually trying to hide from being seen by God or anyone. Pride is just trying to save face. The thing about pride is we don't tend to think of ourselves as prideful. Pride is much more elusive than we typically consider. When the film industry wants to portray someone who is prideful, it's obnoxiously obvious and overdone, but what if pride is much more hidden, even from ourselves, than we suspect?

I hope that the confessions I've offered here can help you also join me in confessing. Confessing our broken and prideful ways. Our continual grab for the next higher rung of power. Confessing our desire to be faster, prettier, more efficient, better qualified, better paid, and all knowing. Confessing the ways in which we've touted equality when it has not been equal. Confessing the ways we've announced justice for all when it's really just been justice for some. Confessing the

---

33. Thompson, *Anatomy of the Soul*, 217.

ways we've believed that God's earth is something to get away from. Confessing the ways we've refused to let our faith be earthbound.

> *God, help our knees to discover your soil. Help us to die to ourselves so that your kingdom may come through love. Give us the grace we need to confront our pride and confess our wrongs. Give us courage to examine our lives in the light of your love and justice in the world, that we may clearly see the reconciliatory work you desire of us.*
> *Lord, please light our way.*
> *Amen.*

Chapter 10 | Dancing in the Moonlight

Look toward heaven and count the stars, if you are able to count them. . . . So shall your descendants be.

GENESIS 15:5

HISTORICALLY, ONE OF THE things that we all had in common was a closer relationship with the night sky. These celestial lights were far more familiar to our ancestors, and though they were very far away, their light helped them figure out just exactly where they were on Earth. Our relationship with the night sky has always played a crucial role in what it means to be a human being on Earth . . . until recently, that is.

Darkness is one of our favorite boundaries to overcome. Since the invention of the light bulb a mere 150 years ago, that "creativity bulb" hanging over our heads has been burning brightly! We've got lights on our cars, porches, bedside tables, and closets. We have lights in our parking lots, office buildings, and streets that burn all night long. We have string-lit patios, ambient-lit showers, sparkling campsites, flashing sneakers, laser pointers, and flashlights galore.

Naturally, humans are equipped with a certain kind of "night-vision" as our eyes adjust to darkness. For the first time in history, that has become a muscle that never gets exercised, and there is speculation as to whether we will lose that trait over time. Earlier in life, when I moved from rural Tennessee to the neon lights of Nashville, one unsuspected discovery was that I didn't need my flashlight at all. Here, everything is already lit! Cities are often very difficult places to see the night sky due to light pollution.

All this light is coming back to haunt us. Researchers are uncovering how light pollution is taking a toll on our bodily health and the health of all creation. This extra light is affecting our circadian rhythm, which affects everything else in our lives.

Our bodies naturally want to sync up with day and night (who would have thought!). Today, that is easier said than done. Many Americans experience sleeping issues even though we have the fanciest beds in history. When you don't sleep well, life gets hard quickly.

The ways in which light pollution, particularly blue LED-type lights that our screens produce, impacts our health have been studied at length. What we know is that these lights are changing the melatonin production in our bodies. There are now links between too much blue light exposure and hormone-related cancers such as breast or prostate cancer. Further studies indicate that light pollution may also increase your risk of diabetes and heart disease.[1]

In the animal kingdom, it is scientifically documented how our excess light is affecting every creature, from baby turtles, to bats, to populations of wallabies, and even to insect pollinators. One study tracking agricultural areas found that their crops were 13 percent less pollinated due to light pollution.[2] We're getting more artificial light but less food to eat!

---

1. Spivey, "Light Pollution"; Walker, "Light Pollution and Cancer"; WGCU Staff, "Connections Between Human Health"; Harvard Health, "Blue Light."

2. Knop, "Artificial Light at Night."

We are a family that loves *Moana*. We've gotten miles out of that movie! As with most things, there is a deeper story being told. A young girl sets out on a quest for self-identity, but she reconnects with her ancestors below and the stars above. Our girls have belted those Lin-Manuel Miranda–inspired "wayfinding" tunes from the backseat of our Prius-shaped sailboat on many trips! It is a beautiful film that works to depict ancient human tethers to the stars from people who were known to be voyagers.

Far from being some fantasy Disney hit, the realities surrounding Indigenous cultures and the night sky are critical. In a paper titled "Whitening the Sky: Light Pollution as a Form of Cultural Genocide," researchers indicate just how serious these issues have become. Aboriginal cultures around Australia and other areas use the stars

> to preserve and inform complex knowledge systems, which are used for things like navigation, food economics, forecasting weather, predicting seasonal change, informing social structure, and serving as a mnemonic for committing information to memory and passing it to successive generations over long periods of time. . . . For Aboriginal and Torres Strait Islander people, the stars encode and communicate history, law, ethics, and moral values.[3]

As artificial light increases, primarily driven through economic growth and urban expansion, the ability to see starlight diminishes and what's being lost are entire ways of life. One group of stars that holds cultural significance is that of the "celestial emu." The celestial emu is a recognizable constellation for Aboriginal Australians such as the Gunnai people. It's noted that it "is not made up of the bright stars, but rather of the dark dust lanes in the Milky Way."[4] Now, infringing light pollution from nearby cities is making this dim star cluster disappear from sight. Beautiful ways of life are being lost and so, too, a culture's ability to be closer to creation.

---

3. Hamacher, "Whitening the Sky," 1.
4. Hamacher, "Whitening the Sky," 1.

This is an example of what's called "slow violence."[5] It is the kind of violence that we have all been affected by, whether we've been aware of it or not. It is the kind of violence that works to separate us from a close relationship with the earth through environmental and even cultural degradation disguised as progress over the long arch of time.

Seeing that great night sky above us isn't just something nice to look at if we get the chance, but it is part of remembering who we are, where we are, and how great our God is!

When God came to Abraham and Sarah all those years ago, those promises happened under a night sky. They're told to "count the stars, if you can."[6]

Seeing the stars is something I miss the most from no longer living in rural spaces. As a boy, there were many nights when, after I had gone out to put wood in our furnace heater, I would just sit for long stretches looking at stars. Today though, when I walk out my Nashville back door at night, I can still count the stars. There are about ten of them.

What does it mean that the further we "progress" here with our transhuman fantasies, the further we distance ourselves from the created tethers God has set in place. These tethers are there to remind us of God's covenant faithfulness, God's everlasting love, and God's greatness. These tethers help us live within our seasons, plant and harvest at the appropriate times, and become people in sync with the world we depend upon. We've become more interested in lighting our own way. But our tethers to artificial light are falling short.

Part of what it means to be an earthbound people and live within our limits begins with simply turning off the lights. How might we again discover the night sky and our place within it? Should we be surprised to discover that re-entering into a right-relatedness with darkness and the night sky makes us healthier people, tethers us to the wisdom of the seasons, and joyfully offers new life to all of creation? (Not to mention, it saves us copious amounts of energy!)

---

5. Nixon, *Slow Violence*.
6. Gen 15:5.

So, get out that star app on your phone. Better yet, just walk outside tonight. What do you see? What can you see? What do you recognize?

May you turn off the lights and screen, get out that telescope, and study the stars that surround you. Learn the seasons and familiarize yourself with where in the universe God has placed you!

TIDAL LOCKING

And God said, "Let there be lights in the dome of the sky to separate the day from the night, and let them be for signs and for seasons and for days and years, and let them be lights in the dome of the sky to give light upon the earth." And it was so. God made the two great lights—the greater light to rule the day and the lesser light to rule the night—and the stars.

GENESIS 1:14–16

Did you know that there is no such thing as zero gravity? Even an astronaut floating in the openness of space, while appearing to be simply directionless, is really being pulled by the gravity produced around her. All mass has a gravitational pull, but in comparison to the mass of a planet, your personal gravitational pull is considerably smaller. All the planets in our solar system are in a gravitational swing dance with our star, the sun. The sun's mass is so great that it is grabbing and swinging entire planets around.

Our entire solar system as a unit is also being grabbed and swirled around in a much greater and larger movement within the Milky Way galaxy, pulled by the gravity of an enormous black hole right at the center.[7] It is estimated that it takes 225–250 million years for our solar system to complete one orbit around this center! Some call it a galactic year. It begs the question—what do you give a solar system on its galactic birthday? Don't worry, you've got some time to decide!

I remember a summer night when Emily, our friend Ryan, and I were driving back to Nashville from an ordination service in Kentucky.

---

7. Sagittarius A* is the name of the black hole at the center of the Milky Way.

The moon was full, and it was dark out. I made the comment, "Did you know that we only ever see the same side of the moon? It's why we talk about there being a dark side of the moon." My wife chimes in: "No, I am confident that the moon turns just like the earth turns, so we must see all sides." To which I responded, "No, that's incorrect because I know for a fact that we only ever see the same side of the moon, so it must not rotate like the earth does." Well, naturally, we went back and forth in this debate for a few minutes. Meanwhile, our friend in the back seat had pulled out his Googling device and looked it up. We were both right.

The beauty of this story is that we were both bearing witness to the truth. The moon does have a dark side that we never see, and the moon rotates just like the earth. Right now, the moon is orbiting around us, just like we, down here on Earth, are orbiting around the sun. Also, like the earth, the moon rotates while orbiting. So, one would naturally conclude that, as this large moon spins and orbits around us night and day, we would eventually catch a glimpse of all its sides. Yet, as it happens, the earth and the moon have been dancing together for so long that, at this point, they are in perfect harmony. The moon rotates in about four weeks' time, perfectly synchronized with its orbit around the earth as the earth is rotating. Dizzy yet? What this means is that the gravitational relationship between the earth and the moon keeps them twirling and spinning together, and the moon is always facing its dance partner. This phenomenon is called "tidal locking."

The technical definition of tidal locking is an astrophysical phenomenon that occurs when an astronomical body's orbital period matches its rotational period. But this definition just doesn't hold within it the beauty of what is occurring here.

For our earth and moon, it is a gravitational love story, now millions of years old. The earth and the moon have spent so much time together, gravity has pulled them closer and closer into a synchronized dance. Over the span of time, or maybe we'll say, later in the evening, the slow jams have started to play. The moon's rotation has slowed until her gaze is right upon her partner. The earth and the moon, in a winding dance, are tidally locked—two lovers who faithfully gaze into the eyes of the other. Now, so long into their union, the moon has had a stabilizing effect on the earth, giving it the all-important axial tilt that creates the possibility for life to flourish. They keep each other steady through time, and as millions turn to billions, this dance becomes even more gentle; in old age, they intimately know each other's movements. The earth's tides, the moon's curves and phases . . . it's a cosmic love story.

What would it look like if, instead of our continual efforts to be more than human, to be unlimited, to be infinite in all ways, we became "locked in" with being who we are made to be? With being here? With being the people God created us to be in the place God created us to be? To be in a tidal-locked slow dance of mutual care as we lock eyes with one another, twirling into space?

I wonder if gravity is more than just God's natural law in place, adding order in the universe—more than just a Gandalf-like "You shall not pass" proclamation to us.

What if gravity is actually love?

Gravity is the way that God creates boundaries, so that we might participate in knowing God and being known by God.

Gravity is the grace we've always been looking for—that's been with us the whole time. It is God's gift to us, holding it all in place, offering purpose and plan, within limits and with "love handles," as we say in the South. Because love needs to be held and to have something to hold. "To have and to hold," we say.

Gravity is a wonderful officiant for us. It is that force that God has surrounded us with, keeping us in earthy bounds with all things, culturally and linguistically shaping us into particular peoples, and eventually descending us to be nutrients for the earth—"to death do us part."

God's covenant faithfulness with us includes creation. Of course, God takes Abraham out and says, "Look at the night sky!" All of this creation is God's! It's all connecting together! And God has a redeeming plan for it all!

Creation needs our presence. The earth needs us to turn our caring attention toward the whole of it. Can we dance with creation and love creation as God intended?

How can we do the inner work of healing if we are hyper fixated on outward escape and embodying absence?

When will we finally be released from this anthropocentric ego-climb and turn our gaze and attention toward the ground on which God has placed us? When that happens, it will be the moment we find stabilization between humans and the earth. It will be a co-flourishing.

Any dance that occurs out of pure self-interest, out of a posture that cries "look at me," out of a grab from lust, power, or greed . . . that's when we lose all harmony again.

One great thing about the moon is that you can gaze right at it, unlike the sun. There is something about the moon that is captivating. If you've ever looked at the moon through a telescope, you can see all the particular nuances of this spherical night-light and imagine climbing around its heights and craters. Better still is the moon's ability to help keep track of time. Humans have been using the moon to mark calendars and seasons for thousands of years. Indigenous lunar observations have given guidance to our entire lives and cultures. These calendars weren't fun hobbies for them but were about their people's survival and flourishing, linking them to deeper patterns within the natural world.

The creation story for several North American tribes of the Great Lakes revolves around a great flood, the falling of Sky Woman, the help of many animals, and the back of a giant turtle. In *Braiding Sweetgrass*, Kimmerer describes this creation story at length and beautifully explores its significance for these original people.[8] These stories are rich and inform us of the deep traditions and Indigenous wisdom that flows through communities who live close to the earth. They

---

8. Kimmerer, *Braiding Sweetgrass*.

are important teachers for us as we discover how to live within limits amidst a culture taken captive by the allure of infinite growth.

For the Lenape, Anishinaabe, or Potawatomi people, Turtle Island is the name for this North American land we live on. Turtles have always been a significant part of Indigenous culture. One of the most fascinating connections lies in plain sight, again on a turtle's back. The Anishinaabe, among other Great Lakes people, follow a lunar calendar observing thirteen full moons in a year. Each new moon has a special name offering knowledge and awareness about the people's relationship with the land. For instance, in early spring, the Sugar Moon (Iskigamizige-giizis) marks the time for maple sugaring; the Blueberry Moon (Miini-giizis) in June indicates when blueberries are ripe for picking; and the Freezing Moon (Gashkadino-Giizis) in November signals when the waters begin to freeze, winter comes, and families gather. In the span of a year, thirteen separate moons guide the people through specific seasons that arrive each with rituals, food, forewarnings, and celebrations.[9] Each new moon comes after a 28-day cycle, concluding in a 364-day year.

If our calendar has more to do with the ebb and flow of national GDP and our own cultural ease, we will miss the treasured beauty, wealth, and wisdom of flourishing within God's created order and provision. We're created to live within these God-ordered rhythms and seasons, not by the artificial calendars of consumption. What if God has hidden this message for us all throughout the creation?

Turtle shells are made of "scutes." These are the distinct sections of the shell that comprise the pattern we see on a turtle's back. Common among many freshwater turtles is a unique pattern of having thirteen larger scute sections on their shell, which correlates to the number of moons! The Anishinaabe people use these shells as a calendar marking their year. They follow, section by section, as each large scute represents a particular full moon. Starting from the top middle, the sections of the turtle shell are traced counterclockwise all the way around to the top again, and then down the middle section; one through thirteen making up their entire year. Our Indigenous friends,

---

9. Giizhik, "Dance of the 13 Moons"; Wiba Anung, "13 Moons Curriculum."

in looking, listening, and living close to creation, uncover the hidden gifts that are right here with us. I believe these are secrets that are rarely revealed to us through any other posture than honor, mutuality, humility, and love.

Upon closer inspection, the surprises keep coming. Around the outer part of the shell are all the smaller scutes that comprise the edge of their "calendar." There are twenty-eight of them.

The signs of our Creator's handiwork are everywhere. Are you looking close enough to see it?

Discovering the ways in which we are made whole as creation is wholly cared for is the joy before us, as we were created to be people of this garden.

Even our bodies testify to this innate wisdom, this is tidal-locking between us and creation. Many cultures have connected moon cycles with femininity and fertility, dating back to Ancient Greece.[10] It is believed by some that, prior to record keeping, a more natural synchronicity may have occurred between women's bodies and the moon. How has gravity played a role in reproduction, hormones, and our physiological health since time immemorial? How has the very moment in which we were born from a lunar-like cycle connected us with this dance between the earth and the moon? Are there quantifiable connections between moonlight, gravity, hormones, and life cycles?

Here is what I'll say: human life is dancing with and within God's creation in ways that we cannot fully see or perhaps comprehend. Our biological clocks and even our well-being are deeply connected with the creatures that crawl upon the earth—the soil, water, air, and gravity—beyond what our data can reveal. Yet, as more research unfolds, the deeper we can investigate the microbes below us and the higher we peer into the cosmos above, we continue to see just how special God's handiwork is and our place within it.

10. Smith, "Correlation Between Menstrual Cycle."

CHAPTER 10 | DANCING IN THE MOONLIGHT

We have a choice. We can choose to see our place here as somewhere we are waiting to escape, or we can take up the hope-embodying work of seeing ourselves through the lenses of mutuality and belonging.

The closer we look at our place here on Earth, our bodies, the solar system, the gravitational pull surrounding us, and the molecules that comprise our being, it becomes increasingly difficult to deny the magnificence of God's handiwork and the beauty within the design. Seeing the ecosystem and entanglement of it all through purely scientific eyes will mean completely missing this deep call to worship the Creator of it all.

Also, not taking the opportunity as people of faith to study and learn the inner workings of this web of life in which we are created constricts our mission, calling, and worship inside a small "spiritual-only" labeled box.

It must be both. The material and the spiritual have always been held together within one good creation. We can learn and appreciate the science and, in that, hold the mystery that is God's cosmic masterpiece in even higher praise! As we discover more, we may have to leave words like *coincidence* behind, while adopting words like *intentional*, *mysterious*, and *providential*.

It is providential and mysterious that, of all the moons and planets within our solar system, our earth and moon are positioned like no other. Our moon, at its diameter, is about 1/400th of the size of the sun. As it happens, the moon is also about 1/400th the distance from us to the sun. As earthlings, this makes the sun and the moon appear as the same size in our sky! This wonder offers us the occasional unique experience of total solar eclipses.[11]

How is it that we can be so quick to use these examples of the wonder of creation to point out what we believe to be a divinely

---

11. Tyson, *Astrophysics for People*.

ordered cosmos and not be just as quick to recognize that, if that is true, we are right where we're meant to be.

NEW MOON

*When you send forth your spirit, they are created,
and you renew the face of the earth.*

PSALM 104:30

Observing the moon's movements was a big part of the ancient Hebrew way of life. They marked time and began each month with a New Moon Festival.[12] One thing that I love about Hebrew is that the language itself refuses to fit our western binary lenses. It's not uncommon for one word to have multiple definitions to help us understand the deeper meaning held within it. In the Old Testament, the Hebrew root word "*h-d-s*" (חדש),[13] which is often translated as "new" (as in "For I am about to create new heavens and a new earth"[14]), is also elsewhere translated as "new moon" (as in "Blow the trumpet at the new moon"[15]).[16]

When we consider something being new today, it doesn't match up with the same line of thinking for the ancient Hebrews. We know there is no such thing as an actual "new moon" or an "old moon," really; we recognize that it's the same moon in its ongoing dance between itself, the earth, and the sun. It isn't being made new—it's just orbiting on close to a twenty-eight-day endless cycle around us. So, this word for "new" isn't about something being made from scratch out of nothing, but it insinuates that something is being *re-newed*.

The prophet Isaiah uses this root word "*h-d-s*" four times near the end of the prophet's book:

"For as the *new heavens* and the *new earth*,

---

12. Num 10:10.
13. In the Hebrew text, there are no vowels. The vowels were added later for differentiation, understanding, translation, and nuance.
14. Isa 65:17.
15. Ps 81:3.
16. Credit to theologian and biblical scholar Laurie Braaten for pointing this out!

> which I will make,
> shall remain before me, says the Lord,
> so shall your descendants and your name remain.
> From *new moon* to *new moon*
> and from Sabbath to Sabbath,
> all flesh shall come to worship before me,"
> says the Lord.[17]

Imprinted within these ancient texts, the Hebrew understanding of "the new heaven and the new earth" isn't the modern idea of "tossing out" anything. There is no delete or discard button for God's creation within the biblical understanding—rather, one that is marked by a contextual setting of *renewal*.

Ultimately, at the end of the New Testament, in the final words of Revelation, are multiple references from these passages as John richly sources from the prophet Isaiah.[18] He writes, "Then I saw a new heaven and a new earth, for the first heaven and the first earth had passed away," and, "the one who was seated on the throne said, 'See, I am making all things new.'"[19] Our creator God is a God who renews. Our God is a resurrecting God, a composting God, a God of redemption. It's no coincidence that what our souls and bodies crave are old growth forests made new again, rejuvenated prairies, unspoiled oceans, glistening tundra, and convivial dunes. Something within us knows that we belong within these places—Eden-like images of creation that have been renewed, places that are formed by the loving hands of God, for the beloved creatures of God, and to the glory of God.

Power that is unable to repair what is broken, power that can't imagine how to redeem, power that is willing to simply discard that which was intentionally created, is a weak, noncreative, and uncaring power.

That is *not* the power of our God!

---

17. Isa 66:22–23.
18. Isa 42:9, 43:19, 65:17, 66:22–23.
19. Rev 21:1–5.

Our God's power is one so almighty that all things can be reconciled. Our God's power is so creative that heaven and earth are part of the redemptive story. Our God is so loving that God put on flesh, came among us, died upon a cross, and was resurrected into that formerly dead body, renewed, in order that everything which was lost may be found. That's power.

Do we know exactly how life will unfold within the final consummation of God's cosmic redemption? No, we don't. But here's what I believe: the new creation is going to be the ultimate God-intended revelation of divine design. It will be the greatest and most magnificent expression and celebration of this colorful web of life! It will be beyond our imagination! The new creation will not be something simply marked by what feels good to us, looks nice to us, sounds harmonious to us, but will be a glorious symphony of everything God has created, the way God created it to be.

Yet, we wonder about how so much that is good will remain. The woodpecker in his duty on the juniper tree. The cardinal in her song. The rivers, undammed, descending from snowy peaks. Here, we will learn anew how to walk with the land rather than pave over it. We'll find silence as it was in the beginning and song as it will be sung in the end. We will eat. We will relearn how to worship while we feast. Every grape consumed will praise the Creator of the vineyard. God will be the light that photosynthesizes new creation and we will taste true wine as it is grown within that light, watered by the streams of life. Birds will rise in number. Oceans will roar loud and deep. Reefs will birth life in full. Bees will pollinate with fervor, and their honey will be the stuff of legend. Mycelium will spread wide and far, and we will bear witness to a topsoil so deep and brown that it can only be expressed within God's final coming. Who knows, even dinosaurs may roam the earth again.

Yes, at the great end–beginning, humans will dance in the true light of our eternal God. All will be in right relationship with each other again, humanity and nonhuman creation. Perhaps, what may change the most in this new creation isn't the nonhuman creation, which has already endured so much of our domineering and colonization, but rather ourselves, who will finally transcend into our intended state of wholeness with God. Heaven–Earth will finally be in ecological balance; this is the kingdom of God.

> *Dear God, we can't do any of this without you. We have nothing without you. Without you there is no saving anything, there is no new creation, and there is no hope. You, God, are the one who makes all things whole and all things new. You are Creator. As we go forward together within the gifts of our created limits, lured by every ladder and mocked by every tower, offer us your fresh and generous gravitational embrace that we might again wake up to the ministry of your love in the world.*
>
> *Amen.*

Epilogue

THERE'S NO SHORTAGE OF questions that still need answering. I hope you have lots of them. There's also a decent chance that this book rubbed you the wrong way. At our core, in our heart, in our gut, we know that there's always more.

    More to learn.
    More to create.
    More to become.
    More to discover.

This kind of "more" is part of the fabric of our humanity. Turning the page to the next chapter has always been a defining characteristic of what it means to be a person. To be created in the image of the

Creator, this creativity is God-given and invites us to become fully alive.

Embracing our earthly boundaries is *not* about denying this sacred spark of becoming inside each and every one of us.

Rather, it is about putting our creative engine to work generating sustainability in our relationships with all creation.

Baked deep within this finite planet we call home is the recipe for regenerative life. The earth, as God has designed it, begets life continually. The natural cycle of birth, death, and new life are the defining characteristics of this ecosystem in which we are a part.

The limitless overconsumption occurring by the few is jeopardizing our human neighbors alongside all other species and forms of life. The solutions are not simply about becoming more "eco" but about recognizing that we are entangled.

I have a pair of jeans with an inscription that's sown on the inside of the waist, close to the button. Every time I wear this particular pair of pants, I pull them up my legs in the morning and read this inscription: "Today is your day."

It's kind of a funny thing that someone had the idea for, but I appreciate it!

I often say that a day is what unfolds between the time I take my pajama pants off in the morning and put them on again in the evening. Pretty much all the *doing* happens within the time frame that I put on my big boy pants and remember that "today is your day."

There is definitely a psychological element to it. It's just hard to be productive working from home if you haven't changed out of your pajamas!

Many days we wish we could just keep those pajamas on because, I think if we are honest, many of us are tired. Our weekly routines involve a myriad of wearing different hats (and pants!), from parent to husband, to pastor, to podcaster, to backyard gardener, to soccer coach, to director of an organization, to home repair person, to landlord, to pizza maker, to a friend who lends a shoulder to cry on. And occasionally, all those hats are worn in a single day! I'm sure that you wear a number of hats, too.

Confession: I have a ridiculous number of hats. If you know me, you know I love hats. Hats are my thing, especially a good fitting cap. On a wall in our kitchen (which I'm sure my wife loves) is a rack that I built from an old wooden crate. I stained it fancily and put antique doorknobs on it to hang several of my regular hats on. When I decide which hat I am wearing each day, I first consider what I'm up to that day. What *vibe* am I going for? If I'm coaching soccer, it's something a little playful, something with a few sweat-stains already waving around the edges. If I'm in that morning-creative-workspace, hanging out in my local spots, it's between my Baja Burrito, Dozen Bakery hat, or a couple of others. If I'm at the beach, it's my Point Loma or Jabroni hat. And on a swanky night out, I might get down my great uncle's hat or my great grandfather's fedora.

The hats serve as a literal embodiment of all the things that make up my life. Yet, if you were to catch me off guard in the evening, playing with my kids on the carpeted floor, you wouldn't see a hat. You would see just some really messy hair. (I've always had lawless hair. The kind that obeys no human code of conduct.) Therefore, hats became even more necessary for socially acceptable adult situations!

Here's the deal. We probably could all use a little more time with our pajamas on and hats off. We could all use a little more permission to be just who we are.

No props.
No filters.
No shoes, no shirt, no problem.
Just you. The human you.

Not trying to impress—not flexing or trying to show off our good side. Messy hair, don't care. Are you with me?

Why is this important for our final pages together? Because at the heart of what I'm hoping you're catching is a spirit of the raw, authentic human condition.

Don't hear me wrong. We most certainly have to put our jeans on, put on the work hat, and get busy participating in the solutions of healing a broken world today; but also, being a finite, tired, messy-haired human is part of the solution. The healing quest that we all must embark on if we are going to help return this planet to a place of balance is an exploration into our frail humanity.

We can be people who believe they belong here on earth, people not obsessed with transcending all boundaries, people who are more interested in becoming less so that those who are hurting can have more, people who love particular people, places, and things, and call them by name, people who Sabbath, people who sing the songs of creation and praise the Creator, and people who love being who they are created to be, where they are created to be.

The processes that are driving climate change and overdrawing our environmental account are embedded in the ways in which we are pushing up against our God-given human creatureliness.

Our unsatiated obsession with crossing every boundary places us at odds with our home and God's order within it. This happens every time we drive a bit faster because we're in a hurry, invest in new body products to hide our aging, get an extra pair of shoes to strut our stuff in, buy that new phone to have those new features, add another commitment into an already jam-packed schedule, fly eight hours to visit that view we've always wanted a selfie with, or just order that lamp that was made in and shipped all the way from the other side of the world because you "needed" it. When you begin to see it, you'll notice how we've made so much of our modern lives about some version of pressing up against and attempting to overcome our human boundaries.

Of course, we find ourselves so tired all the time. All that "transcending" requires a ridiculous amount of resources (all the while, touting a life of ease)! All the propping up, crunching the numbers, creating the content, responding to all the messages, and keeping the image afloat. Whatever work, brand, or persona is yours, to keep it going requires time, energy, income, and whatever you have to do to keep the engine running.

So, can we embody something different? Can we live the kind of lives God created us for down here on the ground?

If today is your day to be an earthbound Christian, how will you live it?

How might we embrace both our God-given spirit of creativity *and* our created earthliness in finding the healing way? How might we participate in the coming of the new heaven and earth through our economics, policies, play, and prayers? How might we bear witness to the good news here "on earth as it is in heaven"?

Professor of Human Factors and Nature Connectedness, Miles Richardson, has written multiple books and published research on humanity's loss of connection with creation. A computer model Richardson developed has tracked data from the last 220 years related to loss of wildlife, urbanization, and, most notably, children's engagement with nature.[1] His findings report that our human connection with nature has declined more than 60 percent since the early 1800s. Adjacent data revealed an almost exact correlation between our loss of earthy language in our publications (words like "river," "moss," and "blossom") and our loss of connection with nature.

The model took the past data and made projections to the year 2125. In conclusion,

> the model simulation reveals a steep decline in nature connectedness . . . primarily driven by urbanisation and environmental degradation. However, the most significant factor is intergenerational transmission: as parents lose connection to nature, their children begin life with lower connection, creating cultural inertia that persists even if environmental conditions improve.[2]

These findings about children are sobering but somewhat unsurprising. We've witnessed this inertia firsthand with the rise of phones and tablets capturing our attention.

1. Richardson, "Modelling Nature Connectedness."
2. Richardson, "How We Lost Touch," 12.

Yet, inversely, this can also be seen as hopeful. We have it within our power to alter it—starting right now! To create new momentum. As a parent, I've witnessed firsthand how children so easily find their way back into engagement and play within creation when given the chance. What's left for us to do, for them and for *us older kids*, is to limit that screen time, curate wild spaces, and maybe even push them out the door at times!

In *Mammon's Ecology*, Stan Goff writes,

> If American churches want a real mission, let us help twenty million more young people to be small scale farmers, urban agriculturalists, permaculture practitioners, truck gardeners, suburban sharecroppers, rooftop growers, food forest designers, hoop house growers, community gardeners, and gleaners.[3]

Could it be that the most meaningful and powerful work we can engage in today is teaching our young people how to live close to the land, to grow food, and tend soil? Is it any wonder, that in order to discover a future of ecological harmony, it begins with ambitious interventions to help our children engage with nature? You know, the kingdom of God belongs to them.

There is one more fascinating bit about this study. Between 1990 to 2020, there was an 8 percent increase in our engagement with the natural world. Richardson states, "There are a number of societal factors that are associated with levels of nature connectedness. Only one with a positive association with nature connectedness has seen a recent uptick, spirituality."[4]

God has cracked the door open; we just have to make our way through it.

Through the doorways ahead, as creation suffers under the heavy weight of pollution, overconsumption, and waste, as climate change continues to unfold, as more species totter on the brink of extinction, God's children have a role to play like none other. As Paul writes, "For

---

3. Goff, *Mammon's Ecology*, 168–69.
4. Richardson, "How We Lost Touch," 10.

the creation waits with eager longing for the revealing of the children of God."[5]

God's desire is for us to participate in creation's healing. God's desire is that "the creation itself will be set free from its enslavement to decay and will obtain the freedom of the glory of the children of God."[6] We are called to embody new realities within broken places.

So, imagine a reality when you had everything you ever needed. But in this reality, everything was solid, everything was local, everything was touched by someone you knew, everything seemed to have a depth of meaning. Imagine in this time that you knew almost every single one of your neighbors, and they knew you. Here, you share everything from childcare and food to tools and clothing. Imagine a time when neither your happiness nor your livelihood depended upon corporate business or the stock market.

Imagine freedom. Not the shallow kind of freedom that we usually talk about—the "I can do whatever I want when I want" sort of freedom—but true freedom. It's a freedom that isn't found in individualism but within community. In this reality, no one is enslaved within Babylonian economies, trapped in systems of brickmaking, but instead our creativity sets one another free. This is the kind of liberty that only comes with being a part of real community, of connecting with the earth, of taking care of what's around you, and letting what's around you take care of you.

Here, in this reality, we trust each other. We're busy running under the assumption that everyone just needs reminded of the image of God within them. Here, we spend our energy teaching our children how to eat meals with neighbors and care for the poor. Here, in this reality, we see the face of Christ in every person, and in the event someone does wrong us, we pray, "Lord, forgive them for they do not know what they do." In this reality, we act out of love. We recognize that our own joy and sorrow are intertwined with the hopes and fears of those around us. Here, in this reality, we're more interested in seeing our neighbors flourish and less interested in keeping score. We're

---

5. Rom 8:19.
6. Rom 8:21.

interested in helping each other, holding each other, feeding each other, and seeking God together.

In this reality, we'll forget about screens and remember rivers.

We'll forget about social posting and remember how to dig a posthole.

We'll forget about coal and remember comfrey.

We'll forget about Amazon orders and remember the Amazon.

We'll forget about chasing happiness and remember the joy of what we already have.

We'll forget the trap of "big success" and remember the liberties of being small.

We'll forget the worries of survival and remember the beauty of the lilies.

We'll forget the hatred of others and remember that there is no other, only more of us.

We will be shaped by love, and all people and all of creation will be revived through it. We will have deeper relationships with all our belongings and our community as we learn again how to repair, sew, grow, cook, and know the people better around us who can, too.

In this reality, it is a time of wealth. It is the wealth of rich soil, nontoxic and nutritious food, equitable access, and equitable work; here, we find true knowledge, true abundance, true education, and true food.

In this reality, we get to see the earth like no one has seen it before. All of creation is living its best life because humans have finally understood their place in it. We've found our true vocations, not as extractors but as stewards. Here, we are more interested in gardening and less interested in mining. We don't possess greed but grace. We live not to become CEOs but servants.

In this reality, we remember what we were created to do with our hands. We remember how to use our time. We decide to shop less and preserve more. We remember how to carve and what to do with clay.

We remember how to live in symbiosis with domestic and wild animals, knowing that their thriving is our thriving.

Instead of mowing, we relearn how to grow beautiful native things. We rediscover what to do with ginger, echinacea, chamomile, turmeric, yarrow, and aloe vera.

In this reality, as we are drawing closer to earth than ever before, we once again find that we are gravitationally native as God intended.

In this new life, we aren't afraid to be slower than the rat race that surrounds us. Thus, it is a life that slows down long enough to taste and touch. This life rejects the onslaught of chemicals that attempt to make our food grow faster and last longer. It is a life that listens well, reads, and dances. It is a life that has time for friends. It is a life that pedals when necessary and isn't worried about taking the night to recharge. It is a life that takes clues from children, who inherently know how to play. It is a life that descends the ladder of ego and does everything it can to lift up the voiceless and oppressed. It is a life that does a few things and does them very well.

An earthbound life enjoys what's in season. An earthbound life isn't afraid to sleep in, to Sabbath well, knowing that our worth isn't tethered to our work. An earthbound life recognizes wrinkles as gifts of having lived long. An earthbound life comes in a body, just like Jesus came in a body, in a town, on a planet.

Jesus certainly lived an abundant life.

Let's be like Jesus. Let's be Earthbound Christian.

> *God, hear our prayer. You are making things new and have called us into that redemptive story. As people bound to the earth, help us to find our humble way forward, announcing your coming and calling one another to repent. Forgive us for all the ways in which we've fallen short of the kind of humanity you desire of us. Help us to follow you, into the kind of life of love that, in childlikeness, wonders at your creation and faithfully stewards its healing. In the name of Jesus, the Creator,*
> *Amen.*

Bibliography

American Bee Journal. "Survey Estimates Over 1.1 Million Honey Bee Colonies Lost, Raising Alarm for Pollination and Agriculture." American Bee Journal, Apr. 1, 2025. https://americanbeejournal.com/survey-estimates-over-1-1-million-honey-bee-colonies-lost-raising-alarm-for-pollination-and-agriculture/.

Anderson, Hannah. *Humble Roots: How Humility Grounds and Nourishes Your Soul.* Chicago: Moody, 2016.

Arendt, Hannah. *The Human Condition.* 2nd ed. Chicago: University of Chicago, 1958.

Barber, Dan. "A Surprising Parable of Foie Gras." TED, Nov. 26, 2008. https://www.youtube.com/watch?v=gvrgDomAFoU.

Bastida, Xiye, and Julia Jackson. "Indigenous Wisdom Can Heal the Planet." The Hill: Changing America, May 14, 2020. https://thehill.com/changing-america/opinion/497849-indigenous-wisdom-can-heal-the-planet/.

Berry, Wendell. *New Collected Poems.* Berkeley, CA: Counterpoint, 2013.

———. *The Unsettling of America: Culture and Agriculture.* Berkeley, CA: Counterpoint, 2015.

———. *What Are People For? Essays.* Berkeley, CA: Counterpoint, 2010.

Botkin, Daniel B. *Discordant Harmonies: A New Ecology for the Twenty-First Century.* New York: Oxford University Press, 1992.

Brockway, Otto, and Ludovic Brockway, dirs. *Eating for Tomorrow.* Santa Cruz, CA: Food Revolution Network, 2024. https://earth.foodrevolution.org/.

Brown, Brené. *Daring Greatly: How the Courage to Be Vulnerable Transforms the Way We Live, Love, Parent, and Lead.* New York: Avery, 2015.

Brumfiel, Geoff. "SpaceX Wants to Go to Mars. To Get There, Environmentalists Say It's Trashing Texas." NPR, Oct. 11, 2024. https://www.npr.org/2024/10/10/nx-s1-5145776/spacex-texas-wetlands.

Canup, Robin M., and Erik Asphaug. "Origin of the Moon in a Giant Impact Near the End of the Earth's Formation." *Nature* 412.6848 (2001) 708–12. https://doi.org/10.1038/35089010.

Carrington, Damian, ed. "Microplastics Found in Every Human Testicle in Study." *The Guardian*, May 20, 2024. https://www.theguardian.com/environment/article/2024/may/20/microplastics-human-testicles-study-sperm-counts.

Carson, Rachel. *Silent Spring.* 50th anniversary ed. Boston: Houghton Mifflin Harcourt, 2002.

Circle Economy Foundation. "The Circularity Gap Report 2024." CGR. https://www.circularity-gap.world/2024.

Clarke, Chris. "Is Coffee Going Extinct? Here's How It Could Impact You." The University of Queensland: Research. https://stories.uq.edu.au/research/2022/coffee-is-going-extinct/index.html.

Clarke, Jodi. "What Is the Gut-Brain Axis?" Verywell Mind, Dec. 5, 2022. https://www.verywellmind.com/what-is-the-gut-brain-axis-5272028.

Creation Justice Ministries. "Truth, Healing and Repair: A Resource for Churches on Environmental Justice with Indigenous Peoples." Creation Justice Ministries. https://www.creationjustice.org/truthhealingrepair.html.

Curtice, Kaitlin B. *Native: Identity, Belonging, and Rediscovering God*. Grand Rapids, MI: Brazos, 2020.

Dahir, Abdi Latif. "Ecotourism Is Being Used to Displace One of East Africa's Long-Standing Indigenous People." Quartz, July 20, 2022. https://qz.com/africa/1278167/maasai-evicted-in-tanzania-for-ecotourism-and-land-conservation.

Danan, Julie. "Rabbi Simcha Bunem's Favorite Sayings." Sefaria. https://www.sefaria.org/sheets/129984.11.

Dawson, Neil M., et al. "Is It Just Conservation? A Typology of Indigenous Peoples' and Local Communities' Roles in Conserving Biodiversity." *One Earth* 7.6 (2024) 1007–21. https://doi.org/10.1016/j.oneear.2024.05.001.

Digital Public Library of America. "Cotton Gin and the Expansion of Slavery." https://dp.la/primary-source-sets/cotton-gin-and-the-expansion-of-slavery.

Duck River Conservancy. "The No. 1 Most Biodiverse River in the Nation: The Duck River." https://www.duckriverconservancy.com/the-duck-river.

Dutfield, Scott. "Light Pollution: Environmental Impact, Health Risks, and Facts." Live Science, Apr. 5, 2022. https://www.livescience.com/light-pollution.

Earth5R. "Women of the Soil: Rural Indian Women Leading an Agroecological Uprising." https://earth5r.org/women-of-the-soil-rural-indian-women-leading-an-agroecological-uprising/.

Einstein, Albert. "Albert Einstein Quote." Today in Science History. https://todayinsci.com/E/Einstein_Albert/EinsteinAlbert-LoveQuote500px.htm#google_vignette.

Ellis, Rose. "Why Female Empowerment and Conservation are Inextricably Linked." Eco-Age, July 3, 2020. https://web.archive.org/web/20210309062844/https://eco-age.com/resources/why-female-empowerment-and-conservation-are-inextricably-linked/.

Fallah, Amy. "Catastrophic 73% Decline in the Average Size of Global Wildlife Populations in Just 50 Years Reveals a 'System in Peril.'" World Wildlife Fund, Oct. 9, 2024. https://www.worldwildlife.org/press-releases/catastrophic-73-decline-in-the-average-size-of-global-wildlife-populations-in-just-50-years-reveals-a-system-in-peril.

Fasih, Suha. "The Hidden Exploitation of Immigrant Labor in Underprivileged Communities." Law Journal for Social Justice, Feb. 5, 2025. https://lawjournalforsocialjustice.com/2025/02/05/the-hidden-exploitation-of-immigrant-labor-in-underprivileged-communities/.

Garnett, Stephen T., et al. "A Spatial Overview of the Global Importance of Indigenous Lands for Conservation." *Nature Sustainability* 1 (July 2018) 369–74. https://doi.org/10.1038/s41893-018-0100-6.

Gatto, Nicole M., et al. "Farming, Pesticides, and Brain Cancer: A 20-Year Updated Systematic Literature Review and Meta-Analysis." *Cancers* 13.17 (2021) 4477. https://doi.org/10.3390/cancers13174477.

Giizhik, Zhaawano. "Dance of the 13 Moons: An Introduction to the Lunar Calendar of the Anishinaabe Peoples." Ojibwe Lessons and Stories by ZhaawanArt, May 15, 2023. https://www.zhaawanart.com/post/dance-of-the-13-moons.

Goff, Stan. *Mammon's Ecology: Metaphysic of the Empty Sign.* Eugene, OR: Cascade, 2018.

Goldman Sachs. "AI to Drive 165% Increase in Data Center Power Demand by 2030." Goldman Sachs, Feb. 4, 2025. https://www.goldmansachs.com/insights/articles/ai-to-drive-165-increase-in-data-center-power-demand-by-2030.

Goodman, Joshua. "Your Seafood Was Probably Produced by Modern Slaves, Bombshell Report on 'Widespread Human Rights Crisis' Finds." Fortune, Nov. 16, 2023. https://fortune.com/2023/11/16/seafood-industry-modern-slavery-forced-work-nonprofit-study/.

Green, John. *The Anthropocene Reviewed: Essays on a Human-Centered Planet.* New York: Dutton, 2021.

Gutiérrez-Li, Alejandro. "Feeding America: How Immigrants Sustain US Agriculture." Rice University's Baker Institute for Public Policy, July 19, 2024. https://www.bakerinstitute.org/research/feeding-america-how-immigrants-sustain-us-agriculture.

Habel, Norman C. *The Birth, the Curse and the Greening of Earth: An Ecological Reading of Genesis 1–11.* The Earth Bible Commentary 1. Sheffield, UK: Sheffield Phoenix, 2011.

Hamacher, Duane W., et al. "Whitening the Sky: Light Pollution as a Form of Cultural Genocide." *Journal of Dark Sky Studies* 1 (2020). https://arxiv.org/abs/2001.11527.

Hartmann, William K., and Donald R. Davis. "Satellite-Sized Planetesimals and Lunar Origin." *Icarus* 24.4 (1975) 504–15. https://doi.org/10.1016/0019-1035(75)90070-6.

Harvard Health. "Blue Light Has a Dark Side." Harvard Health Publishing, July 24, 2024. https://www.health.harvard.edu/staying-healthy/blue-light-has-a-dark-side.

Hatton, Tim. "Why Did Humans Grow Four Inches in 100 Years? It Wasn't Just Diet." Live Science, May 6, 2014. https://www.livescience.com/45376-why-did-humans-grow-four-inches-in-100-years-it-wasnt-just-diet.html.

Haynes, Caleb Cray. *Garbage Theology: The Unseen World of Waste and What It Means for the Salvation of Every Person, Every Place, and Every Thing.* Lynchburg, TN: McGahan Publishing House, 2021.

Haynes, Caleb Cray, et al. *Keeping Creation: A 5-Week Study.* Kansas City, MO: The Foundry, 2023.

Hickel, Jason. *Less Is More: How Degrowth Will Save the World.* London: Penguin, 2022.

Historic Maury County. "The Lost Cantaloupe Capital." Historic Maury County, Nov. 14, 2019. https://historicmaurycounty.com/2019/11/14/the-lost-cantaloupe-capital/.

Holmes, Pete. "Neil Degrasse Tyson." You Made It Weird with Pete Holmes. YouTube, Apr. 19, 2023. https://www.youtube.com/watch?v=cdyHzmv_HlY&t=4357s.

How to Feed the World 2050. "Global Agriculture Towards 2050." Food and Agriculture Organization of the United Nations, Oct. 12–13, 2009. https://www.fao.org/fileadmin/templates/wsfs/docs/Issues_papers/HLEF2050_Global_Agriculture.pdf.

Intergovernmental Panel on Climate Change (IPCC). *Global Warming of 1.5°C: IPCC Special Report on Impacts of Global Warming of 1.5°C Above Pre-Industrial Levels in Context of Strengthening Response to Climate Change, Sustainable Development, and Efforts to Eradicate Poverty.* Cambridge: Cambridge University Press, 2022. https://doi.org/10.1017/9781009157940.

IPCC. "AR6 Synthesis Report: Climate Change 2023." https://www.ipcc.ch/report/sixth-assessment-report-cycle/.

Jackson, Justin. "Increased AI Use Linked to Eroding Critical Thinking Skills." Phys.org, Jan. 13, 2025. https://phys.org/news/2025-01-ai-linked-eroding-critical-skills.html.

Jackson, Tim. *Prosperity Without Growth: Foundations for the Economy of Tomorrow.* 2nd ed. London: Routledge, 2017.

Javaid, Maham. "Race to Build Nuclear Reactor on Moon Raises Galaxy of Legal Questions." *Seattle Times*, Aug. 12, 2025. https://www.seattletimes.com/nation-world/race-to-build-nuclear-reactor-on-moon-raises-galaxy-of-legal-questions/.

Jenner, Lauren C., et al. "Detection of Microplastics in Human Lung Tissue Using μFTIR Spectroscopy." *Science of The Total Environment* 831 (2022) 154907. https://doi.org/10.1016/j.scitotenv.2022.154907.

Jensen, Derrick, et al. *Bright Green Lies: How the Environmental Movement Lost Its Way and What We Can Do About It.* Politics of the Living Series. Rhinebeck, NY: Monkfish, 2021.

Johnson, Ayana Elizabeth, and Katharine K. Wilkinson, eds. *All We Can Save: Truth, Courage, and Solutions for the Climate Crisis.* New York: One World, 2021.

Karamcheva, Nadia, et al. "Trends in the Distribution of Family Wealth, 1989 to 2022." Congressional Budget Office, Oct. 2, 2024. https://www.cbo.gov/publication/60807.

Kearnes, Matthew, and Thom van Dooren. "Rethinking the Final Frontier: Cosmo-Logics and an Ethic of Interstellar Flourishing." *GeoHumanities* 3.2 (2017) 1–20. https://www.researchgate.net/publication/316229433_Rethinking_the_Final_Frontier_Cosmo-Logics_and_an_Ethic_of_Interstellar_Flourishing.

Kelly, Martin. "What Were the Top Causes of the Civil War?" ThoughtCo., May 18, 2024. https://www.thoughtco.com/top-causes-of-the-civil-war-104532.

Kennedy, John F. "We Choose to Go to the Moon." Rice University. https://www.rice.edu/jfk-speech.

Kimmerer, Robin Wall. *Braiding Sweetgrass: Indigenous Wisdom, Scientific Knowledge, and the Teachings of Plants.* Minneapolis: Milkweed Editions, 2020.

———. *Gathering Moss: A Natural and Cultural History of Mosses.* Corvallis, OR: Oregon State University Press, 2003.

———. *The Serviceberry: Abundance and Reciprocity in the Natural World.* New York: Scribner, 2024.

Knight, Camillah Agak. "The Impact of Technology on Contemporary Slavery in the 21st Century." Platform for Peace and Humanity, Aug. 23, 2020. https://peacehumanity.org/2020/08/23/the-impact-of-technology-on-contemporary-slavery-in-the-21st-century/.

Knop, Eva, et al. "Artificial Light at Night as a New Threat to Pollination." *Nature* 548 (2017) 206–9. https://doi.org/10.1038/nature23288.

Kornreich, Ar, et al. "Rehabilitation Outcomes of Bird-Building Collision Victims in the Northeastern United States." *PLOS One* 19.8 (2024) e0306362. https://doi.org/10.1371/journal.pone.0306362.

Lamb, Avery Davis. "The EPA Has Abandoned Reason. Now We Build Arks." *Sojourners*, Aug. 14, 2025. https://sojo.net/articles/opinion/epa-has-abandoned-reason-now-we-build-arks.

Le, Linh. "The Modern Slaves: Parallels in the Economic Justification of Slavery, Undocumented Immigrants and Skilled Foreign Workers." *The DePauw*, Jan. 21, 2025. https://thedepauw.com/the-modern-slaves-parallels-in-the-economic-justification-of-slavery-undocumented-immigrants-and-skilled-foreign-workers/.

Leasca, Stacey. "A New Study Reveals a Potential Link Between Pesticides and Prostate Cancer—Including Those Used on Corn, Soybeans, and Citrus." Food & Wine, Nov. 6, 2024. https://www.foodandwine.com/pesticides-prostate-cancer-risk-8739772.

Leschin-Hoar, Clare. "Was Your Seafood Caught with Slave Labor? New Database Helps Retailers Combat Abuse." NPR, Feb. 1, 2018. https://www.npr.org/sections/thesalt/2018/02/01/582214032/was-your-seafood-caught-with-slave-labor-new-database-helps-retailers-combat-abu.

Leslie, Heather A., et al. "Discovery and Quantification of Plastic Particle Pollution in Human Blood." *Environment International* 163 (2022) 107199. https://doi.org/10.1016/j.envint.2022.107199.

Levis, Carolina, et al. "Contributions of Human Cultures to Biodiversity and Ecosystem Conservation." *Nature Ecology & Evolution* 8 (2024) 866–79. https://doi.org/10.1038/s41559-024-02356-1.

Li, Pengfei, et al. "Making AI Less 'Thirsty': Uncovering and Addressing the Secret Water Footprint of AI Models." Cornell University arXiv, Mar. 26, 2025. http://arxiv.org/abs/2304.03271.

Linthicum, Robert C. *Building a People of Power: Equipping Churches to Transform Their Communities*. Eugene, OR: Wipf & Stock, 2015.

Madeira, Erin Myers. "Want to Save the Planet? Empower Women." The Nature Conservancy, Mar. 6, 2018. https://www.nature.org/en-us/what-we-do/our-insights/perspectives/want-to-save-the-planet-empower-women/.

Malik, Tariq. "Katy Perry Just Became the 1st Pop Star to Sing in Space—But Lance Bass, Beyonce, Lady Gaga, Sarah Brightman, and Justin Bieber Had Their Chance." Space.com, April 15, 2025. https://www.space.com/space-exploration/private-spaceflight/katy-perry-just-became-the-1st-pop-star-to-sing-in-space-but-lance-bass-beyonce-lady-gaga-sarah-brightman-and-justin-bieber-had-their-chance.

Manuel, John. "DDT and Breast Cancer Revisited: New Findings in an Old Debate." *Environmental Health Perspectives* 115.10 (2007) A505. https://ehp.niehs.nih.gov/doi/full/10.1289/ehp.115-a505b.

Marsh, Rene, and Laura Paddison. "Elon Brought 'the World's Biggest Supercomputer' to Memphis. Residents Say They're Choking on Its Pollution." CNN, May 19, 2025. https://www.cnn.com/2025/05/19/climate/xai-musk-memphis-turbines-pollution.

Maury County. "Yanahli Park." Maury County Parks and Recreation. https://www.maurycounty-tn.gov/584/Yanahli-Park.

Meister, Ever. "What Does Climate Change Mean for Coffee?" Trade, April 22, 2022. https://www.drinktrade.com/blogs/education/coffee-going-extinct.
Montgomery, David R. *Growing a Revolution: Bringing Our Soil Back to Life*. New York: Norton, 2018.
Moore, Jason W., ed. *Anthropocene or Capitalocene? Nature, History, and the Crisis of Capitalism*. Oakland, CA: PM Press, 2016.
Moore, Timothy, and Heidi Gollub. "Fatal Car Crash Statistics 2024." *USA Today*, Jan. 16, 2024. https://www.usatoday.com/money/blueprint/auto-insurance/fatal-car-crash-statistics/.
Morrissy-Swan, Tomé. "Why Your Morning Coffee Is Facing Extinction." *The Telegraph*, May 30, 2023. https://www.telegraph.co.uk/food-and-drink/drinks/why-your-morning-coffee-is-facing-extinction/.
National Geographic. "Indigenous Peoples Defend Earth's Biodiversity—But They're in Danger." Nov. 16, 2018. https://www.nationalgeographic.com/environment/article/can-indigenous-land-stewardship-protect-biodiversity-.
———. "Wolves of Yellowstone." https://education.nationalgeographic.org/resource/wolves-yellowstone.
National Ocean Service. "How Much Oxygen Comes from the Ocean?" https://oceanservice.noaa.gov/facts/ocean-oxygen.html.
Ndasi, Samuel Ade. "Protecting Ancestral Lands: MRG's Plea for Sengwer and Ogiek Rights at ACHPR." Minority Rights Group, May 24, 2024. https://minorityrights.org/protecting-ancestral-lands-mrgs-plea-for-sengwer-and-ogiek-rights-at-achpr/.
Nicoletti, Leonardo, et al. "The AI Boom Is Draining Water from the Areas That Need It Most." Bloomberg, May 8, 2025. https://www.bloomberg.com/graphics/2025-ai-impacts-data-centers-water-data/.
Nixon, Rob. *Slow Violence and the Environmentalism of the Poor*. Boston: Harvard University Press, 2013.
NOAA Fisheries. "Successful Fish Passage Efforts Across the Nation." June 4, 2025. https://www.fisheries.noaa.gov/insight/successful-fish-passage-efforts-across-nation.
Nolan, Davis. "Water Pipeline Proposed to Preserve the Duck River." WKRN News 2, Mar. 27, 2025. https://www.wkrn.com/news/local-news/water-pipeline-proposed-to-preserve-the-duck-river/.
Paine, Thomas. *Common Sense*. Thomas Paine Society. https://www.thomaspainesociety.org/common-sense.
Peñalver-Piñol, Arnau, et al. "Occupational Exposure to Pesticides and Endometrial Cancer in the Screenwide Case-Control Study." *Environmental Health* 22.1 (2023) 77. https://doi.org/10.1186/s12940-023-01028-0.
Perkins, Tom. "Exposure to Combination of Pesticides Increases Childhood Cancer Risk—Study." *The Guardian*, Mar. 5, 2025. https://www.theguardian.com/us-news/2025/mar/05/pesticides-childhood-cancer-study.
Poole, John. "Beulr Update After Shark Tank: Attendance App's Success Story." Shark Tank Success, Oct. 1, 2025. https://sharktanksuccess.com/beulr-update-after-shark-tank/.
Pringle, Eleanor. "Over the Past 30 Years the U.S.'s Top 1% Got Richer, and Now Hold Nearly a Third of the Nation's Wealth." Fortune, Oct. 8, 2024. https://fortune.

com/2024/10/08/congressional-budget-office-wealthiest-one-percent-nation-wealth/.

Project Drawdown. "Indigenous Peoples' Forest Tenure." https://web.archive.org/web/20250903104924/https://drawdown.org/solutions/indigenous-peoples-forest-tenure.

Ragusa, Antonio, et al. "Plasticenta: First Evidence of Microplastics in Human Placenta." *Environment International* 146 (Jan. 2021) 106274. https://doi.org/10.1016/j.envint.2020.106274.

Rahman-Jones, Imran. "AI Means Google's Greenhouse Gas Emissions Up 48% in 5 Years." BBC, July 3, 2024. https://www.bbc.com/news/articles/c51yvz51k2xo.

Raworth, Kate. *Doughnut Economics: Seven Ways to Think like a 21st Century Economist.* White River Junction, VT: Chelsea Green, 2017.

Reiserer, Alec. "How to Feed 10 Billion People." The OPEC Fund for International Development, Aug. 1, 2023. https://opecfund.org/news/how-to-feed-10-billion-people.

Reynolds, Kevin, dir. *Robin Hood, Prince of Thieves.* Burbank, CA: Warner Brothers, 1991.

Rice, Doyle. "North America Faces a Sprawling 'Pollinator Crisis,' Study Says." *USA Today*, Mar. 28, 2025. https://www.usatoday.com/story/news/nation/2025/03/28/north-america-pollinator-crisis-study/82649992007/.

Richardson, Miles. "How We Lost Touch with Nature." Finding Nature, Aug. 11, 2025. https://findingnature.org.uk/2025/08/11/model/.

———. "Modelling Nature Connectedness Within Environmental Systems: Human-Nature Relationships from 1800 to 2020 and Beyond." *Earth* 6.3 (2025) 82. https://doi.org/10.3390/earth6030082.

Rodriguez, Adrianna. "Texas' Lieutenant Governor Suggests Grandparents Are Willing to Die for US Economy." *USA Today*, Mar. 24, 2020. https://www.usatoday.com/story/news/nation/2020/03/24/covid-19-texas-official-suggests-elderly-willing-die-economy/2905990001/.

Rohr, Richard. *Breathing Under Water: Spirituality and the Twelve Steps.* Cincinnati, OH: St. Anthony Messenger, 2011.

———. "We Learn by Doing It Wrong." Center for Action and Contemplation, Mar. 27, 2023. https://cac.org/daily-meditations/we-learn-by-doing-it-wrong-2023-03-27/.

Rollins, Peter. *The Idolatry of God: Breaking Our Addiction to Certainty and Satisfaction.* New York: Howard, 2013.

Rosi, Eleonora, et al. "Exposure to Environmental Pollutants and Attention-Deficit/Hyperactivity Disorder: An Overview of Systematic Reviews and Meta-Analyses." *Environmental Science and Pollution Research* 30 (2023) 111676–92. https://doi.org/10.1007/s11356-023-30173-9.

Science and Space News. "Flying Cars Are Coming in 2026: All You Need to Know About the AirCar." Science and Space News, Aug. 16, 2025. https://scienceandspacenews.com/2025/06/03/flying-cars-are-coming-in-2026-all-you-need-to-know-about-the-aircar/.

Scorzafava, Lauren. "Light Is Energy: Estimating the Impact of Light Pollution on Climate Change." DarkSky International, Aug. 2, 2022. https://darksky.org/news/light-is-energy-estimating-the-impact-of-light-pollution-on-climate-change/.

Sea Turtle Conservancy. "Artificial Lighting." https://conserveturtles.org/threat/artificial-lighting/.
Silva, Daniella, and Phil McCausland. "Feds Bust 'Modern-Day Slavery' Ring amid New Immigration Enforcement Effort." NBC News, Dec. 10, 2021. https://www.nbcnews.com/news/us-news/feds-bust-modern-day-slavery-ring-new-effort-immigration-enforcement-rcna8273.
Smith, Rhianna-lily. "Correlation Between Menstrual Cycle and Lunar Phases Identified." Technology Networks, Apr. 19, 2024. http://www.technologynetworks.com/proteomics/news/correlation-between-menstrual-cycle-and-lunar-phases-identified-385949.
Snyder, Howard A., and Joel Scandrett. *Salvation Means Creation Healed: The Ecology of Sin and Grace*. Eugene, OR: Cascade, 2011.
Spielberg, Steve, dir. *Jurassic Park*. Universal City, CA: Universal Pictures, 1993.
Spivey, Angela. "Light Pollution: Light at Night and Breast Cancer Risk Worldwide." *Environmental Health Perspectives* 118.12 (2010) A525. https://doi.org/10.1289/ehp.118-a525.
Starr, Noah. "Santa Maria." Nashville: Unpublished poems, @offeringsforthepeople, 2023.
Strebig, Neil. "Unpacking How Elon Musk's xAI Supercomputer Project in Memphis Unfolded Over the Past Year." *USA Today*, June 5, 2025. https://www.usatoday.com/story/money/business/development/2025/06/05/elon-musk-xai-supercomputer-grok-memphis-tn/83599473007/.
Taylor, Stuart Ross. *Lunar Science: A Post-Apollo View*. Oxford: Pergamon, 1975.
Thombs, Ryan P. "Does Renewable Energy Production Displace Fossil Fuel Production in the U.S.? A Panel Data Study of Fossil Fuel-Producing U.S. States, 1997–2020." *Journal of Environmental Studies and Sciences*, Mar. 11, 2025. https://doi.org/10.1007/s13412-025-01013-8.
Thompson, Curt. *Anatomy of the Soul: Surprising Connections Between Neuroscience and Spiritual Practices That Can Transform Your Life and Relationships*. Carol Stream, IL: Tyndale, 2010.
Thoreau, Henry David, and Joseph Wood Krutch. *Walden and Other Writings*. New York: Bantam, 1981.
Tickell, Josh, and Rebecca Tickell, dirs. *Common Ground*. Ojai, CA: Big Picture Ranch, 2025. https://commongroundfilm.org/.
Trebeck, Katherine, and Jeremy Williams. *The Economics of Arrival: Ideas for a Grown-Up Economy*. Bristol, UK: Policy Press, 2019.
Tyson, Neil deGrasse. *Astrophysics for People in a Hurry*. 1st ed. New York: Norton, 2017.
———. *Starry Messenger: Cosmic Perspectives on Civilization*. New York: Henry Holt, 2022.
Ultimate Longevity. "Grounding Research: 20 Medical Thermography Case Studies." https://www.ultimatelongevity.com/earthing-grounding/thermography/thermography.shtml.
UN Environment Programme. "How Chernobyl Has Become an Unexpected Haven for Wildlife." Sept. 16, 2020. https://www.unep.org/news-and-stories/story/how-chernobyl-has-become-unexpected-haven-wildlife.
United Nations. "Artificial Intelligence: How Much Energy Does AI Use?" July 4, 2025. https://unric.org/en/artificial-intelligence-how-much-energy-does-ai-use/.

———. "Seagrass: 10 Facts About an Ocean Plant Under Threat." Feb. 24, 2023. https://unric.org/en/seagrass-10-facts-about-an-ocean-plant-under-threat/.

———. "Universal Declaration of Human Rights." https://www.un.org/en/about-us/universal-declaration-of-human-rights.

———. "World Must Sustainably Produce 70 Per Cent More Food by Mid-Century—UN Report." Dec. 3, 2013. https://news.un.org/en/story/2013/12/456912.

UN Women. "How Gender Inequality and Climate Change Are Interconnected." April 21, 2025. https://www.unwomen.org/en/articles/explainer/how-gender-inequality-and-climate-change-are-interconnected.

Vigliotti, Jonathan, and Sarah Welch. "More Than a Century After Their Land Was Ravaged by the California Gold Rush, Yurok Tribe to Reclaim Territory." CBS News, Dec. 16, 2024. https://www.cbsnews.com/news/redwood-national-park-land-returned-yurok-tribe/.

Wagner, David L., et al. "Insect Decline in the Anthropocene: Death by a Thousand Cuts." *Proceedings of the National Academy of Sciences* 118.2 (2021) e2023989118. https://doi.org/10.1073/pnas.2023989118.

Walker, William H., et al. "Light Pollution and Cancer." *International Journal of Molecular Sciences* 21.24 (2020) 9360. https://doi.org/10.3390/ijms21249360.

Wesley, John. *Primitive Physick: Or, an Easy and Natural Method of Curing Most Diseases*. 12th ed. Farmington Hills, MI: Gale ECCO, Print Editions, 2018.

———. "Rule of Life." UMC Discipleship Ministries, Aug. 11, 2011. https://www.umcdiscipleship.org/resources/rule-of-life.

WGCU Staff. "The Connections Between Human Health and Blue Light Pollution." WGCU: PBS and NPR for Southwest Florida, Nov. 19, 2024. https://news.wgcu.org/podcast/gulf-coast-life/2024-11-19/the-connections-between-human-health-and-blue-light-pollution.

Wiba Anung. "13 Moons Curriculum." https://wiba-anung.org/index.php/our-work/13-moons-curriculum/.

Wilkinson, Katharine. "How Empowering Women and Girls Can Help Stop Global Warming." TED, Nov. 2018. https://www.ted.com/talks/katharine_wilkinson_how_empowering_women_and_girls_can_help_stop_global_warming.

Wirzba, Norman. *Love's Braided Dance: Hope in a Time of Crisis*. New Haven: Yale University Press, 2024.

———. *This Sacred Life: Humanity's Place in a Wounded World*. Cambridge: Cambridge University Press, 2021.

Wittenberg, Ariel. "'How Come I Can't Breathe?': Musk's Data Company Draws a Backlash in Memphis." Politico, May 6, 2025. https://www.politico.com/news/2025/05/06/elon-musk-xai-memphis-gas-turbines-air-pollution-permits-00317582.

Wright, N. T. *Surprised by Hope: Rethinking Heaven, the Resurrection, and the Mission of the Church*. New York: HarperOne, 2008.

WWF. "'System in Peril': Average Wildlife Populations' Size Declined by 73% in Just 50 Years, Warns WWF." Oct. 10, 2024. https://www.wwf.eu/?15334891/System-in-peril-Average-wildlife-populations-size-declined-by-73-in-just-50-years-warns-WWF.

Younger, Sally. "NASA Helps Find Thawing Permafrost Adds to Near-Term Global Warming." NASA, Oct. 29, 2024. https://www.nasa.gov/earth/nasa-helps-find-thawing-permafrost-adds-to-near-term-global-warming/.

Zhao, Shiye, et al. "The Distribution of Subsurface Microplastics in the Ocean." *Nature* 641 (2025) 51–61. https://doi.org/10.1038/s41586-025-08818-1.

Zero by Fifty. "What Did I Do With . . . ? Designed for the Dump." Zero by Fifty Missoula. https://www.zerobyfiftymissoula.com/wdidw-designed-for-the-dump.

www.ingramcontent.com/pod-product-compliance
Lightning Source LLC
Chambersburg PA
CBHW062017220426
43662CB00010B/1374